# Successful Relocation to Costa Rica: Proven Strategies & Advice

Tarik .A York

*Successful Relocation to Costa Rica: Proven Strategies & Advice : Successful Relocation to Costa Rica: Proven Strategies & Advice*

## *Funny helpful tips:*

*Harness the power of digital health platforms; they're centralizing patient data and enhancing healthcare delivery.*

*Incorporate healthy fats like avocados and nuts; they support brain health and provide sustained energy.*

## _Life advices:_

_Stay vigilant about hydration, especially during intense workouts; replenishing lost fluids is crucial._

_Stay financially literate; understanding money management is key to long-term stability._

# Introduction

This is your comprehensive companion to embarking on a new chapter in the beautiful country of Costa Rica. Whether you're planning a short vacation, considering a move, or dreaming of long-term living, this guide has got you covered.

Before you take the leap, it's essential to understand the intricacies of Costa Rican life. You'll encounter the diverse stories of individuals who have already made the transition, providing valuable insights and wisdom to help you plan your own journey. Additionally, the guide offers exit strategies to keep in mind should you ever need to make a change in your plans.

Crime and safety are crucial concerns for anyone relocating to a foreign country. This guide addresses these topics, giving you the tools to make informed decisions about your security and peace of mind. You'll also discover helpful advice on what to bring with you and what to leave behind, easing the transition into your new life.

Navigating Costa Rica requires a deeper understanding of its culture and customs. You'll learn about the unique aspects of the country, from its road conditions and driving experiences to the charming beach communities and the adventure-packed Caribbean region.

Practical matters like budgeting, transportation, and housing are extensively covered, offering insights into living on a budget, working in Costa Rica, and choosing the ideal residence to suit your needs. You'll also gain valuable tips on obtaining a driver's license, banking, and dealing with real estate matters.

The guide doesn't shy away from real-life experiences. From medical concerns and obtaining legal advice to dealing with plumbing issues and setting up utilities, you'll be well-prepared for the ups and downs of daily life in Costa Rica.

Living in a tropical paradise comes with its fair share of adventures, and this guide prepares you for the unexpected. Whether it's dealing with a stomach bug or getting a colonoscopy, you'll find stories of resilience and adaptability.

As you venture further into the guide, you'll gain valuable insights into different industries, including mini-golf, ice cream shops, and the restaurant business. These firsthand experiences will inspire you to explore various opportunities and create a sustainable living in Costa Rica.

Discover the wonders of Costa Rica through road trips, exploring the Central Valley, Arenal, the Pacific Coast Highway, and the Osa Peninsula. Each destination offers unique experiences and hidden treasures, showcasing the diverse beauty of the country.

Throughout the guide, real questions sent to the "Happier" platform provide answers to common concerns and challenges faced by those living in Costa Rica. Whether it's about healthcare, dental care, or embassy assistance, this guide ensures you have access to essential information.

This is more than just a guide – it's an immersive experience that delves into the heart of Costa Rican life. As you embrace the beauty of the country and overcome its unique challenges, you'll be well-prepared to live your dream in this vibrant and enchanting paradise. Bon voyage!

# Contents

# Part I: Getting Started

# The Unofficial Guide

My sister loves her unofficial, kid-friendly guide to Disney World. Essentially, it tells you where to find the shortest lines, what the best places are to watch fireworks, and how to avoid getting trampled when Mickey Mouse comes out for pictures. I think the directions to the nearest bathrooms are what appeals most to dads, since they tend to hide there while little Jimmy throws a tantrum.

My dad would have loved an unofficial Disney guide since it probably would have warned him not to stand on top of a bench— unwisely positioned under a spiked, wrought-iron lantern— to get a better view of the Electric Light Parade. What transpired next was my dad suffering a head wound that was not very kid-friendly at all. Nothing like a geyser of blood squirting out of someone's cranium while "It's a Small World" pipes into the crowd.

Luckily, Disney's first responder came in the form of an anthropomorphic dog sporting a tall hat and turtleneck. Goofy was kind enough to escort my father to the nearest first aid center where a qualified nurse wrapped his head in a turban of gauze and propped him against a lamppost on Main Street. We drove straight back to New Jersey the next day.

The good news was that my father's blood loss left him surprisingly indifferent to the shenanigans that went on in the backseat of our Chevy Impala. Consequently, my sister and I got to smack each other with wild abandon for twenty-four glorious hours. I couldn't imagine a better ending to our family vacation.

This book is my unofficial guide to navigating Costa Rica, along with a little humor and a few life lessons thrown in. I'll be including the things that I feel are most important, answering the questions people ask most often, and leaving out the things that you could easily find on the Internet. My goal is to inform but not overload, while sharing some laughs along the way. If you are looking to buy a teak farm, I'm sorry. I can't help you with that. But if you are interested in moving here, or even traveling throughout the country, you may find some of these chapters useful.

If you haven't read my previous two books, *Happier Than A Billionaire: Quitting My Job, Moving to Costa Rica, and Living The Zero Hour Work Week* and *Happier Than A Billionaire: The Sequel*, then my occasional tangents may surprise you. I have a tendency to share a lot of my life, especially all the funny (and not so funny) things that my husband ropes me into. Some have made accusations that my stories never happened, or that I've exaggerated. But I can assure you, once you decide to really start living—and take a chance on adventure—you tend to find yourself in one crazy predicament after another. This is my blueprint so that you can create all of your own incredible stories that no one will believe.

These adventures were exactly what I was searching for when embarking on this crazy odyssey, and I suspect you too are searching for something similar. You might have even ordered this book without telling your spouse. My husband, Rob, started researching our escape before he ever officially announced the plan to me. He knew where we should be long before I ever considered it.

I applaud you and want you to know that there are plenty more of us out there. It wasn't until I became an expat (expatriate) that I met so many interesting people looking for a different kind of life. They did exactly what I did, and had equally interesting (if not better) stories.

This book is designed for everyone. For those who've already bought tickets and are making Costa Rica their home, and for those who read a chapter a night under the covers after they put the kids to bed. There is nothing wrong with dreaming of moving here, and armchair travel can take you many places you may never get to see in a lifetime. Through great books I've imagined living in Tuscany, climbing the tallest mountains, and traveling into space. Reading has given me more joy than I can possibly quantify. Therefore, this book is dedicated not just to those who want to live the *pura vida* (common phrase in Costa Rica meaning "full of life" or "going great") lifestyle, but also to those who want to imagine the adventure. Because in many ways, I'm still doing that.

So come along and I'll try to keep you from smacking your head into jagged lanterns. But remember—sometimes you're going to have to do that to see the parade.

# The Person with a Story

In the summer of 1964, my mother traveled throughout Europe. She saved for years and went with a few girlfriends, one of whom fell in love with a French waiter. The man became their own personal tour guide of Paris. Sadly, her girlfriend gave a teary goodbye to her new love when she boarded the plane back to the United States. They never saw each other again. I am enamored by these stories. These women did something I secretly longed for; they had a story to tell.

My brain overflowed with wanderlust while working in my office. I ached to be one of those globe trekkers that recited clever anecdotes next to the cheese platter at parties: "If it wasn't for that extra granola bar and Zippo lighter, I would never have made it out of there alive."

Unfortunately, my adventures were more along the lines of cleaning out gutters and plowing snowy parking lots. Not the nail-biting cliffhanger that gets you invited to the after-party. It was then I decided to carve out a plan. From henceforth, my stories would be about airplanes and mountains, bugs and oceans, odd fruit and equally odd people. Moving to Costa Rica accomplished these goals, and then some.

After writing my first two books, I received emails from people with dozens of questions about moving to Costa Rica. They wanted information on more practical matters that I hadn't covered. What I thought was just a fun narrative about two people leaving the rat race turned into something bigger. Although getting chased by killer bees and wading through crocodile-infested waters was entertaining, these people were looking for "how to" information on gaining residency and getting their driver's license. It is because of them that the *The Costa Rica Escape Manual* was born. It was a challenging birth, with lots of mood swings and binge eating in the middle of the night. But I knew I had more to say, even if my husband was looking forward to the day that I would have less to say… specifically about him.

"Go ahead. Write this book, but maybe we could make this installment less about the dopey things I do," he pleaded. I nodded but knew deep inside I could never resist writing stories about my husband.

When I told my dad over the Christmas holiday that I was writing a "how to" book on Costa Rica, he gasped. I wasn't sure why the news had elicited such a reaction, but I figured it was polite to return an unwarranted gasp with an equally discernible one. There we stood next to my mom's glazed ham, gasping at one another for what felt like an unrelenting amount of time, until he finally explained his irritation.

"Nadine, I've read these books," he said. "Lord knows I've tried to get through them, and let me express my concerns. To put it simply, nobody reads them." There are times when it's hard to tell how my father feels about a certain topic. This was not one of them.

"Okay, Dad, I'll consider that," I replied, trying to end the conversation as quickly as possible. It appeared I was ruining our festive Presbyterian Christmas, one overflowing with long-upheld traditions of stoic silences and subliminal resentment. To think, I was under the impression I was actually livening up the place with talk of my travel guide.

"The type is always small," my dad said. "And when you add the glossy white of the stiff pages, it becomes even more difficult and aggravating to read. In summary, they are heavy, boring, and awkward. Once you make the supreme effort to read it, there is nothing but a dull textbook quality as you peruse the standard sections: hotels, sights, weather, and criminal activity. On and on they drone. In the end, they all end up in the corner of one's garage."

"Received the message, Dad. Loud and clear," I moaned. But he was unforgiving. After this pep talk, I had little confidence beginning this project.

"Perhaps I should listen to him," I thought. He's a smart guy, a man who would skim the whimsical pages of *Soviet Life* during his leisure hours after work. While other families discussed their day, my father would lecture on the inevitable fall of Communism. It's no surprise that my spontaneous dissertations on rationed cooking fuel never garnered a bigger crowd during gym class. A bunch of pinko commie sympathizers for sure.

All this made me wonder if this *Escape Manual* would end up like other poorly received sequels, such as *The Godfather III* or the *Rocky* installment where he goes back to his old working-class neighborhood after filing for bankruptcy. Somehow the Balboas are so broke, Adrian is forced to wear her black-rimmed glasses again. She even ends up working at her old job in the pet store, spending an inordinate amount of time feeding turtles and staring at the ground. This could be my future if I wasn't careful.

Therefore, to avoid having this book get demoted to a corner of your garage as my dad predicted, I decided that I'd make this road trip exciting. We'll be taking a tour of the country, selling our junk, shipping some things, finding housing, and boarding a plane with our pets. We will apply for residency, wait for residency, and reapply together. Perhaps we'll stop by and visit a doctor. Hopefully, we won't be spending too much time in any hospital. But don't worry—if you need medical attention, I'll drive you to the best facility outside San José. That's if the roads haven't destroyed my car by then. It smells like the transmission is burning. If not that, something else is on fire. Eventually, the entire engine is going to blow. But even that doesn't stress me out anymore. Since moving here, I've found that my anxiety is nowhere near the levels it was when I was working. It's one of the greatest gifts Costa Rica has given me.

We'll even be visiting some luxury homes. At the end of the Accommodations chapter, I've included the "wow factor": links to fabulous houses so that you can snoop around and peer into other people's kitchens. It's the perfect way to enjoy the experience of an open house without ever leaving the couch.

Before we begin this road trip, remember to pack your sense of humor. We may encounter some frustrating times as we embark on this journey, but I promise we will have equally hilarious moments. Navigating a foreign country while sorting out cultural misunderstandings can be funny if you take a second to look at the bigger picture. It's one of the reasons my husband and I have had such a positive experience here. Rob can laugh at anything. Me? It's a skill I've had to learn.

If you've been following my adventures, you know that everything wasn't always hammocks and palm trees. There were many formidable situations that tested my last nerve. I never knew where the last nerve was located, but if I were to ask my mom there is no doubt she could tell me exactly how to find it. (Apparently, I had been hanging off hers between the ages of thirteen through seventeen.) But I never considered calling it quits. I knew that if I could just laugh at the ridiculousness of it all, the obstacles would eventually work themselves out.

Although *The Costa Rica Escape Manual* has a nice ring to it, my husband felt we should call it *Costa Rica: Results May Vary* because our experience will be vastly different from yours, and yours will be different from the next guy's. He also suggested *My Husband Is a Genius*, which quickly got placed on top of my things-that-are-never-going-to-happen pile—a pile that includes chapter ideas such as: *First Aid and Duct Tape: Your Personal Guide to Affordable Healthcare*, *How to Safely Hide Firearms in Fireplaces*, and *Fix Anything With Bungee Cords and Underpants: A Love Story*.

Varying results are something you will have to get used to while living here. One agency will never know what's going on with the other, and you can never predict what may or may not transpire. Something you thought would take an hour might take the whole day. So pack a lunch and a very entertaining book. I recommend the *Happier* series for maximum mind-numbing enjoyment.

A perfect example of bureaucratic confusion is when we applied for residency. Before you can finalize the paperwork, you have to pay into the CAJA (healthcare and social security system). When we went down to their office to open an account, I was told you have to be a resident first. But you can't become a resident until you enroll in CAJA. You will encounter situations like this regularly. And don't be surprised when another expat, with similar credentials, just parades right by you and opens an account.

In the end, you'll win some and you'll lose some. Some things will be easy while others will be challenging. Moreover, predicting what may take a day and what may take many months is nearly impossible. But trust me, there will be times when the magic fairy of Costa Rica will rain her monkey dust down upon you. You may get lucky and easily obtain residency, or have a phone line that rarely goes down. You could be the only one on the block that still has electricity during an outage, or someone who never loses their water supply. Although you will rarely have all of these things at once, when it happens you will shout out "pura vida" with gusto.

One way or another, you'll have a story to tell. And shouldn't we all have more stories, more French waiters we tearfully wave goodbye to while boarding a plane? (Costa Rica fact: 10% gratuities are usually included on your restaurant bill. See that, Dad? Useful information cheerfully presented without any difficult pages to turn.)

I can't guarantee you a perfect plan, but this trip will beat sitting in rush-hour traffic. Now let's get started. Find your passport and order your airline ticket. Tell your boss you're taking a much-needed vacation, and make sure to pack enough sunscreen for the entire family because it's super expensive here (another fun fact skillfully delivered without any noticeable side effects).

But it's important to remember—and I can't stress this enough—results may vary.

# Exit Strategies

There is no doubt that Rob and I did something drastic. We weren't happy, and we had to do something about it. But the difficulty is that knowing you have to change your life is not enough. To get to where you want to be, you actually have to figure out the part on *how* to change it. For me, the only way out was to start fresh and begin a new and uncomplicated life in Costa Rica, but untangling the complexities of one's life is challenging. Perhaps this is where you are right now. You look around and think, "I need to find an exit strategy. Where do I begin?"

There are many different exit strategies, and you should consider them all. You don't have to do what Rob and I did to find the perfect solution. Who says you need to be all-in in the first place? I went that route because I was totally burnt out. I'm not even sure how I found myself in such an unhappy place. It's amazing how quickly you can lose touch with what is most important in life when you concentrate too much on the superfluous stuff surrounding you. Costa Rica helped me find balance. Now all the things surrounding me are monkeys and parrots. Seriously. As I'm writing this, there are monkeys outside my window, and a flock of parrots just flew overhead. This is how my day begins. It's like waking up to the best day ever, every single day.

Let's consider the ways you can design a similar plan. I've met some people who take a year's sabbatical to travel and search for a different lifestyle. If that doesn't work, others elect to spend a few months out of the year in Costa Rica: the snowbird option. I like to call it the *expat-lite* lifestyle. For many, this is the perfect amount of time in Costa Rica. The obstacles you run into are not that upsetting since you will be returning home in a few months anyway. It's such a great choice for those who can afford it.

Then there are those who simply come down for a vacation every year. Costa Rica has resonated so deeply with them, they look forward to returning. I love meeting these people. They don't have the ability to move here permanently, but they love it nonetheless. They take advantage of all the fun activities and leave refreshed and ready to tackle their jobs again.

Many of these decisions depend on finances and how much risk you are willing to take. I've met people who have made it work and others who return home after six months. Your road need not mirror anyone else's. Make it your own. Results will vary, but you will have a better shot if you understand that there's no guarantee that things will work out.

Take a moment to develop a different plan for each of these scenarios:

1. A two-week vacation.
2. Spending a month.
3. Spending three months (that way, you can leave before your visa runs out).
4. Spending half the year.
5. All In: The big move.
6. Or no move at all! Simply dreaming about it is good enough.

Consider how you can finance each of these. When we first moved here, we were able to stick to a budget of $1,000/month. However, that was when we resided in Grecia. Now that we are at the beach, products are more expensive and there are a lot of activities we find ourselves doing. You may require a bigger budget, or be able to squeak by on less.

There are other questions to ask yourself, some that are more personal and might take a while to answer. Like this one: what exactly are *you* looking for?

Are you ready for retirement and looking for an adventure? Or do you want to find another job in a foreign country? (That is not the easiest route and I talk further about it in a later chapter.) Are you unhappy at home and feel a change in latitude will help? Do you have enough money to float for a while, but you will eventually need to find a job or open a business?

Knowing exactly where you are, financially and emotionally, will help to make this trip a little easier. For me, I wanted the adventure. I wanted a different way of life but knew that I couldn't live like this forever without finding some sort of income down the line. But I was willing to take that shot. Others may think this option is too risky. I don't blame them. Rob and I did something so outrageous that I think back and wonder how we were brave enough to see it through.

Everyone you meet will tell you their story, and many of these people will insist that their way was the right way. We have all made mistakes when moving here, but that is exactly what happens when you commit to making the move. It's part of the journey, and unavoidable.

It's about this time in the book that I should be leaving big gaps of space for you to write your "notes." I can never understand why travel guides do this; I've rarely written anything in a book since college. And even then it was probably a doodle.

Anyway, note sections burden me with feeling like I should be jotting down ideas. Way too much pressure, especially for those reading this on a Kindle, where you can't write anything clever if you wanted to.

Enjoy the ride, and let's discuss what is near and dear to everyone considering a move to Central America: crime. Am I going to get kidnapped?

# Book'em, Dano: Crime in Costa Rica

"Is there a lot of crime in Costa Rica?"

I know that there is a good portion of you who skipped straight to this chapter. It's the number one question most people ask, and the reason I put this topic toward the front of the book. Upon my own investigation on relocating to Costa Rica, all the crime-related ranting on the Internet immediately terrified me. It almost stopped me from moving here… almost.

What I have since learned is that when someone is negative on a topic, they're going to write a lot about it. Happy people don't do this because they are too busy being happy. They are off doing happy things and don't feel the need to write about it since they think you are having a similar experience. So I'm going to give you my take on crime, from the perspective of someone who is very content living here. I should also point out that I've never been a victim of any crime. But there is always a possibility my house will be cleaned out by noon, and if that happens, I'll be sitting on my floor, pounding away on my invisible laptop, and possibly painting a completely different picture of this subject.

There is a good amount of petty theft in this country. If you leave your backpack lying on the beach unattended, chances are it will disappear. However, a friend recently forgot her purse on the beach for a good fifteen minutes. When we ran back to retrieve it, remarkably, no one had stolen it. We've even forgotten things on the beach, only to find them lying there an hour later. But don't count on this. I'd advise you to watch your things closely when out and about.

In my husband's attempt to thwart crime, he shoves our phone and keys into a Ziploc bag. He then buries it in the sand and places an unassuming coconut on top to mark the spot. I applaud him for being so creative. I call this the "Idiot's Coconut Scavenger Hunt Game." We end up spending the remainder of the day digging under every coconut searching for our car keys.

However, sometimes my husband does have good ideas. Rob stockpiles broomsticks in assorted lengths in the back of our car. When staying at a hotel, he wedges them in the tracks of sliding-glass doors. It has proven more effective than most of the locks I've seen. It also has proven effective in stopping any friendly conversation with people when forty broomsticks roll out the back of our SUV.

I don't blame anyone when they are a victim of crime. I hear a lot of people saying, "Well, they shouldn't have left their things unattended on the beach." This is true, but it's still terrible when someone's vacation is ruined because of incidents like this. I feel for these people. It must be awful to have your possessions stolen in a foreign country. Everything looks different, communication is an issue, and it can be a scary experience even if it is just your hotel room key.

I can easily be the one forgetting my purse at a restaurant or dropping a wallet. It can happen to any of us so go easy on that tourist who decided to leave her suitcase with that creepy guy on the corner; the one who said he worked for the hotel. She's probably a nice lady from Minnesota who doesn't even lock her car doors back home. This might even be her first time out of the country, so pat her on the shoulder and reassure her that everything will be okay. A little compassion goes a long way.

Speaking of locking car doors, I find one of the most prevalent crimes in Costa Rica is to have your car broken into, especially if you have bags or suitcases noticeably lying on the seat. When we travel throughout the country, if we stop to eat at a restaurant, we always take our bags inside with us. And don't be embarrassed by this, you'll see plenty of people doing the same thing.

I once met a college student at the US Embassy who'd had his passport stolen. He'd stopped at a popular fast food chain and decided to leave his backpack in the car. When he returned ten minutes later, the bag was gone. So please, no matter where you park, take your bags with you. You'll be surprised what a crook will break a window for, and you'll be equally surprised at how long it takes to fix a broken window in Costa Rica. Ask my German mechanic, Claus, about ordering the right part for your car. "For me... it can take veeks if I can't find zeh right model." So do what I do: have your husband haul all your stuff inside.

As far as your car getting stolen, it does happen. Rob installed three kill switches throughout our car, which basically makes it impossible for anyone to start it, including us. He also attaches two Clubs to the steering wheel. Do you remember the Club? We have two of them. On occasions, our car is more secure than the Popemobile. In fact, if the Popemobile ever goes on sale Rob will be first in line to buy it. The bulletproof glass and climate-controlled interior would be an excellent way to tour the country.

Unfortunately, all our little locking devices do not make for a quick getaway. I end up trapped in the sweltering passenger seat for fifteen minutes while Rob disengages all his doodads. Inevitably, he forgets one and we sit there trying to figure out why the car isn't starting. It's like my own personal sweat lodge. I can easily lose five pounds this way. It's my favorite way of unloading unwanted electrolytes while I dip in and out of consciousness. (I'd like to add here that my friends Sandy and Ian have no Club or kill switches installed on their cars. Ian never leaves anything in his car and keeps his windows open. That way they won't break them in their search for a suitcase or wallet. Sandy's car barely starts, so she's not too worried about theft. In fact, she might welcome the crime.)

If you have read my previous books or blog, you know my husband takes crime prevention seriously: a little too seriously if you ask me. Rob is one beef jerky away from becoming one of those "preppers." The kind of person who thinks bedlam is lurking just outside the door—which it is, in the form of my husband.

He recently researched online for a pair of shoes he wants me to start wearing. Hidden in the heel of the wedge sandal is a stun gun. If I am ever in a dangerous situation, all I have to do is karate kick the ruffian in the face and Taser him with this fancy footwear. I am not averse to this. It sounds like a great way to introduce myself, while getting a good hamstring workout. Perhaps this should be the opening performance at my next book-signing gig. He also mentioned something about a baton that shoots tear gas, which is a splendid idea. I can only imagine good things coming from that.

Now here is something you rarely hear about in other countries: Your car can get kidnapped and held for ransom. This is how the crafty plan works. Shortly after noticing your car is missing, you get a polite call from the thief asking you to meet him at the local hardware store. For a small sum, he will return your car and you can be on your way. Consider this a nice day out with your wife, and a chance to dart into that hardware store to see if they sell the Club. (All kidding aside, you should always go to the police first.) On the scale of crime, I rate this pretty low. I'd rather this happen than have my home burglarized. You'll never get a polite phone call after that occurs.

Having someone break into your house is not all that uncommon. This happens not only in tourist areas, but in the mountains as well. What's interesting about this is that they may come once and grab your TV, and then return a week later for your microwave. It's like a pesky neighbor that keeps coming back wanting to borrow your hedge clippers. Many times these thieves don't have cars so they only take what they can carry.

Is there more crime in Costa Rica than other countries? I'm really not sure, but statistically speaking the answer is no. However, many crimes go unreported. The difference here is that if your house is getting robbed, it could take three hours or three days for the police to arrive. There are few tax dollars to pay for a large police force, so personal responsibility is paramount. That is why you see fences or walls around houses and bars on windows. It persuades the crooks to consider another house, perhaps one without any security.

I suppose if reporting a crime makes little difference in the end result, fewer people will report them. Therefore, the statistics may not be at all that accurate. In addition, filing a police report at OIJ (Organismo de Investigación Judicial) is problematic. The closest police department may be miles away and their hours can fluctuate. This can be irritating especially for those that have home insurance, which requires a police report to make a claim. And yes, you can get insurance here. My friend was reimbursed after her home was robbed. It took her three months to get the police report, but she eventually got a copy. There is a rumor that OIJ is opening a branch in Tamarindo, so I'm sure more people will be making reports. That's encouraging.

On the flip side, just the other day a home was robbed in Potrero. A family had rented it for a week, and when they returned from the beach one day, they found someone had entered through an open window and stolen their belongings. The tourists called the police, who promptly showed up and found the bandits. The tourists got all their possessions back. This is a perfect example of why I say, "results may vary." I'm happy to see that things are changing and there is a quicker response to these issues.

There are options such as hiring a private security firm. (S.E.S. is a great one if you are living in the in the Flamingo area.) They're an armed response team that will rush to your home when you call or even when your alarm goes off. In this country, alarms are never programmed to call the police, but you can easily have one installed. When it is activated, it will call the private security firm. This is a great way to feel more secure knowing that if anything happens, someone will show up looking for you. Some people I know are happy using this service and probably wouldn't live here without it, while others never think about crime and leave everything open to chance.

Overall, an ounce of prevention goes a long way and most likely you will be fine. But it's also important not to underestimate what can happen if opportunists know you have valuables in your home. I recently heard of a woman who moved here with $250,000 worth of jewelry. Someone got wind of it and stole it while she was out buying a safe for her jewelry. Ladies, listen up. If you have a quarter of a million dollars' worth of gems, please put it in a safe deposit box at the bank. Also, I'm assuming if you own a quarter million dollars' worth of gems, you have a pretty nice pool. Give me a call. I'll be the incognito woman driving up in the Popemobile with a big bald guy carrying a tear gas baton. I promise to kick off my Taser shoes before diving into the deep end.

I know plenty of people who take no precautions as all. "I don't want to live my life like that," they say. I respect their decision. The house we rent has bars; I feel good about it. After a week, you don't even notice they're there. Rob has all sorts of sensors around the house that can alert us if someone is walking around at night. It's the reason I call our place the Thunderdome: two men enter, one man leaves. Please call before visiting.

It all depends on your comfort level. I am not here to convince you to live as I do. I am just sharing what works for me. I suppose one could say that we haven't been a victim of crime because of the precautions that we take, or maybe because we've been lucky so far. It's a hard call. All I can say is I live a very happy life in Costa Rica and wish for you to have a happy one as well.

On a side note, in my attempt to live a happy life, I don't watch the news anymore. I find it just makes me crazy and paranoid. No matter what country you live in, crime segments get high ratings and the programs take advantage of this. No one wants to hear about that happy woman who moved to Costa Rica and wrote a book. It's a shame because I believe it's a great news story and should be featured every night after the weather report.

Now that we've gone over my take on crime in Costa Rica, here are some rules Rob and I live by:

1. Never leave any bags in the car.
2. Do not walk around with expensive jewelry.
3. Always lock the doors to your house and car.

4. Do not sleep with windows or doors open. I know that ocean breeze feels nice, but too often it makes it easy for people to slip in and out without you waking up. This is a common home invasion scenario. At first it feels kind of nice, like the housekeeper cleaned up a bit. Until you realize, it was the burglars that were doing the cleaning.
5. Be careful at night. We don't go out to clubs or bars and stay until the wee hours. But if you do, be careful when leaving. Especially if you are that drunk guy flashing money and buying drinks for random people. (You know who you are.)
6. If you read online that the soccer field in the middle of town is a problem at night, please don't take a short cut and try to walk through it at three in the morning. If there are known places that crime happens, don't take a chance walking through them.
7. Most of all, always give the appearance that you are alert and aware of your surroundings.

These are my seven lucky rules, but I'd like to point out that for a place with such a small police presence—and no army—it is still known to be one of the happiest countries.

So let's move on and talk about the process of moving here. See all that junk you own in your house? If you were like me, you probably have way too much of it.

Next up, shipping your stuff to Costa Rica. Garage sale, anyone?

### Links

OIJ agency for reporting crime: www.poder-judicial.go.cr

S.E.S Security: Email Donald or Patricia at: privatesecuity_ses1@hotmail.com

If you are in the Guanacaste area, Brian Howard is an excellent installer and supplier of alarms: gtesecurity@gmail.com

# Stuff: Keep It or Start Over?

"Is it better to bring my possessions or buy new in Costa Rica?"

Life can often feel like the game Twister: Spin the dial and your right arm lands on green, your left leg on yellow. Some of these moves work out, while others turn your life upside down. There are times when all you want to do is call it quits and have a do-over. This is where I found myself when contemplating the move abroad. I wanted a spin of the dial that would change everything for the better, but boy, did I have some things to work out first.

In my first book I wrote about my robotic martial arts hamster. When you turned it on, it played *Kung Fu Fighting* while flamboyantly twirling nun-chucks. I can't remember why I bought it; perhaps it was a gift to my husband. All I know is that it made me laugh, and when I'd come home from a long day at work I'd turn it on and stare at it much like Jack Nicholson in *One Flew Over the Cuckoo's Nest*.

Moving across town or across borders causes one to take a thorough inventory of one's life. What was once buried in a box in the attic becomes painfully visible. It grows in weight and dimensions. It will require padding, packing, and lifting. That candlestick you received as a wedding gift from your freshman-year college roommate now glares back at you as if to ask, "So, what are you going to do with me?"

Now multiply that question by a thousand. This move is going to cost you time, energy, and money. Decisions must be made and there are two trains of thought: keep it or start over.

I knew that beginning a new life in Costa Rica would not be easy, and having all of these possessions to worry about was not going to make it any easier on me. Where would I put them since most rentals come furnished? Are there storage units in Costa Rica? How much are these storage units per month and how many months will I be storing these items? Will the climate destroy my furniture before I find a place for it? Is it bad to own a leather couch in a cloud forest? (Answer to that: yes.) Could these items serve my family and friends much better right here in my community?

When I rented my furnished home on the mountaintop in Grecia, we had a significant mold problem. The bamboo furniture grew mold like a Chia pet. If you are looking for rolling green pastures in your living room, I would suggest following your husband's advice and leaving the windows open as a cloud rolls in. It was like the hills in Scotland but without the bagpipes. Now I know why Mel Gibson painted his face in *Braveheart*; it was covered in mold.

Now that I'm living in Guanacaste (in the driest part of the country), mold is not as much of an issue. Just your basic cleaning every week will solve that problem. You can see how climate plays a major role in how durable your furniture, or that collection of cute leather sandals and purses, will be.

You don't realize how much your belongings tie you down until you free yourself from them. My big move to Costa Rica was a huge transitional phase in my life. I had to reassess my inventory and make some hard decisions. I knew that if my heart was in this adventure, I would have to let go of many things; some metaphorical, some physical, all a necessity. What I owned did not own me. I had to believe that there was a bigger story ahead, and that this story had to be a lighter one.

I gave nearly everything away and it brought me more happiness than keeping it ever could. I trusted my instincts and knew that this was the right decision. The only thing that brought me to tears was giving away a ficus tree my husband had given me in college. Now I live in a place where there are ficus trees growing everywhere, some so large they reach over the road and form thick, shady canopies. I smile every time I see one. It's so much more rewarding watching one growing in the forest than in my living room.

To think, when I was working I thought that owning possessions was a reflection of success. Little did I realize that I was happier with less stuff. In college I was enjoying some of the best moments of my life, and the things that mattered the most were the experiences and interactions that were shaping my future. And it's these new experiences that keep your life exciting. Maybe it's the reason people lose inspiration as they grow older: living a life with fewer surprises. I believe travel can bring you back to that intoxicating place. The place where tasting a strange fruit or looking out at a remarkable vista makes you feel energized once again.

If you are ready to experience living in a foreign country, it's important to ask yourself some questions about why you want to. Is it your plan to recreate your life in a new country at a discount price? If this is the case, I would discourage you. It's difficult and expensive to replicate the life you lived at home here in Costa Rica. You may be setting yourself up for a very frustrating experience. It is possible to live on less money, but you will have to adopt at least some of the techniques local people use to reduce their cost of living. If you love Froot Loops and can't imagine a world without them, be prepared to have a very large grocery bill.

It's common to overhear heated rants about someone's inability to find their favorite cheese in Costa Rica, or the outrageous cost of imported soymilk. I tend to zone out quickly during these encounters. I would love to remind these people that there are bigger rewards than affordable cottage cheese. Dozens of species of hummingbirds taking baths in my sprinkler comes to mind. I watch them all morning as they rustle their feathers under the cool water. Or the scores of green dragonflies that frequent my backyard midafternoon and all but disappear before dusk. There must be some give and take for an expat. If you are willing to let some things go, you'll be pleasantly surprised by the incredible gifts that will take their place.

This attitude shift may not come immediately; it takes some time. Within three months I was starting to get the hang of things. For others it could take over a year. It's important to be open to the process, and to always look on the brighter side of things when you find out your favorite cookies cost close to a mortgage payment.

(Tip: Buy the cheaper non-imported version or bake them yourself. Better yet, choose the dollar pineapple. Get healthy and save money simultaneously.)

By eliminating the clutter from my life, I was able to make more room for new experiences. I became more appreciative of the beauty right in front of me and less stuck on old habits of accumulating useless items. I also became much more aware of how much I take from this world. It's nice to recognize how little I really need to be happy. Sometimes you need to strip apart your life to uncover what was there all along.

Now you know the reasons why Rob and I sold or gave away everything (including that robotic hamster) before moving here. But let's be fair and take a look at someone who did the opposite. My friends Darlene and Frankie—who you remember from my first book —moved most of their things here. The next chapter will take a look at why they did it and if they have any regrets.

# You Can't Convince Me Otherwise, I'm Keeping My Stuff

"I found a non-furnished house to rent in Costa Rica and I plan on shipping my furniture. Will this be difficult?"

You've decided to keep your stuff and ship it down to Costa Rica. Good for you. It will be nice to have all of those top-of-the-line appliances that are too expensive to replace here. What I would do for a food processer right now. These items are about double what they would cost in a town near you, so I'll wait until I go back to the States to purchase one. Look for me at the airport; I'll be that jerk holding up the security line because I shoved a Cuisinart in my carry-on.

When bringing products into the country for personal use, there is a tax exemption of $500 per person every six months. Rob once asked our landlord to lug a weedwacker onto the plane. Not exactly the easiest thing when traveling with a wife and two small children. I'm surprised I haven't been evicted yet.

As a result, while passing through customs his bags were taken out of the line and inspected. It was then he had to show the agent the $200 receipt for the weedwacker. Our landlord got a stamp indicating that he used up that amount of his tax-exempt status.

Once Rob realized it was that easy, he asked him to bring a couple inflatable kayaks the next time he visited. The expression on my landlord's face was priceless. Later that day, I hid the weedwacker for reasons of personal safety.

I've been lucky in regard to bringing things into the country. I've only been stopped once at the airport for luggage inspection. Rob had packed vanilla-flavored protein powder and it exploded in our suitcase. For a moment, I considered the possibility that my husband might have really tried to smuggle a kilo of cocaine. I mean, do we ever really know our spouse? My dad—who watches every crime show available with his cable subscription—can give you numerous examples of husbands doing all sorts of seedy things to their Pollyanna wives. This might explain the prolonged stares my dad gives Rob and my brother-in-law during the holidays. It's just a matter of time before they screw up as far as my dad is concerned.

As I was strategizing my ingenious getaway that included hiding inside a bucket in the janitor's closet, the customs officer called off his cronies upon tasting the delicious vanilla powder. It was quite a relief.

You eventually discover while living abroad that the square footage of anyone's luggage is more valuable than a Manhattan apartment overlooking Central Park. This is the best way to bring goods into the country and can save you a bundle in the long run. This is also an excellent way to eliminate a potential flood of houseguests. An old friend from grammar school invites himself over for two weeks? Ask him to pack thirty pounds of maple syrup in his luggage. This will ensure that he vacations in the Dominican Republic.

It's important to note that this tax-exempt status also applies to products you order online and have shipped to Costa Rica. You just need to have someone file exoneration paperwork. This can cost upwards of $35 so it is best to reserve it for a big-ticket item. Sandy just ordered rubber rings for her blender to replace the ones her dog used as chew toys. She ordered them online and when they showed up, she had to pay the tax before she could retrieve the package. It wasn't that big of a deal. The washers only cost $2.50, but she had to pay an additional $1.50 in taxes. Totally affordable if it is something this cheap, but it will all start to add up if you do this every time you need something.

In addition, used clothing and books are not subject to any tax, so feel free to bring those copies of *Happier Than A Billionaire* with you on vacation to Costa Rica. What a bargain!

Surprisingly, shipping containers are responsibly priced if you are looking to move a large amount of possessions to Costa Rica. As a rule, plan to pay $1,500 for a twenty-foot shipping container, while a forty-foot container will cost closer to $2,000. But that's just for the container. Remember that even used goods and electronics are subject to taxes ranging from forty to ninety percent. Also, take into account that there will be charges to move your things to the nearest seaport, so all of this adds up quickly.

If you want to ship a smaller amount, you can hire a freight consolidator. They will lump shipments together and store them at a warehouse. This is more affordable. In both cases, you will need to retrieve your items within ninety days of their arrival.

Let's assume that you have already moved to Costa Rica and are waiting for a shipment. At some point, you will need to get to customs to retrieve the items your wife packed into the shipping container. How did I know your wife was in charge of the packing? Because that's what we do unless we want the wedding china shoved under the Rubbermaid container full of automotive tools. There has not been one carton of eggs, loaf of bread, or container of protein powder that has made it safely home when Rob was responsible for packing it. Some things are best left to his neurotic wife.

Once at customs, things really get interesting. Think of it as the worst Valentine's Day date ever. Of course, you go in with the best of intentions. You wear a clean shirt and make sure there is nothing stuck in between your teeth, only to find that your date is solely interested in talking about her plantar fasciitis in excruciating detail.

You might have to make a few trips to the customs office in San José so make sure you have all your paperwork ready:

1. A copy of the main page of your passport, as well as the page with the entry stamp from when you last entered Costa Rica.
2. A detailed list of the contents of the container and their declared value.
3. All the paperwork from the shipping company.

How do they determine what is a fair tax for each item you shipped? Well, look no further than the fascinating periodical called *The International Convention on the Harmonized Commodity Description and Coding System*. You may want to get under the covers and lower the lights for this. Make sure there are no pointy lanterns in your perimeter since I'm predicting you will be suffering from an acute case of narcolepsy in about thirty seconds. This is exactly the type of information my dad warned me about writing. "Heavy, boring, and awkward" doesn't begin to describe the following.

The *HS*—as the cool kids like to call it—is the classification system that establishes the tariffs owed on each item. There are sections for furniture, and subcategories under them for whether the furniture is used in kitchens or offices. There are entries for soccer balls and batteries, water filters and windshields. The list goes on and on. After researching this, I was going to title this chapter, *Where's the Nexium?,* but Rob said you would never buy this book with chapter names like that. The good news is that books are tax-exempt, so carrying the HS manual into the country will not cost a thing.

You may want to hire a customs broker to do some of the dirty work since this is going to get complicated. This is a perfect example of when being fluent in Spanish would come in handy. Your paperwork will reflect other taxes as well like the C.I.F. fee (cost, insurance, and freight), consumption tax, sales tax (13%), and the oddly named Tax Law No. 6946 (1% tax on the C.I.F. price). Are you still with me? What you should take from this chapter is that it will cost more than you think, so it's worth carefully planning what you want to ship. If there are things you can do without, sell or donate them.

You may find that there seems to be no rhyme or reason to a lot of this. Your neighbor may pay half the amount in tax for his new bedroom set that you did for your ten-year-old IKEA bookcase. You will scratch your head and try to understand the logic behind this, but you'll soon realize that there is nothing you can do about it now. When it comes to shipping your things, results will *definitely* vary. (You'll be scratching your head a lot while living here, so be careful to not bore a hole straight into your brain.)

You are going to win some and lose some, but shipping things does have its merits. At least, you will have comfortable furniture. Costa Rican furniture builders do not always use the highest-grade foam in their cushions, and this may result in couches that are uncomfortable. There are a few pieces in our living room that are built with dimensions better suited for a dollhouse. I find it delightful; however, Rob can't squeeze into any of it. This leads me to believe that either Rob, myself, or both of us are oddly proportioned.

My friend Darlene shipped her couch and it's my favorite thing in the country. It's so dreamily comfy, I wish I had one like it. Although she was happy to have her belongings in Costa Rica, Darlene's shipping experience was mixed.

"Before I moved here, I rented out my condominium in Florida to a tenant that wanted it unfurnished," Darlene explained. "I had already planned on shipping my belongings, but this gave me extra incentive to bring it all down.

"I did some research and talked with a woman who furnished a three-bedroom house in Escazú. She shopped around San José, and it cost her close to $15,000 once it was all said and done. Although that might be on the upper end, it still makes you consider the cost of furnishing a new place.

"She also complained about Costa Rican appliances. I love to cook and I didn't want to be working with crumby equipment. I suggest people who live here consider a gas stove. Electric is so expensive, and it was costing me a fortune to use my electric oven. Eventually, I ended up buying a gas stove and I love it! A propane tank was installed outside my house. This has cut my electric bill in half. The smartest thing I ever did.

"In the end, my twenty-foot container cost $5,000. But where I took a hit was with the moving company. They wrapped everything in bubble wrap, charging me an additional $1,800.

"Even before I broke ground on my house, my container made it to Limón, where it was shipped straight to Alajuela. The taxes for everything ended up being an affordable $900, but I've heard of people paying more or less for similar things.

"The most important thing I can stress is to take very good inventory of your belongings. Many things ended up damaged: my microwave and refrigerator were dented. Some of my personal possessions disappeared, even silly keepsakes that were not worth anything.

"In the end, the company returned $1,000 for the missing or damaged items. It wasn't the worst experience, but it wasn't the best. Results will definitely vary when you do something like this. But even with all the headaches, I love having my furniture and all the appliances that make cooking a joy."

I think the best part of shipping your things could be having a little piece of home once you get here. Sometimes that can make this transition easier. Your dog, Fido, will have his favorite pillow, and if Fido is happy, everyone else will be happy, too.

Now that you have your comfortable furniture and a happy dog, how are you going to get him all the way to Costa Rica? Next up: Fido flies the friendly skies.

### Links

The Costa Rican Customs Department (Direccion General de Aduanas) is overseen by the Costa Rican Department of the Treasury (Ministerio de Hacienda):
www.hacienda.go.cr

I don't have any first hand experience with a shipper, but I have friends who had great experiences with Barry at Ship Costa Rica.
barry@shipcostarica.com

# Fido Leaves the Rat Race *

Let's be honest, Fido could use a vacation. He wouldn't mind a change of scenery, and he's ready to trade those backyard squirrels for a family of monkeys howling overhead.

If you're like me, you would never consider leaving your pets behind. I told my husband at the beginning of this adventure that my critters were coming along, and I didn't care how much it cost. Since Rob wasn't comfortable driving the Pan-American Highway all the way from the United States to Costa Rica with a cat, a dog, and all of what was left of our possessions, it was clear we would be flying our pets.

Luckily, Costa Rica does not have a quarantine policy like many other countries. You can get your animals right away from the airport. All you need is to have your papers in order:

1. An international certificate from your veterinarian is required, stating that the animals have had their proper shots. Your veterinarian should be familiar with this paperwork, and should be conducted within 2 weeks of the departure date. It should be made out in duplicate since you will be handing over one of these sheets to customs. Dogs require the following shots: distemper, hepatitis, leptospirosis, parvovirus and rabies vaccinations. Your pet must be vaccinated for rabies between 21 days and one year prior to entering the country. Cats require only a rabies shot.

2. These papers then need to be endorsed by your state's US Department of Agriculture office. Many times this office can be found in your state's capital.

3. Be aware that each airline has their own rules in regards to transporting animals. Check with them

before booking your trip to ensure you have the proper paperwork.

I'm surprised there aren't more class trips to the US Department of Agriculture. It's an admirable institution, one whose waiting room is a Library of Congress full of reading material. Most of the selection describes in great detail the many ways skipping through a cow pasture in Acapulco—and unknowingly dragging the fecal material into the country— could wipe out our entire nation's food supply. And kudos to their eye-opening investigations concerning venereal diseases in cattle. If only the place had a Keurig machine, I could sit there all day.

Now that you have your papers endorsed, what's next? If your pets are traveling in the cabin with you, you shouldn't run into too many problems. You just walk off the plane with them. If your pets are traveling in the cargo area, they may end up at the customs warehouse. An import permit from the Animal Quarantine Offices (SENASA-Departamento de Cuarentena Animal) will be required. The cost is roughly $20. There may be other fees as well. Sandy paid $200 to get her dog out of "customs jail."

This is one of the main reasons most people fly with their pets. If the pets are unaccompanied, they are considered cargo and you will most likely need to hire a pet specialist or "broker." They will take care of everything at the customs warehouse.

This may seem nerve-racking, but the biggest snafu in all of this is dealing with the airline. Each one has different procedures with regard to transporting animals, but they all focus on one important thing:

- You should fly your pet at times of the year when the weather isn't too hot or too cold. This may completely change the timing of your move. I know it did for me.

Out of all the elements that Fido will be subjected to, heat is the most dangerous. Other factors that may affect your departure date will include how many other passengers are shipping their pets. Some airlines have guidelines that only allow one animal in the cabin at once. Since my cat was small enough to fit under my seat, the airline kept delaying my flight in order to accommodate him. This was one of the biggest decisions of our lives and it was being dictated by my cat.

It is imperative you check with your airline about their pet policies. Sandy had an easier time flying into the Liberia International Airport with her dog, since all the animals arrive through baggage claim there. If that is the case, it may be worth investigating arriving at that airport instead of the one closer to San José.

So now that you've decided to check Fido as luggage and he is ready for his flight, let's make sure his crate is big enough for him to stand up and turn around. The airline will not allow a pet to fly if it does not have adequate room. It's a good idea to attach a battery-operated fan to your animal's crate. You should also provide water, a wet towel, and a comfortable blanket. Keep in mind the water may spill in shipping, but at least he will be able to lick the wet towel.

As for driving down, I suppose this is possible. I've met people who drove all the way from California down the Pan-American Highway. Some did it on motorcycles; others in VW vans that look like they just came from a Grateful Dead concert. It sounds like an amazing adventure, but I have no personal experience with this and can't give any advice on it.

What happens once you land in Costa Rica? That depends whether your pet comes out as baggage or gets sent to customs. Since our cat flew under the seat with us, getting him through customs was not a problem. However, getting my dog, Clementine, back was not as easy. A fidgety guy walked up and informed us that "it will take a long time… such a long time" to get our dog back without his help and our cooperation. And that cooperation will cost $30 to $60 depending on your negotiation skills.

Overall, it was stressful but it worked out. I couldn't imagine my life without my pets and I am happy to say that they both arrived safely. Incidentally, my beautiful dog, Clementine, passed away a few months ago. It's something that I couldn't bear to write about. I share a lot of my life, but losing her was an insufferable blow. She was a piece of home and a dear friend who made all the obstacles bearable. I remember the day I picked her up from the pound. I asked the associate for a dog that was hard to place. Poor Clementine had been abused; her tail had been broken and amputated. She was curled in a corner while other dogs nipped at her. I fell in love the moment I saw her.

"That's the dog for me," I said. Rob and I had discussed getting a dog, and while Rob had always wanted one, he felt we were not ready because of our small apartment. So when he got home from a fishing trip, he was especially surprised to find that I had adopted an antisocial, scared, amputated-tail dog from the shelter. Of course after telling Rob the story, he fell in love with her too. My cat had passed away a year before, so my darling Clementine was the last piece of this journey that still connected me to my home in the States.

I miss her terribly. I think about the life she had the last five years, and it brings a smile to my face. Although she was an older dog, she really thrived once she landed in Costa Rica. It just goes to show you that no matter where you start in life, you can always have a great finish. A dog from the shelter got to live alongside a volcano. She had the chance to breathe fresh mountain air, travel to the coast, watch monkeys swinging from the trees, and even be chased by temperamental magpies in my backyard. Clementine reminded me that life goes by quickly, and we should soak up as much of it as we can while we are still healthy enough to do so.

I have wonderful memories of her, and I know that I'll carry those little paw prints of love with me forever. If I listen hard enough, I can almost hear her nails clicking against the tile floor. But that sound is dimming. It once followed me everywhere but now I strain to hear it. I'm afraid that one day I will forget what it ever sounded like.

And that is the story of my dear shelter dog, Clementine.

## Links

Pet Information from the US Embassy in Costa Rica: http://costarica.usembassy.gov/catsdogs.html

National Animal Health Service: www.senasa.go.cr/senasa/sitio/

# Airports *

There are two international airports in Costa Rica: Juan Santamaría International Airport and Liberia's Daniel Oduber International Airport. The Juan Santamaría airport is located near San José, and is commonly referred to as the San José airport. There is a Hampton Inn Express directly across the street that provides shuttle service. The Liberia airport is closer to the North Pacific coast, with a Hilton Garden Inn across the street that also provides shuttle service.

Flights to the San José airport are generally less expensive, but once you land, be prepared for a six-hour drive to North Pacific tourist towns like Tamarindo, Playa del Coco, or Playa Hermosa. However, the San José airport is a good choice if you are traveling to Central Pacific hotspots like Jacó, Manuel Antonio, and Dominical.

Please note: When booking a flight to the Liberia airport in Costa Rica, be aware that there is also a Liberia Airport in West Africa. This is why I keep Rob off the computer and I schedule all our flights. If he booked our trip, I can only imagine his explanation for screwing up and us landing in Africa: "It's not Costa Rica but I bet they have a two-for-one excursion to Sierra Leone. And they don't use the metric system. This is my kind of place!"

Upon arriving in Costa Rica, the plane may not taxi to a gate (this mostly happens at the Liberia airport). Consequently, you will have to walk down a flight of stairs onto the tarmac. Rob always enjoys this. I think it makes him feel like Mick Jagger. Exiting the aircraft in this manner can be difficult for those having health issues or even traveling with heavy carry-ons. Keep this in mind and let the flight attendants know ahead of time if you will require assistance.

Upon entering the airport, you'll proceed to immigration. The workers are usually very friendly and try their best to keep the lines moving. Hand them the immigration form provided by your flight attendant, as well as your passport. You should have easily filled this form out on the plane—or you could act like my sister and flip out because she couldn't find one pen in her purse. This is hard for me to imagine. My sister has three children and carries the largest purse in the Northern Hemisphere. I'm surprised it's not on wheels. She did pack Dramamine, gum, wipes, crayons, Benadryl, gummy worms, and travel Yahtzee, but alas… no pen. She eventually found a purple pencil and was reprimanded by the man sitting next to her, who said that it had to be filled out in blue or black ink. She drank wine for the remainder of the flight.

An updated passport is a must if traveling to Costa Rica. A couple of years ago, while sitting in the airport, I noticed a flustered Canadian family of five. Their flight had just landed, and immigration officials were refusing them entry into Costa Rica because their passports were expiring within six months.

- Be aware that your passport must be within six months of its expiration date upon entering the country. If not, you will be asked to leave. Trust me, this happens; I saw it with my own eyes.

My husband and I tried to help by making multiple phone calls on their behalf. I felt so awful. Here I was, someone who writes lovingly about this country, watching a nice family—one that spent thousands on this trip— get turned away. Please check your expiration date before scheduling your trip.

People have contacted me stating they were able to enter the country with a passport expiring in a couple months. This is a perfect example of "results may vary." Even if the laws have changed, it doesn't mean the immigration officer knows about it. So do what you feel is best, but if I were you, I wouldn't roll the dice on ruining your vacation over this. Plus, do you want to sit on a plane wondering if you're able to enter the country?

Let's assume your passport and paperwork are all in order and you cruise through immigration: now it's time to get your luggage. Be aware that if the baggage carousel is overcrowded with suitcases, a worker will start taking them off and putting them aside in order to make room. There were times I couldn't find my bags, only to discover that they had been piled alongside the conveyor belt. If you have an oversized bag, it may be in a totally different location. Ask someone carrying a surfboard; they will show you where to find your oversized bag, while at the same time giving tips on how to live here for just ten dollars a day. These tips may include sleeping in a van, but surfers always have a good attitude and it's fun to see a group of people so eager to get to the beach.

Going through customs is a relatively painless process. If you only have a few bags, you rarely get stopped. People with many bags are more likely to get pulled aside for inspection. As with any airport, inspectors will be searching for drugs. They are also making sure people are not trying to avoid import taxes by smuggling items into the country for resale.

Recently, a friend of ours had several suitcases crammed with five hundred pairs of socks designated for a local charity, and he was expected to pay the import tax. He was supposed to have received an exception, but apparently there was a problem with the paperwork. Who pays these taxes and who gets a free pass is determined solely by the custom agents working that day.

Another thing you may want to do is remove all price tags from your clothing before you pack. If you leave the price tags on, it may appear as if you're planning to resell the garment. Be sure to cut those tags and take new items out of their original packing.

When returning to the airport for your flight home, you'll have to pay a per person exit tax. There is a special window for this. Be sure to pay this tax before getting in line for your boarding pass. This tax is $29 but may go up by the time this book is released. After paying the exit tax, you will receive a form similar to the immigration one you had previously filled out on the plane during your inbound flight to Costa Rica. Turn the exit tax receipt over, grab a pen, and fill this out before queuing up in front of the airline counter.

This tax can be paid in advance at the Bank of Costa Rica, but it is actually quicker to do it at the airport. It is better to pay with cash or a debit card. If you pay with a credit card, it is considered a cash advance and you may receive a charge on your credit card statement (mine was ten dollars).

I learned the hard way that it is not a good idea to pay this entire tax in loose change. I tried it, thinking it was a great way to get rid of heavy coins and make a new friend in the process. As it turned out, it was a great way to get the cashier to walk away for a ten-minute coffee break while discussing what to do with the idiot who just dropped a huge bag of coins on her desk. Needless to say, no friendship bracelets were exchanged.

Now that you have gone through immigration, retrieved your bags, and made it through customs, how will you get to your resort? Navigating the tricky maze of taxis, gypsy cabs, shuttle buses, and rental cars without losing your mind is an art unto itself. In the next chapter, we'll discuss how to get you to that beachside hammock in no time.

Let's Recap:

- Planes may not take you directly to the gate.
- Your passport should not expire within six months.
- Cut off all price tags to avoid paying unnecessary import taxes.
- If you can't find your luggage, look to see if there are any bags piled alongside the conveyor belt.
- When leaving Costa Rica, there is an exit tax that should be paid before standing in line for your boarding pass.

Special Considerations:

- When leaving the country, families with small children are directed to another line before going through security. They will scrutinize the child's passport and may ask you questions. This is to prevent human trafficking and I applaud Costa Rica for doing this. You may even see signs throughout the country stating, "Our children are not for sale." We have a long way to go on this issue, but the first step is recognizing it occurs.
- Liberia airport food is expensive—*really* expensive

## Links

Hampton Inn Express Hotel across the street from the San José Airport: http://hamptoninn3.hilton.com/en/hotels/costa-rica/hampton-inn-and-suites-by-hilton-san-jose-airport-SJCAPHX/index.html

Hilton Garden Hotel across the street from the Liberia Airport: http://hiltongardeninn3.hilton.com/en/hotels/costa-rica/hilton-garden-inn-liberia-airport-SJOLAGI/index.html

# Transportation *

There is nothing more thrilling to me than walking out of the airport in a foreign country for the first time. Fun is in the air as you imagine a concierge at the curb waiting with a tropical drink. Unfortunately, this is not going to happen. Your dapper host is actually part of a mob of taxi drivers frantically trying to get your attention. Not one will be holding a piña colada, unless he's drinking it himself.

Before we talk about the taxi drivers, let's back up a minute and discuss other methods of transportation available to you. If you are a backpacker or just a bargain-lover, there is a public bus stop outside the Juan Santamaría Airport. It is located outside the terminal in front of the El Coco gas station. It's a good idea to know some Spanish because the bus driver most likely will not understand English. Make sure to ask where the bus you are boarding is headed. Although the sign may say San José, the driver may have forgotten to update it and your bus may actually be headed in the opposite direction. Liberia Airport's bus stop is about a mile away from the terminal, so plan accordingly. The weather in this area is hotter than in San José. Make sure you have water available before leaving the airport.

If public transportation is not for you, there are also private shuttle buses. Interbus is one company that services a large variety of locations such as Playa Hermosa, Tamarindo, Flamingo, Conchal, Samara, Monteverde, La Fortuna, Jacó, Manuel Antonio, and Puerto Viejo. They may even drop you off at your hotel. It is a safe option, but wait time can be extensive. These buses are often expecting passengers coming into the country on many different flights. Your bus will not depart until all of its customers have arrived. The good news is you can see these buses throughout the country and they always appear to be clean and air-conditioned.

I recently found a great option if you plan on landing at the Liberia airport. Tamarindo Transfers & Tours (aka Tamarindo Shuttle) is best known for offering the most competitive rates for airport shuttle between Tamarindo and Liberia airport. Their vehicles are clean and air conditioned. Depending on their schedule, they will also drop you off in other locations in the area. They're really nice and helpful, so send them an email before you arrive to see if they can accommodate your schedule.

If you are planning to rent a car, rental agencies have shuttles available that will take you directly to their offices. Most agencies are only a couple miles away from the airport. I enjoy renting a car since I like to travel on my own schedule and the best things are often off the beaten path. I get many emails asking which rental company is the best, and I honestly do not have an answer to that. I have heard of rental agencies charging additional insurance to people's credit cards without their knowledge. Make sure you go through the contract thoroughly and ask specifically about additional costs.

Most times tires are not covered in insurance contracts because potholes are brutal in Costa Rica. I had a friend who drove from Grecia to Dominical and blew out all four tires along the way. It's not surprising that there are many tire (*llantas* in Spanish) repair shops all around the country. Fancy spoilers with little clearance are another thing rarely covered in these insurance contracts. Also, when renting a car, or even a moving van, in any country, it is important to go over every nick and scratch on the car before you drive off. It is not uncommon to return a car and be blamed for a dent that was already there.

Before you consider any of these options, check to see if the hotel you are staying at provides transportation. I would highly recommend doing this. Even if it seems a little more expensive than a shuttle, there is nothing better than walking off a plane and seeing your ride waiting for you. It's stressful enough flying, who needs the added aggravation of figuring out how you're getting to your destination? You should be thinking about swim-up bars and dazzling lavender sunsets.

If you're not using any of the above options, perhaps a taxi will work best. Let's try to break down the taxi system in Costa Rica. It's going to be tricky, but if you follow some basic rules you should be fine.

As in most countries, there can be unlicensed gypsy cab drivers waiting at the airport. They will approach you after you leave the airport and will try to steer you to their cabs. You should avoid this. It is better to get safely to your destination than to haggle for the cheapest fare. I am not saying gypsy cab drivers are bad people. Most are just trying to make a living, but without a license there is no way to know the intentions of your driver.

A licensed taxi driver should be wearing a blue badge, dark brown pants, and a white shirt. Many drivers will approach you so be prepared! They'll be driving orange cars and working off their meters (*la Maria*). All public drivers are registered with a special code that can be found on the dashboard. You should write this number down. If you forget anything in the cab, or have a problem, you will be able to identify the vehicle you were riding in. The driver should not be asking for personal information. Do not give your passport number to any taxi driver. There are reasons your hotel may need this information, but not your cab driver.

I have had many experiences with taxi drivers. Some were good and some were bad. But you can limit your risk by following the above rules.

If you would rather not drive or deal with a taxi, there is another option: a personal driver. And I have just the guy for you.

**Links**

Interbus:  www.interbusonline.com

Tamarindo Transfers & Tours: www.tamarindoshuttle.com

Shuttle Reservations: (506) 2653-4444 or in the US at (848) 480-6096

# Your Personal Driver, Plastic Surgery & Girls Gone Wild

I was first introduced to Daniel, a personal driver, by one of my readers, Deborah. She has visited Costa Rica many times, and this trip was for a little nip and tuck. She enjoyed *Happier Than A Billionaire* so much, she wanted to treat my husband and me to dinner. We all got together at her beautiful hotel, the JW Marriott in Guanacaste.

"Just a warning. I'm a little banged up so don't freak out," she warned.

Not knowing what to expect, I imagined meeting a head-to-toe-bandaged woman sucking a liquid appetizer through a straw. Maybe even removing some of her stitches if the situation called for it. Since taking out Rob's abdominal staples after his hernia surgery, I feel confident in using my medical degree from the University of YouTube to help others.

"Are you *Happier Than A Billionaire*?" a man asked as we were walking into the hotel. "Deborah is waiting for you at the restaurant. Follow me."

He escorted us down a flight of stairs and toward three giggling women sitting at a dinner table. "You must be Nadine," Deborah hollered. One of her hands was holding ice to her bandaged face while the other was gripping a glass of wine. This was a clear sign I was in for a memorable experience.

We spent most of the evening listening to tales of plastic surgery in Costa Rica. One of the women proudly explained—in a thick southern accent—the liposuction procedure she had just received. On a side note, I love southern people. I just learned from a friend in Alabama that when a southerner says, "Bless her heart," that's not necessarily a good thing. And if they say, "Bless her *little* heart," that's a polite way of calling someone an idiot. I think this is fabulous, and much more dignified than calling someone a putz or meatball.

Deborah's friend was more than eager to tell us all about her surgery. "Sugar, they sucked the fat right out of my rear end. Shoot, if my friend had the guts to get a facelift, I wasn't going to leave there without smoothing out some of my problem areas," she explained. "They sucked out two gallons! Can you imagine that?"

"Not two gallons, two liters!" Deborah reminded her.

"Two gallons… two liters… what's the difference? I can't wait to put on my bikini."

It reminded me of the time I went on spring break and all of my girlfriends got tattoos. I chickened out. But instead of leaving with nothing, I decided on a belly button piercing.

"I don't want it to be subtle," I told Mr. Happy. (Seriously, that was the tattoo artist's name.) "Give me something that will stand out."

Mr. Happy attempted to pierce my navel two times, and each episode resulted in me passing out. However, the third time was a charm. It turns out my idea of standing out resulted in Mr. Happy taking the initiative and adorning my belly button with a scrotal ring. If you haven't had the distinct pleasure of knowing the dimensions of a scrotal ring, let me just say it is markedly bigger than your standard naval ring. It's like the hula hoop of the piercing world. Needless to say, my belly button didn't enjoy this rebellious stunt and six months later I had a raging infection. The scrotal ring was removed permanently, but for a short period in time I was that girl who went wild on spring break.

While listening to the gals tell their surgery stories, I saw the man I met earlier scrutinizing the bill, making sure we were not overcharged. The women finally explained that he was their personal driver, Daniel Campos. He is Costa Rican and has been a licensed taxi driver for years. Deborah hired him full-time to take her to and from her doctor appointments in San José. Once she recovered, Daniel drove the whole gang to Guanacaste.

The first thing I noticed was that Daniel was very attentive and was an excellent translator. "He's been wonderful," Deb said. "He's even assisting us up and down the stairs since we had the surgery."

Once she returned home, I asked Deb if she was satisfied with his service and she was kind enough to send a detailed account of her experience.

"We took the red-eye from Ft. Lauderdale to San José and arrived at 12:30 a.m. Our hotel was only three miles away, so I figured even if we got a crooked taxi driver he couldn't drive us around in circles for too long. There was a long line of cabs waiting. While I was queued up on the line, I noticed one of my girlfriends bolting away with a driver carrying her bags. I caught up to them and immediately asked the driver how much the trip would cost. He replied in English, "My name is Daniel, and my cab has a meter so you do not need to worry." I was relieved after hearing that.

"He took us directly to the hotel and the fare was only ten dollars. We had one free day before going under the knife so we thought we should book a tour or do something fun the next morning. We asked Daniel for options and he offered to take us to several places that were not too far away. He suggested La Paz Waterfall Gardens where we could see beautiful plants and animals. He also said they have a great buffet. We wanted to sleep in so we arranged for him to pick us up at 11 a.m.

"Daniel is an excellent tour guide and told us the history of the areas we were driving through. We arrived at La Paz Waterfall Gardens safely, had an excellent lunch, and walked around the grounds. After a wonderful day, Daniel drove us through the countryside.

"Daniel is from Alajuela and was excited to drive us around his hometown. We shopped at a small market and stopped for cocktails. Daniel went out and got us all coco frios for a dollar apiece.

"The next day I had my facelift. While my friend was getting liposuction performed, our other girlfriend decided to get her teeth fixed. She received six crowns. After she was finished, Daniel picked her up and took her on a tour of San José, stopping at a local restaurant—known as *sodas* in Costa Rica—for a typical Tico (nickname for Costa Ricans) lunch. It was only four dollars.

"Daniel drove us to all of our doctor appointments. Once we were well enough, he took us on a tour of the beautiful churches in Sarchi, Grecia, and Heredia. We even stopped at an allegedly haunted hotel in Grecia and tried to get the caretaker to let us in to take pictures. (No dice but Daniel tried!) Daniel made us feel right at home in Costa Rica as opposed to a fish out of water, flopping around town.

"Eventually we were well enough to take the long trip to Guanacaste. We made reservations for three nights at the JW Marriott. I had originally planned on renting a car but once we hooked up with Daniel, we decided to forgo the rental and use him as our driver for the entire week. It ended up considerably less than renting a car and it was great not having the anxiety of navigating a foreign country while bandaged and bruised.

"When we finally made it to the beautiful JW Marriott resort, we said goodbye to Daniel and retired for the night. He was prompt the next day and proceeded to take us on a tour of Tamarindo and Flamingo. We learned later that he had slept in his car by the beach fighting off mosquitoes, even waking up to a couple making whoopee on the hood of his car. After that we decided to he would sleep in the screened-in porch off our hotel room. We were really becoming attached to Daniel. He became like a long-lost Costa Rican cousin, and he was a doll to put up with us American plastic surgery dames!

"Although Daniel was not expecting or requesting to become our guest, it was our pleasure and he really made it a trip to remember. To this day I still consider him my friend.

"There was one more thing that made this trip memorable: meeting an incredibly funny and happy couple who wrote a book about following their dreams. We enjoyed great food, drinks, and too many laughs for my new-and-improved face!"

While writing this book, I found it difficult at times to suggest businesses and services. I have heard good and bad stories about personal drivers, but Deborah was very pleased with Daniel. In addition, I had a chance to see firsthand how attentive he was at the hotel. I wouldn't hesitate to contact him if you prefer to travel the country as Deborah and her friends did.

You may even go home with a new face or relieved of two *gallons* of fat.

Next Up: Costa Rican Currency. Am I rich?

**Links**

Daniel Campos:  www.facebook.com/Yoamocostarica2013

# Sloth Money

There is something about being on vacation that invokes the twelve-year-old boy in many men. (I hear you snickering at restaurants.)

"Costa Rican money is called colons?" they say while trying to figure out how to pay a bill. I can always appreciate a little gastrointestinal humor: however, the money is not colons but colones (pronounced "cologne-ez"). I like to think of it as the Chanel No. 5 of currency.

You're going to love Costa Rican money: It'll have you believing you're a millionaire. It's all champagne and caviar dreams from here on out. Unfortunately, you *will* have millions in Costa Rican currency, but it will not be enough to rent the Bellagio penthouse.

- Here is a phrase you should remember for paper currency: Take off three zeros and multiply by two.

Let's repeat that. Take off three zeros and multiply by two. That's *roughly* what your money will be worth in dollars. (Currency fluctuates weekly, so check Bank of Costa Rica's Internet site for an exact exchange rate.)

For example, if you have a bill marked 1000, take of three zeros and multiply by two. You are actually holding a $2 bill. And don't get too excited when the ATM spits out a stack of 10,000 colones. Take of three zeros and multiply by two. Each bill is only worth about $20 dollars.

Costa Rican currency comes in the following values.

Paper Currency:

1000   ($2)
5000   ($10)
10000 ($20)

20000 ($40)

• There is a different formula for coins: take the value of a coin and divide by five.

Coin Currency:

5    (1¢)
10   (2¢)
25   (5¢)
50  (10¢)
100 (20¢)
500  ($1)

It is very easy to use the bank machines in Costa Rica, and often you will be given the choice of dollars or colones. Just check with your bank to see what kind of fees will be deducted. Often, there is a minimal charge of 3% to perform an international transaction. However, it is nice to avoid waiting in line at a bank to exchange money, and the independent booths at the airport usually don't give the best rates anyway. So feel confident that your credit and ATM cards might be all you need as a tourist when traveling throughout the country.

> • Before traveling overseas, contact your bank and credit card companies and notify them about your planned trip. This will prevent them from denying an international transaction for fear the card was stolen.

Most businesses and vendors will accept a 500 colon coin as one dollar, regardless of small fluctuations in the market. Keep an eye out for the 500 colon coin. Although slightly larger, it looks like the rest of your change but it is worth roughly a dollar.

Ladies, you will need a good understanding of Costa Rican coins because you will be getting a lot of them back as change, all of which will end up in *your* pocketbook. Since I've known my husband, he unapologetically hands me not only his loose change, but anything he doesn't want to carry… which is everything. Sometimes he finds a rock—one that he thinks would look nice in our garden—and passes it to me. It's only a matter of time before he tosses me the tailpipe that is presently hanging off our car.

By the end of this trip, your purse is going to weigh fifty pounds. This is good because if someone tries to pinch your camera, you won't need those Taser shoes that Rob keeps talking about. Just swing your bag like a pendulum and smack the miscreant in the nuts. It's my plan of action if ever presented in a sticky situation. You can find me practicing this maneuver whenever I'm walking through the market. Not only is it a great crime prevention measure, but it also keeps Rob a comfortable distance away from me, thus preventing him from handing me more stuff to carry. To avoid back spasms and trips to your chiropractor, try unloading your loose change during your travels.

It can all be a little confusing, but if you remember that a 500 colón coin is worth roughly one dollar and stick with the "take off three zeros and multiply by two" rule when handling bills, you shouldn't get frazzled when paying a check.

For example, if your dinner cost 35,000 colones take off three zeros and multiply by two. The price is roughly $70. Most places will give you the colón and dollar price, but when presented with a check that has as many zeros as the national debt, just stay calm and use the above formula.

Dealing with foreign currency is always confusing. Whenever I pay a large bill (anything over $100) I ask for the clerk to write the number down for me. Many will repeat the total so fast that I still often don't understand. It's incredibly embarrassing, but mostly everyone has been very patient repeating the numbers in Spanish. It's like an episode of *Sesame Street* wherever I go.

Now that we got all the complicated stuff out of the way, let's get to the best part of all this. As we all know, Costa Rica is a happy country. How can I prove it? There are monkeys, sloths, and butterflies on the back of their bills. If there were a beauty contest for currency, Costa Rica would win. Take that, Panama.

Now that you understand Costa Rican currency, I would like you to dog-ear this page in order to make my dad happy. Or if you are reading this on an e-reader, highlight this whole sentence. Whatever you do, please don't stick it in your garage next to that other book about moving to Belize. Keep it in good shape for when you sell it at the flea market for ten cents.

Or price it in Costa Rican currency... fifty colones.

# The Roaring Twenties

When I started this adventure, I felt like I was the only one who would dare to quit the rat race. Although many of the people around me were unsatisfied in their lives, no one seemed crazy enough to do what I was about to do.

Most people said, "Come on, Nadine, everyone gets burnt out. But skipping off to a foreign country is not a good idea. You'll regret it."

I was also told, "You'll be back in a year." That one was the worst, as if I was running off to join the circus. It was rare to find anyone who said anything encouraging. At times I felt like Rob and I were alone on an island.

Since writing *Happier Than A Billionaire*, I'm contacted by many readers who share their own personal stories and dreams with me. After many emails, I found that they can usually be categorized be the person's age. Incidentally, within these age groups are defining factors such as enthusiasm, health, and energy levels. I can usually predict how the rest of an email will read once someone tells me their age.

Throughout this book are examples of these emails, and maybe you will fit into one or more of these categories. Even though many of the concerns or questions may be different than yours, there may be something that resonates with you. Everyone is looking for a happier life. Let's start with someone in their twenties:

*Dear Happier,*

*I read your book and I'm so stoked on moving there. I am twenty-two and graduating college. I don't have any money to pay for it so I decided to try something crazy. I'm attempting to barter my way to owning a house/bungalow in Costa Rica. I started four days ago with two action figures and I'm now in possession of some antique books. Hopefully the trades will keep coming.*

*Ultimately, I just want you to know that your books and blog are wonderful and I hope you keep it up for those of us who dream about living as you are!*

*Charlie*

I remember my twenties quite well. It was a carefree time full of enthusiasm, parties, and student loans. I had a lot of friends and thought the future was bright. It was as if I could do anything.

The email above is similar to many I receive from twenty-somethings who are looking for adventure. They don't see any obstacles in their path. Their energy is at its highest, as are their health and tolerance levels. They can't imagine it *not* working out.

These individuals will backpack, stay at hostels, couch surf, and do many creative things that I never considered. They want the experience so much that they don't particularly care about any potential problems, and when they hit an obstacle they simply hop over it.

"I'll deal with each worry as it comes," they say. This naiveté is something that we often lose in adulthood. As we age, we try to prevent obstacles before they occur. I've learned that a little bit of naiveté goes a long way when planning this move. In fact, planning too much may give you so much anxiety you never end up doing it.

I also get emails from this age group that express the harsh realization that they hate their profession. "I don't think I want to do this for the rest of my life," they confide.

Some might view this as irresponsible, but I see it as being honest with oneself. There is nothing wrong with questioning the road that you're headed down. Many of us have these doubts, but we fear telling anyone because of the reaction we might receive.

It was by far the hardest thing for me to admit: everything I worked for didn't make me happy. My life didn't "fit" anymore and I wanted to trade it for a different one, a life I wasn't even sure existed. The reactions weren't particularly positive when I finally told others, but I still believed that there had to be more for me in this world.

Try to remember what the twenties felt like: when it wasn't unusual for a friend to yell out "road trip" without much of a thought on the destination. All you knew was a story was about to unfold, and you wanted to play a leading role in one of the chapters.

As you continue reading this book, allow that naiveté to reemerge. Throw a little caution to the wind. Don't let the endless narrative of questions and jitters stop you from enjoying the journey. The air is full of happiness molecules, so loosen your anxiety belt a couple notches and take a deep breath. It may feel so good that you consider taking that belt off permanently.

# Part II: Where the Rubber Meets the Road

Or as we like to say in Costa Rica, where your flat tire hits the pothole.

# Costa Rica: The Original View-Master

In 1977, I was given a View-Master for Christmas; a nifty toy that made it possible for children to view 3D pictures by means of cardboard reels. It was a clunky, red model that had the characteristic toxic smell that all kids grew to love. We weren't scared of a little gene mutation in the 70s; we sniffed, licked and inserted various plastics in our mouths with a passion rarely seen outside of that generation. Heavens, we were a stupid bunch.

Some of us had a more daring palate than others. Take Herman Schmeil. He constantly sucked on the leg of an unfortunate G.I. Joe, gliding it back and forth across his mouth as one would a toothpick. Occasionally, he'd stop by the swings, pull the faded limb out of his mouth, and lean in as if he had some urgent cafeteria gossip to share with the rest of the gang. I can't remember what he said, but I always hid my *Charlie's Angels* dolls behind my back just in case he might have had a hankering for go-go boots. Back then when you lost a doll to Herman, it was gone for good.

After school, I enjoyed hiding in my closet with a flashlight, slowly inserting cardboard reels of 3-D pictures into my View-Master. There I'd get lost in my imagination: traveling by jeep to an African safari, cozying up with my friends Snoopy and Woodstock, or being magically transported onto the Tea Cup ride at Disneyland. With each downward *cha-click* of the spring-loaded handle, a new picture was revealed. I don't think there was any toy I loved more than the View-Master. The only drawback was that the pictures turned an odd shade of red overtime, making each scene appear as if it had been shot on the surface of Mars.

I bring this up because even as you drive from the airport you quickly understand why Costa Rica is the original View-Master. There are dozens of shades of greens across the mountaintops, each popping off the other as if ready to shoot into the air like fireworks. Vendors along the side of the road will have stands stacked with fruit: strange red balls with funny looking spikes shooting out, or mangos piled high with their yellowish juices bursting from their skins.

Look up! Toucans and parrots cruise over the treetops, making one feel like a welcomed guest. Each one more beautiful than the next; a 120 pack of Crayola crayons scribbled across the sky. Everything in high definition, sharper and more vivid than anything you could have imagined.

Every new place you see will feel like another reel of your View-Master. Cha-click: The peaks of ocean waves sparkle like aquatic stars. *Cha-click*: The sun sets, flooding the sky with an afterglow of pastel colors. *Cha-click*: The dark brown fur of howler monkeys freckled by little specks of leaves as they jump from branch to branch. It makes one wonder if anyplace in this world is as lovely, or if maybe it feels that way because there is more to this package than what one first sees. Spending time in Costa Rica gives you the chance to unravel some of these surprises.

One can find riches in every corner of this country. It may be at the gas station, where scarlet macaws fly overhead, or at the roadside souvenir shop, where a coati wonders around the picnic benches. None of this requires battery power or a sophisticated smartphone to enjoy. It's all there, right in front of you.

Sometimes I wish I could climb back inside that closet and tell my seven-year-old self that there are really places this spectacular and that the slides are only a small part of the world. One day I will see things that would make these 3D pictures feel like old sepia prints. I can almost hear my mother's footsteps across my bedroom floor before she opening the closet door and handed me a glass of RC Cola. Of course it was a *warm* glass of RC Cola, because back then my parents believed that ice was the catalyst to all ailments ranging from whooping cough to flat feet. I never had a cold drink until I turned seventeen. What's odd about this is that my parents always offer cool beverages to their grandchildren. Perhaps it's because the Cold War is over that they choose to celebrate with such uncharacteristic fanfare.

My mother seemed to enjoy it when I disappeared in that closet. It gave her some time to take a bath or finish reading a book. But maybe that wasn't the only reason she encouraged this. There are unspoken things most parents understand: childhood is fleeting. Flashlights and dark closets don't hold much of an appeal to a kid after the age of ten. A child's imagination fades away in such tiny increments that no one actually realizes it's gone until that View-Master is abandoned inside a box in the attic.

I've taken mental snapshots throughout my journey, and I hold these memories close. I revisit them when I'm having a particularly bad day, to remind me that there are bigger things in this world that will be here long after I'm gone. I can hear that characteristic *cha-click* as I run through my favorites, the ones that convinced me to move here. I can almost taste the salty water as Rob and I played in the waves, deciding that we were really going to do it: leave our old life for one with endless possibilities in a country we hardly knew.

We will be starting our road trip, so remember to take these quick pictures and log them away for when times get tough. Believe me, they often fix what is ailing you. And don't worry about how old this reel gets: it'll never turn red.

# Road Trip: The Central Valley

"Where is the best place to start? Is it better to live near the capital or at the beach?"

Now that you have a pocket full of funny money, let's discuss some of the more populated places to live or visit in Costa Rica. The Central Valley is a large area in the middle of the country where most of the population resides and is sometimes referred to as the Central Plateau. In reality, it is neither a valley nor a plateau, since it contains both types of landscapes. You will find the culture, climate, plants, and animals will vary greatly while traveling through this region.

This area includes the provinces of Alajuela, Heredia, San José, and Cartago. If you are a volcano lover, this is the place to be: Poás, Barva, Turrialba, and Irazú volcanoes are just a drive away.

Some of these mountain ranges are so tall and majestic you'll want to race straight to the top. The Juan Santamaría International Airport is also in the Central Valley. It's where I started my adventure and where you may be starting yours as well.

If you love the idea of living with no air conditioning or heat, this area may be right for you. It's also the best place to be near some of the best hospitals. And if you're searching for a mall, where you can simultaneously shop for a gun and spray mace into your own face like my husband did, you have a better chance here than anywhere else in the country.

- San José: Where the streets have no names

San José, the capital of Costa Rica, is about twenty minutes from the airport depending on traffic. Like most towns in Costa Rica (big and small), this bustling city has no street signs (but rumor has it they are installing some). This will probably have you scratching your head in disbelief. Directions are always a nightmare, usually starting with something like, "turn right at the blue building… I think it's still blue… or it might be yellow now." I'm not ashamed to say I've had major anxiety attacks while lost in San José. My husband, on the other hand, just eats peanuts and patiently waits for my meltdowns to end.

Instead of driving, it's a better idea to hire a taxi. A good driver can make an ordinary trip spectacular. Daniel, the taxi driver I previously mentioned, often takes tourists through San José, stopping at some of the more memorable attractions:

- The National Theatre of Costa Rica
- The National Museum of Costa Rica
- The Museum of Pre-Columbian Gold

You will probably notice stone spheres in front of museums, and throughout your travels in Costa Rica. These are considered icons of Costa Rica. Some can be as small as a few inches in diameter while others are as big as six feet. At first glance, I thought they were lawn ornaments. But this is not your typical gnome or plastic flamingo. These have major historical significance.

The spheres trace back to the Isthmo-Colombian area and are believed to have been carved between 200 BC and 1500 AD. They were initially found by workers clearing land for banana plantations. And what did the workers do when they found them? They blew them up, thinking there was gold inside!

It seemed tragic this happened until I remembered my husband telling a story about his childhood friend, Kenny O'Kelly, who filled a kiddie pool with gasoline and then tossed a fiery G.I. Joe into it. It created a mushroom cloud of flames that eventually attached itself to the side of his house. The fire department was called and he was grounded for two months. (Kenny is now a highly decorated police officer.) So it appears every generation, including Herman Schmeil's and Kenny O'Kelly's, had its share of nitwits who couldn't see the value of things.  (A 1974 Vintage G.I. Joe with Kung-Fu Grip, that was not sucked on or set afire, is now worth $300.)

No one is quite sure why the spheres were sculpted. It could have been to worship war gods or as a symbol of power. Either way, they are amazing. Costa Rica may not have the Valley of the Kings, but it does have a growing archeological presence. Take that, Egypt. Costa Rica has balls! Stone ones at that.

- Cartago

Cartago is considered one of the oldest towns in the country and was the capital until 1832. It sits at the base of the Irazú Volcano, Costa Rica's largest and highest active volcano. You can drive or hike to the top and see the Diego de la Haya crater. On a clear day, you can see both the Atlantic and Pacific oceans.

Much of Cartago was destroyed in 1732 by the eruption of Irazú Volcano. In the city's central plaza, you'll find the Santiago Apóstol Parish Ruins. It is not actually a true "ruin," but an unfinished building that was damaged in the 1910 earthquake. It's worth a visit to take some pictures and stroll around the lovely gardens.

While in Cartago, stop by the huge white cathedral, the Basílica de Nuestra Señora de Los Ángeles, where a pilgrimage occurs every year on August 2nd. According to legend, a girl found a statue of the black virgin (La Negrita) in 1635 and took it home. The next day it miraculously appeared on the same rock where it was found. This rock is now located in the cathedral. Hundreds of thousands of people come here every year to pray for miracles.

- Guayabo de Turrialba—Now this is a ruin

If you are interested in archeology, Guayabo is a must see: an archeological site located at the base of the Turrialba volcano. It dates between 1000 BC and 1400 AD and not much is known about it. It's one of the most memorable places I've visited in Costa Rica.

The site is located in a dense forest containing ancient bridges, foundations of homes, and petroglyphs that date back three thousand years. A sophisticated aqueduct system carried water throughout the city, which, was estimated to have ten thousand inhabitants at one time. But my favorite artifacts are the stone roads that lead into the forest. These roads are so well crafted, one might think they were gazing at the Roman Forum. We tend to believe civilization started with the Roman Empire while in reality, other cultures where developing their cities long before Rome ever existed.

It is truly a mystical experience to stand in these ruins and look up at the Turrialba Volcano. Since it is not yet a huge tourist attraction yet (half of it hasn't even been excavated), you will have plenty of quiet moments to reflect on what life was like in this newly unburied town.

- Grecia—You knew this was coming

If you read my first book, you already know that I started this grand Costa Rican adventure in Grecia. The reason Rob and I started there was because of the unremarkable decision to buy a car. It's probably the most unglamorous reason to move anywhere.

Grecia is well known for its many car lots. We thought we would stay in Grecia for six months and move on to the beach. But we fell in love with the town and realized there is so much to do in this part of the country. Not to mention we needed to get our driver's licenses (which you have to do at the San José facility) and start the residency process. I talk more about getting a driver's license later, but here is a fun fact:

- You must be a resident now to obtain a driver's license. Your country's driver's license is fine for 90 days and can be extended if you leave the country.

By now you know I love this town. If I write about it anymore, I fear someone will think I work for the Grecia Chamber of Commerce. But indulge me a bit more so I can tell you a few more facts about this cute town and why it is a great place to visit or live.

Grecia is unique in that it lies at the foot of a number of mountain ridges. I remember driving through the town and looking up at all those hills. I'd never considered living in the mountains before, but once in Grecia, I couldn't imagine living without these views. There are days the clouds feel so close, you can reach out and touch them.

Each ridge has a different feel, but they all have one thing in common: the higher you go, the cooler it gets. It's not rare to experience a drop in temperature of ten degrees within a fifteen-minute drive. If you would like to avoid buying a car, the bus service here is excellent on any of these ridges. You can also choose to live in town so that you can easily walk to the market and local amenities.

If you are just visiting, the metal church in the square is a great place to stop for pictures and to a take a quick stretch. It was imported from Belgium in the 1890s and is located in the center of town, surrounded by beautifully manicured gardens. Across the street is an ice cream shop. Grab a cone, sit on one of the park benches, and watch the children as they sprint around the fountain.

It's fun to watch how people interact, and it doesn't take long to notice that the pace is very different in Costa Rica. People walk slower, stop to talk to one another, and smile at you as they walk past. You'll instantly begin to feel a connection with the community. I think it's one of the things we tend to lose in a fast-paced society. We forget to stop and smile. Grecia reminded me how much I missed that. I smile a lot more now; I have to thank Costa Rica for that.

Rob and I used to drive up and down many of Grecia's mountain ranges on our scooter. One of our favorite spots was San Luis de Grecia. It is a lovely town, and the views get more spectacular the higher you go. There are a couple little places to stop for coffee at the top.

If you're in the mood for a walk and some bird-watching, you can find Bosque del Niño park at the top of the San Isidro de Grecia ridge. This is near where the kinkajou from my first book jumped onto our windowsill and scared the bejeezus out of me. You'll find this park full of wildlife, and it's a wonderful place to hike or have a picnic.

On the weekends, don't forget to check out the farmers' market across from the Judicial Building. The market is open on Friday after 3 p.m., and all day Saturday. The prices are great and it was the main reason we could live on such a tight budget. We bought most of our food there. I would frequent the same vendors and they were always nice to us. It's also a great place to work on your Spanish. It's a shame my husband told everybody there he was going to punch them instead of pay them (I taught him the wrong word for "pay," which is remarkably similar to "punch"). It may be the reason everyone was so nice to us. They must have had a fiesta when they heard we were moving to the beach.

Just like at the park, the pace at the market is slow. People stop dead center in a crowded aisle to say hello to a neighbor or a friend. They'll kiss each other on the cheek and hold up traffic behind them. Nobody huffs and puffs. It's a wonderful way to live.

- Poás Volcano

When in the Grecia area, a trip to Poás Volcano makes for a great day. Since Grecia is situated right below it, we traveled there weekly on our scooter. The higher you climb, the colder it'll get. The weather can be unpredictable, and it's important to always bring warm clothing if you are planning to visit the crater.

I can't begin to tell you how fabulous this experience can be. Imagine standing on top of the world looking down at a massive aquamarine lagoon that is steaming with sulfuric acid. And get this: it is a thousand feet deep, making it the deepest volcanic lagoon on earth. Tell that to the guy at your boss's Christmas party who bragged about his noble adventures at an all-inclusive resort in Jamaica. Once you tell people you looked down the crater of a volcano, that story about a poolside Zumba class doesn't sound quite so interesting.

Even though it looks like the most inviting swimming hole you've ever encountered, the water's pH is zero, which means there will be zero left of you if decide to swan dive into it. To the dismay of my husband, there will be no pool-hopping on this outing.

Fun Fact: Occasionally, the pressure builds up causing the steam to shoot over eight hundred feet into the air. I'm pretty sure that would scare the heck out of me, but then again, a six-inch cricket got caught in my hair this morning causing a generous display of hysterics. So really, anything can set me off.

- Park hours are from 8:00 a.m. to 3:30 p.m., but the best time to see Poás Volcano is right when it opens. At this time on most days, there will be less cloud cover. If you get one chance to visit this volcano, shoot for 8 a.m.

The entrance fee to the park is ten dollars and well worth it. The trail to the crater is paved and wheelchair accessible. The walk up feels mysterious, the vegetation so verdant it looks like the movie *Jurassic Park*. You'll come across a big plant nicknamed the Poor Man's Umbrella. It's closely related to the giant rhubarb, and its leaf is so big, it could actually be used as an umbrella. After being caught in the rain so many times up there, I can tell you from first-hand experience that it really works.

Once you're done viewing the crater, you can walk down the trail to Lake Botos. It's an extinct crater which is now a beautiful lagoon surrounded by lush vegetation. Don't be surprised to see dozens of hummingbirds darting in front of your face as you hike. Over eighty species of birds call this area their home. You'll also notice that plenty of orchids and colorful flowers brighten this path. It is truly a magical place.

Before leaving, check out the park's café and souvenir shop. It's the perfect stop for a hot cup of cocoa. They also have a large-screen projection television where you can learn about the history of the volcano and its various eruptions.

Although Poás Volcano has been relatively quiet lately, there was activity in 2009 resulting in minor "phreatic eruptions." Considering I was living at the base of this volcano at the time, you would think I would fully understand what that means. All I can say is this activity probably happened on the day I turned to Rob and said, "Is it snowing out? And what stinks?" It was the sulfuric acid erupting from the volcano, and its ash raining down upon us.

I remember riding our scooter up to Poás and feeling a sense of freedom. It was at a time when I was still unsure of the move and feared how my future would unfold. But it's amazing what a volcano can do for your disposition. Nature has a way of pulling you into its magic. It's hard to have anxiety or feel depressed when you are standing on top of a volcano.

After an excursion to Poás, you can have breakfast at one of the miradors along the mountain ridge just below the entrance. *Mirador* means balcony or viewpoint in Spanish. They're usually perched high on a ridge with stupendous views. You will come across many while driving throughout Costa Rica and I urge you to stop at one. But make sure you bring your luggage inside with you; lesson one in avoiding crime.

- La Paz Waterfall Gardens

If you still have time, another fun thing to do is to visit La Paz Waterfall Gardens. It is located on the southern side of Poás Volcano and is worth the steep admission of $36 for adults. On the way, you will drive through rolling hillsides. It's one of the reasons this area is called the Switzerland of Central America. You'll pass cows grazing in Kelly-green pastures and people selling strawberries on the roadside. The weather can be so cool and foggy it may be hard to believe that you're still in Costa Rica. On other days, it can be so sunny that you can't imagine there was ever a cloud in the sky.

La Paz Waterfall Gardens is open from 8:00 a.m. to 5:00 p.m. There are five spectacular waterfalls to see and many exhibits to explore. My favorites are the huge butterfly garden and the free-range frog exhibit. It's here where you'll see colorful leaf frogs and poisonous blue-jeans frogs. It's worth every penny.

A large aviary houses toucans, scarlet macaws, and painted buntings. If you are a bird lover, this is an excellent place to see many species. It's always more fun to observe them in the wild, but La Paz Waterfall Gardens does an excellent job of caring for these birds while making it a great experience for their visitors.

It is important to note that many of the animals at the La Paz Waterfall Gardens were donated by the MINAE, the Costa Rican Ministry of Wildlife, and were confiscated from people who held them illegally. "In many cases the animals were abused and in near death condition when we received them," heir website states. "We have rehabilitated them and combined them into sociable groups where they have become families." It's unfortunate, but these animals rely on humans and it would be too dangerous to release them into the wild.

When you are done viewing the exhibits, end your day with exploring the five waterfalls. I would suggest a decent level of fitness for this. There are metal stairs that are often wet, so it's important to watch your step. Platforms are built alongside the waterfalls and are wonderful places to stop for a picture. I think this is the only time I've ever worn a winter coat in Costa Rica. It was a cold day and we'd just come from seeing the volcano. I've been up to the area enough times to know that it can get chilly enough that a warm jacket is necessary.

If you feel like spending the night, the Peace Lodge is located inside the park. It's pricey but incredibly luxurious. It has the distinct honor of being the location where Trista and Ryan's honeymoon was filmed (stars from the television show *The Bachelorette*). A little piece of trivia that Rob says not one guy will know what I'm talking about. If you ever want to see Rob disappear for an hour, turn on *The Bachelor* or *The Bachelorette.* It's like I'm single again.

- Escazú

Whenever I'm in Escazú, the theme song from *Mary Tyler Moore Show* plays in my head. This is a happening town that feels much like many in the United States. You can get anything here. Your computer crashes? No problem, someone can fix it. You feel like eating onion rings tonight? There are plenty of fast food restaurants that you can choose from.

I call it "Little New Jersey" because there are many restaurants, fast food joints, car dealerships, and stores. Walmart and PriceSmart are a stone's throw away. Escazú even has a Starbucks. How's that for assimilating? And if you feel like you are having heart palpitations from that venti cappuccino, take a drive over to CIMA, one of the best hospitals in the country. It's all one-stop shopping here. From the looks of things, Costa Rica's economy does not appear to be slowing down. Every preconception I had about living in Costa Rica changed after a drive through Escazú.

Unfortunately, all these amenities come with a higher price tag. Rob and I couldn't afford to live here so we crossed it off our list. But if you have the budget for it, it's a great place to call home, especially if you want to feel like your life hasn't changed too much.

**Links**

San José:

- Marriott (outside San José) www.marriott.com/hotels/hotel-photos/sjocr-costa-rica-marriott-hotel-san-José/
- Intercontinental (type in San José, Costa Rica): www.ihg.com/hotels/us/en/reservation
- Best Western Costa Rica: www.bestwesterncostarica.com/

Atenas:
- Vista Atenas: www.vistaatenas.com/
- Poco Cielo Resort: www.pococieloresort.com/

Grecia:
- Mango Valley: www.mangovalley.com
- Mangifera Hostel

Poás Volcano Information:
http://en.wikipedia.org/wiki/Poás_Volcano

La Paz Waterfall Gardens: www.waterfallgardens.com

# Hostels, Buses, Sodas & Traveling on a Budget  *

People travel on all different kinds of budgets. Some desire all-inclusive resorts while others go rogue. My friend Donovan fits into the latter category. He's one of those free spirits that will stuff only the bare essentials into his backpack and head out to wherever the road may take him. If someone handed him a plane ticket to anywhere in the world, Donovan is the kind of guy that could pack in sixty seconds and jump in that person's car for a ride to the airport.

I admire this type of person who can just grab their passport and go. It's all about the journey, a new place and the chance to experience something different. Everything beyond that is icing on the cake for these folks, and maybe that is the true meaning of pura vida!

I asked Donovan to share his experiences traveling throughout Costa Rica using his method: taking public transportation, staying in hostels, eating in sodas, and getting the most out of life on a limited budget. If you're the type of traveler that doesn't mind surprises and has a go-with-the-flow attitude, this may be your perfect way of traveling throughout Costa Rica.

"I arrived at the San José airport on Tuesday, July 28, 2015. I decided to stay at La Riviera Hotel Bed & Breakfast because it looked really nice online, and they offer a free shuttle from the airport. With rooms starting at eighty-nine dollars per night, this would be the most expensive stay of my trip. If you include the free shuttle, it is still a score and it was a great place to recharge my batteries.

"On Wednesday, July 29, I took a bus to La Fortuna and what a mess! There was a transit strike. Not a score! However, keeping a positive attitude when traveling on the fly is key. I eventually made it to Arenal Volcano Lodge Hostel. At nine dollars and change per night, it was not the Ritz but not terrible either. The next morning I ate breakfast provided by the hostel at a very reasonable 2500 colones (about $5), and booked an excursion: "The Two Volcano Extreme Hike" by Red Lava Tours. The tour runs about $75 but includes a visit to the top of Chato Volcano, a swim in its beautiful green lake, lunch, two hanging bridges, Danta River Waterfall, lots of wildlife, Arenal Observatory's Museum, and sunset on their incredible observation deck as well. This was both a challenging and exhilarating hike.

"The next day I tried to find transportation to Tamarindo. Red Lava Tours came through once again with very specific details and a great combination of bus routes. One traveled from La Fortuna to San Ramón, which got me one step closer to Tamarindo. The cost was negligible, and it was a beautiful drive through winding mountain roads. After arriving in San Ramón, I took a taxi to the highway, where I would attempt to catch a direct bus to Tamarindo. I waited four hours, but it never came! I then decided to take a bus to Santa Cruz instead, and continued from there to Tamarindo via taxi. In times like this, it is important to be flexible and stay positive. It's all part of the journey.

"I arrived in Tamarindo at about eleven in the evening and was faced with the daunting task of finding a place to stay. I went first to Hostel Pura Vida, where I had stayed last year, and asked if they had a bed available. No luck. Turned out that the hostel next door, Botella de Leche, had a vacancy. They also had a pool and air-conditioned rooms which Pura Vida lacked. Score! It was around sixteen dollars. Four bucks more than Pura Vida, but worth it. I slept quite well that night. I got up the next day and had no plan except to relax, find some food, and eventually try and contact Rob and Nadine from *Happier Than A Billionaire*.

"I ended up sleeping late and then relaxing around the hostel. I found a place called La Bodega and had an early afternoon 'breakfast' for about six dollars. They proclaim to be all organic and the food was great. I then spent a good chunk of the mid- and late afternoon just hanging around the beach, shopping, and snapping photos. I caught some really nice shots on the beach, including a few nice sunset pics. You can find some of them on my Pixoto page.

"I woke up the next day and again had no real plan except to relax and find some food.

I enjoyed another meal at La Bodega organic restaurant and had a brief chat with the owner, who was originally from Texas. I ordered a plate that included Greek yogurt, organic granola, tropical fruit (banana, watermelon, pineapple, and papaya), organic bread with ginger and hibiscus jelly, and an iced green tea with mint. It was a satisfying meal that gave me energy for hanging out on the beach and taking more pictures.

"Later I found a neat little burger/sandwich shop that stays open very late, maybe even all night. I think I was there until around three a.m. Friday morning. I ate there again late on Saturday night. The cost was reasonable, but touristy Tamarindo is surely more expensive than most of the country.

"Being a devout Catholic, on Sunday I tried to go to church three different times. I saw a website that said there was Mass twice in the morning, and once at five p.m. It turned out there was no Mass on this morning at all. Someone told me there was only the five p.m. Mass, but when I got there I was told it was actually at six p.m. We all waited until about six fifteen, but no priest showed up.

"I got a ride back to my hostel with a nice woman from the Southern United States, decided to say 'pura vida,' and enjoyed a great meal under an ocean-view canopy at a restaurant called La Palapa. The prices were reasonable for Tamarindo, food was great, and the atmosphere was amazing. Later that evening I did actually hook up with Rob and Nadine. They picked me up, showed me their potential building site, treated me to dinner, and Rob and I sang 'Hotel California' during karaoke up at The Club At Mar Vista. It was a fun night, and Nadine even wrote about it on her blog.

"On Monday August 3, after my third night at La Botella de Leche Hostel , I gathered my things together and started to figure out how I would get to Manuel Antonio. I asked the lady at the hostel's front desk for some advice, and figured out that I could take the San José bus as far as Orotina. I could then get off and walk a few minutes to a different highway, where I would have to catch the southbound bus to Manuel Antonio.

"As it turned out, I got off at the wrong place and the bus to Manuel Antonio didn't stop where I was. I needed to be a few kilometers away. I jumped on another local bus, which took me to the correct stop for just around one dollar. This stop was at a roadside market where farmers were selling their goods: fruits, vegetables, honey, jellies, bread, etc. Since I had woken with a cold, I decided to buy a small jar of honey. My cold was annoying but not terrible. It was just hard to slow down with so much beauty and adventure surrounding me.

"As I was exiting the bus in Manuel Antonio, I discovered there were travelers from France getting off with me and who were also looking for a place to stay. The three of them and I walked to a couple of hostels to see if any had vacancies for the night. We found one called Vista Serena that had a private room with a twin bunk bed as well as a full-sized bed. This was perfect for the French trio and they quickly grabbed that room. Two slept in the full bed while the third took one of the bunks. They offered me the open bed in their room so their cost would be lower, and I would have a place to stay. I took that deal; everyone wins!

"On Tuesday, August 4, my annoying cold was still an issue. While everyone else went into the park, I stayed at the hostel to rest. This was one decision I regret from the trip. I was in Manuel Antonio for three days and I never saw anything except the hostel. On the plus side, it had a gorgeous view of the Pacific, two nearby markets, and a restaurant where I walked to get a casado (local dish usually containing beans, rice, salad, and your choice of chicken, fish, beef or pork). That evening there was a spectacular sunset, which I photographed from a few different vantage points. The pictures turned out great, which helped me feel a little better.

"On Wednesday, August 5, I started planning out my trip back to San José. I had the opportunity to speak with other travelers from the United States that had found a hostel in Alajuela near the airport. It was reasonably priced and had free airport drop-off. Score! I emailed them and reserved a room as well. We all got on a bus to nearby Quepos, where we would get a connection that went straight to downtown San José. Once there we grabbed a cab to Maleku Hostel, which was right across the street from the new Hospital San Rafael in Alajuela. Dorm-style rooms there start at fifteen dollars per night. Our cab ride would've been crazy expensive had there not been three of us splitting the cost. The great thing about staying in hostels is that everyone is usually helpful, and we are all there for the same reason: trying to explore Costa Rica without breaking the bank.

"On Thursday, August 6 , it was time to say goodbye to my new American travel buddies and say hello to some new ones. One was a young man from Minnesota who was on the same return flight that I was. I spent the day checking out the surrounding bits of Alajuela, walked to a Radio Shack to buy a new phone charger because mine crapped out, and found a cool little soda where I ate lunch for about six dollars.

"Later that afternoon I met up with a Facebook friend whom I've only spoken to online. She is a friendly Tica who speaks no English. We had a lot of fun despite our language barriers. Maybe that was even part of the fun! While she speaks no English, she quickly discovered my Spanish leaves a lot to be desired as well. We met at RostiPollos, a chicken joint next to the casino near the airport. With true Tica hospitality, she paid for dinner and my taxi. Arguing was futile and also kind of hard since I speak Spanish like a first-grader.

"Sadly on Friday August 7, my Costa Rican adventure came to an end. I packed up my gear, checked out of my room, and walked down the street to a nearby soda for one last casado. When I got back to the hostel, my two new American friends were there waiting for me. We all checked our luggage and decided what we should keep or leave behind. A friendly worker at the hostel helped us get transportation back to the airport.

"While I would not recommend my "Donovan" method of traveling through Costa Rica to everyone, if you are looking to save a little money, like meeting new people, can go with the flow, and have an adventurous spirit, it could work out great for you. While buses did not always show up on time, and my cold slowed me down just a little, it is a trip I will never forget. As soon as I have the chance to do it all again I will be on the next flight to Costa Rica!"

I am so thankful to Donovan for the invaluable information he has provided. If you dream of visiting this beautiful country, but feel you will never have enough money, you might contact Donovan on his very own Facebook page, entitled 365 Things To Do In Costa Rica. Maybe you too can travel on pennies a day using the Donovan Method!

## Links

Donovan Facebook: https://www.facebook.com/365CostaRica

Donovan's Pixoto Page: http://www.pixoto.com/donovantwaddle

La Riviera Hotel Bed & Breakfast: https://www.larivierahotel.com/homepage

Arenal Volcano Lodge Hostel: https://www.facebook.com/arenalvolcanohostel

Red Lava Tours: http://www.redlavatouristservicecenter.com/en/activity/37277/amazing-two-volcano-extreme-hike

Botella de Leche: http://www.labotelladeleche.com

La Bodega: http://labodegatamarindo.com/menu

La Palapa: http://www.lapalapatamarindo.com

Vista Serena: http://www.vistaserena.com

Maleku Hostel: http://www.malekuhostel.com

Happier Than A Billionaire post about meeting Donovan:
http://www.happierthanabillionaire.com/2014/08/31/panning-for-gold

# Working in Costa Rica *

Some of the most common emails I receive are over concerns about finding work in Costa Rica. "Is it easy to find work as a mechanic, hairdresser, etc.?" There are a few things you need to know before considering employment in Costa Rica.

There are only two ways to obtain legal employment here: a work permit or permanent residency. A work permit can be difficult to get since the employer must fill out extensive paperwork and there are fees involved. You can apply for permanent residency two years after fulfilling temporary residency status. A permanent residency application can take up to a year to be approved, so all in all, you can be here three years before being able to work legally for someone else.

It is possible to earn a living without permanent residency or a work permit: you can be the manager of your own business. This will legally entitle you to pull dividends from your business every week. This gets a little confusing, so I interviewed people who I knew had done this for themselves.

Tim and Kim are a married couple that own Bolas Loco Mini Golf in Tamarindo. Kim is a soft-spoken woman who used to be an investment banker. She loved her job and this made me immediately suspicious.

"I don't get it, Rob, I've never met a person who loved being an investment banker," I whisper.

"It's because she's Canadian," Rob replies. That didn't make any sense, but we have had interesting interactions with Canadians in the past. When we first moved to Costa Rica, we looked at a rental where the Canadian owner insisted that he show us the commode.

"As you can see, we have Canadian toilets," he said. He proceeded to flush the toilet while Rob and I waited for something special to happen, like the possibility that a hockey puck would

80

shoot into the air. We stood over it like two geniuses, only to determine that it flushes just like a regular toilet, which makes me believe that this guy had an uncanny affection for his crapper.

When Tim and Kim invite us over for dinner, I learn that in addition to owning the mini-golf course, Kim also runs a consulting business helping other expats navigate the red tape involved in opening their own business. She is incredibly gracious with her knowledge, describes some of the hoops you'll need to jump through, and highlights the people you will need on your side to get your business off the ground.

"The very first thing any person should do when starting a business in Costa Rica is to hire an attorney. He or she will open a new corporation for you. There are many different kinds of corporations, and your lawyer will open one that is appropriate for that specific type of business. The attorney will then register the corporation at the tax ministry, an important step that allows the owner to charge for services and pay Costa Rican taxes.

"The next step is for your attorney to apply for permits. You will absolutely need an operating permit. Depending on what kind of business it is, and if it has a restroom, you may need a health permit as well. The bathroom will also need to be handicap accessible." Apparently some businesses would rather not go through the hassle of obtaining this health permit. It's not uncommon to have to walk three stores down the street to use the toilet after dining at a restaurant.

"For example, at our mini golf we sell soda and ice cream. In order to offer these items, we needed a 'soda' health permit. We could not even get an account with Coca-Cola without one.

"Liquor permits (which we do not have) are more complicated. You used to be able to rent one for hundreds of dollars per month, but rumor has it our municipality will soon be issuing some for a much more reasonable fee. I can't be certain of this since you always hear different rumors, but this is a hopeful one."

"But what about figuring out specific tax deductions for your employees?" I ask. "This can be difficult in any country?"

"There are many things you need to know," Kim replies. "For instance, 9.3 percent of each employee's salary needs to be paid in toward CAJA, to cover social security and health care benefits. We then have to add 25 percent out of pocket toward CAJA as well. This is a big number and something you need to pay close attention to when hiring employees. We also must contribute toward workers compensation, a charge that is determined by the occupation of your employees. My employees are categorized as cashiers, but if they were construction workers or armed security guards their workers' compensation fees would be much higher."

"Another thing I would like to add," Tim interjects, "is that we also contribute to vacation pay. This is mandatory. Employees get a two-week paid vacation after working one full year. There is also a bonus that employees receive called an aquinaldo. An aquinaldo can be calculated by taking a total of the worker's salary from Dec 1 to Dec 1 and dividing it by twelve."

"What if you need to fire people?" Rob asks.

"Very complicated in Costa Rica. If an employee has worked less than 90 days, you can fire them for any reason. However, you will still need to pay a prorated portion of their vacation and aquinaldo. After 90 days, it becomes even more complicated."

"We recently needed to let someone go," Tim says. "We had just cause, so we thought we only had to pay her vacation and aquinaldo. But she fought us and in the end we had to give her severance pay as well. I would suggest business owners present employees with written warnings that they must sign when they are not performing their job properly. After several infractions, you'll have a record of your employee's job performance. This is important information if your worker should fight you in court for severance."

"I think it's wonderful you came here and are making a living. You are doing what many people dream about. What advice would you offer to someone wishing to embark on this same journey?"

"Be persistent and expect challenges. There were moments we thought we might not get over an obstacle, but we kept at it and here we are. With the right people on your side, you should be able to follow your dreams and make a living. We are perfect examples of that."

"So are you glad you left investment banking?" I ask Kim.

"You know, I liked my position and I felt like I was doing great work. But to be honest, there were days I hoped the floor would open up and swallow a few people."

I'm not as suspicious of Kim anymore, and neither she nor Tim gave us a tour of their distinguished toilet. They're my kind of Canadians.

# How to Make a Living: Mini Golf and Ice Cream  *

Now that Kim and Tim have taught us about the logistics of starting a business in Costa Rica, let's find out what they did to make their dreams become a reality.

"I loved reading your book and immediately saw my wife and me in your stories," Tim says. "We, too, wanted to change career paths and do something different. We longed for an adventure, preferably in a place that was not cold."

Canadians are funny when they mention snow or chilly weather. Their eyes go dark while describing snow drifts, white-out blizzards, and the many ways you can slide off the road and never be heard from again. Winter is a serious topic for Canucks. It's best not to complain to them about scraping any ice off your car or shoveling six inches of snow. Until you've been buried by an avalanche, you have absolutely no winter bragging rights.

"Mini golf wasn't our first idea. We were actually going to buy a stand-up paddleboarding/adventure tour business. That fell through. Our next idea was to purchase a catamaran."

"Do you guys know how to sail?" I ask.

"Uh… no," Tim replies.

Kim laughs. "It was ridiculous, but, heck, it sounded fun, so we were going to go through with it. We negotiated with the seller, and I eventually insisted he present his bookkeeping."

Tim smiles and grabs Kim's hand. "This is when things got interesting, and why I say my wife is a genius."

"So I glance over the books, which were strange since they looked hand drawn and there were many expenses that weren't listed. I had already calculated how much gas was used. The owner said he had two motors and did at least five tours a week. But that expense wasn't listed anywhere."

"Nor were many, many other expenses," Tim says. "It turns out this business just didn't have the paperwork history we needed for us to feel comfortable about going through with it. I'm thankful for her background in finance. I tend to be the dreamer, and you really need someone with their feet on the ground for things like this."

Tim and Kim are a lot like Rob and me. Considering my husband has fallen off the scooter twice, I'll take the award for having my feet on the ground while Rob's are somersaulting through the air.

Tim scratches his head and raises a finger. "I almost forgot. We also considered doing property management, but that business already sold by the time we inquired about it. I think we dodged a bullet on that one. It's something I have no interest in doing. We were really struggling, but one day while we were driving through Tamarindo I turned to my wife and said, 'You know what's missing? It's mini-golf.' "

I can't stress how many times I've heard a similar story from successful business owners. Some of their best ideas appeared when relaxed, had been here a while, and were just casually driving through an area. It often takes some time before an "ah-ha" moment. Your best chance for developing a successful business comes when you have already been living in an area long enough to understand its needs.

"So we found a piece of property, but before we bought it Kim made sure we already had the permits we would need in order to build the mini-golf business. My wife is brilliant. I'm so lucky to be married to her."

I agree with Tim, she is brilliant. He should hoist her on his shoulders and carry her throughout the mini-golf course. These are the exact qualities that are needed when you consider opening a business here: patience, perseverance, and flexibility. Kim stayed clearheaded and made sure she wasn't left holding a piece of property she could not do anything with.

"We did face challenges," Tim says. ""When we showed our two-dimensional construction plans to the builders, they were puzzled. It's hard for a Tico to envision the need for a miniature windmill.

Once we made three-dimensional plans, they slowly began understanding our vision. Finally, we made a model mini-golf course out of Play-Doh. Well, it wasn't even Play-Doh, but something Kim made in the kitchen. That's when everything fell in to place."

"What's next for you guys?" I ask.

"We started selling ice cream at the farmers' market. It's going really well and I've even sold a few ice-cream cakes in town. After looking around and realizing no one makes them here, we have found a new niche and we are exploring this new business opportunity today."

So that's the story of Kim and Tim, a lovely couple enjoying their life in Costa Rica. One golf ball and ice- cream cone at a time.

**Links**

http://www.bolaslocas.com/
https://www.facebook.com/BolasLocasMiniGolf

# Housing: The Trade-offs

"I'm not sure how to go about finding a house to rent. What towns would you suggest? And is there a big difference between living in the Central Valley as opposed to on the coast?"

So you've finally decided to sell your stuff and move to Costa Rica. Unless you want to "sleep in a van down by the river," you will need somewhere to stay. A good way to start is to come down a month before the big move for as long as you can get away. Check Craigslist, but from my experience those listings can be very expensive. They are mostly designed for short-term tenants, and the prices reflect that. I have had better luck connecting with realtors. Many not only sell houses but have a database of rentals as well. A good realtor can put you on the right track toward finding a home that's perfect for you.

I really like Brooke Bishop from Go Dutch Realty. Her expertise is in the Grecia and Atenas area. She is a nice woman from Michigan and is very honest. She knows a lot about trees, and will stop periodically in order to tell you about them. I remember asking Rob what he thought about her after we first met.

"I think she's cool," he said. "I've never met a bad person who talks that much about trees. It's a good sign."

He had an interesting response, and I can't be one hundred percent certain if this holds true in every case. But Rob lives by a different code, one that also involves never wearing flip-flops in the event you need to defend yourself. Every time I urge him to wear them, he will say something like, "I'm not going to be a fish." Whatever that means.

"Have you ever watched a guy fight while wearing them?" he asked me after I bought him a pair. "He always ends up getting decked."

"But I like flip-flops," I replied. "And we live at the beach."

"You can't run in those things! All I'm saying is it doesn't make for a fast getaway."

"Rob, we don't have a fast getaway. It takes us twenty minutes just to take the Clubs off the car and disengage all the kill switches."

"Trust me. Wear your sneakers. What if there's an earthquake? Have you ever tried to climb up a fifty-foot crevice in the earth wearing flip-flops?"

Rob enjoys sharing these life lessons with me at least three times a week. It reinforces how much he cares for me, while at the same time filling me with intoxicating paranoia when choosing footwear.

I'm not sure how Brooke feels about flip-flops, but she can help point you in the right direction when looking for housing. There are many options: apartments within houses, houses, and even guesthouses behind those houses. What is important is that it fits your needs.

The best deals often are down the worst roads. It's a trade-off, but not too bad if you have a decent vehicle. We'll talk more about this later, but four-wheel drive comes in handy for many reasons.

It's surprising that even on some of the worst roads there are bus stops. If you are not planning on buying a car, you will still be able to get into town. It *is* possible to live here without ever purchasing a vehicle.

When Darlene and Frankie built their house, they chose a lot near a bus stop for two reasons: if they had to rent out the house it would be attractive to people without a car. And they would also have access to transportation if for any reason they couldn't drive anymore.

As I previously mentioned about Craigslist, you will find that some rentals are more expensive because they are for short-term tenants. It is possible to meet with these landlords and try to haggle for a better deal if you sign a one-year lease. It never hurts to negotiate. Just ask Rob: while at the car dealership, he negotiated our $12,000 Mitsubishi Montero all the way down to $12,000. The stench of failure still lingers in the backseat.

Rent fluctuates widely throughout the country. In Grecia, the rents range from $300/month to $2,000/month. Some have views that are amazing. Others are downwind from chicken farms. Results will vary, but for some this area is paradise. I call Brooke and ask her why she enjoys working here.

"I love it," Brooke replies. "The best thing about this area is the climate; no air conditioning or heat are needed. The temperature is always perfect in my house."

I have to agree with Brooke. It's an incredible feeling as you walk from inside to outside your home and experience no temperature change at all. It's usually constant until October rolls around; this is the height of the rainy season. It can pour every day for the entire month. But it's a small inconvenience since the dry season is right around the corner.

"Another great thing about this area is the proximity to the airport and San José," she continues. "Both are less than an hour away. In Grecia, you can pretty much get anything you need: fresh mozzarella, meats, and one of the best farmers' markets in the area. I also think it is worth mentioning the smaller towns next to Grecia: Naranjo, Sarchi, Palmares, and Atenas. They are all fun places to visit, go out to eat, and poke around in the shops, all while not dealing with too much traffic."

- Atenas

Atenas is about a half hour from Grecia and also has a fantastic farmers' market. We used to drive through this town on our scooter and stop at a mirador to order breakfast. The temperatures are a little warmer here, but some people prefer that over the cooler temperatures of the mountains.

- Fun Fact: Rumor has it that *National Geographic* once announced Atenas as having the best climate in the world.

Atenas has fantastic homes on mountain ridges and stunning estates in town. What's nice about living here is that you are very close to the Autopista del Sol Highway, a highway that originates near San José and ends in Orotina. It makes for a quicker drive to the southern Pacific beaches. The tolls on this road are the highest in Costa Rica and can be upwards of three to four dollars. It doesn't bother me since the last time I visited the United States, it cost me $28 to drive from New Jersey into Brooklyn.

Some problems were reported when the Autopista del Sol Highway first opened. Commuters witnessed mudslides and sharp curves that were extremely dangerous. But a phone call was made to Spain, the country that built it, and they have since returned to fix it. I wish I'd been there for that conversation.

"Atenas is loaded with expats so it's great to assimilate," Brooke says. "There are lots of property managers, which can be very helpful if you are planning to purchase real estate but cannot be here year-round. The new road to Escazú makes it is easy to get to San José within thirty minutes."

Starting your relocation process closer to San José has many benefits. As I mentioned, it is easier when starting your residency process. Having immigration only an hour away is a real plus since you will most likely be making more visits to this office than you ever anticipated. On a recent attempt to get my cedula (residency card) renewed, due to a small glitch in my paperwork they wouldn't mail it to the Tamarindo Post Office. It was six-hour drive to immigration to get things cleared up, and a tiring six-hour drive back. How I wished I was still living in Grecia during that trip.

- Nothing says I love you like an oxcart—Sarchi

Sarchi is the home of one of the biggest oxcart manufacturers in Costa Rica. It's fun to stop by the town center in order to view the huge, colorful ones on display. Oxcarts used to be the only means of transporting coffee beans across the country. Like having a well-engineered car today, it was important then to have a well-crafted oxcart. Painting them served an important purpose. Each region had their own design so one could identity where the driver was coming from by the pattern on his wheels. It gives one a nostalgic feeling to see so many here still using these carts to transport things short distances today.

Located a short distance from Grecia, Sarchi is the home to many artists. One can find an assortment of beautiful souvenirs here. Even though we lived in a furnished home, we could not resist buying rocking chairs made in Sarchi. Each one is unique. They are made from high quality wood, and the seats are made from strips of leather with intricate designs embossed into them. Chances are you have seen these chairs for sale at the airport if you visited Costa Rica.

"I love the listings I have in Sarchi," Brooke says. "What I like most is that it is a really quiet town. You almost never have traffic or lines at the bank, and the Sarchi Botanical Gardens are fun to explore. If you are looking in Sarchi, I would suggest you consider Naranjo as well. I don't have as many listings there, but it's a wonderful coffee town with less expats. The people are very friendly and there are plenty of stores in town to keep you busy.

"Not only is it incredibly beautiful, the Ticos here are the best. They are also more likely to understand and speak English. Most of the older Ticos in Naranajo are or were farmers. People here acknowledge that education is the key to a better life. My husband comes from a family with lots of brothers and sisters. Families are becoming smaller today and there seems to be a shift away from farming and toward professions requiring a college degree."

- San Ramón

Another area to consider is San Ramón. The weather can be cooler and rainier, but that depends on your exact location. It is a half hour northwest of Grecia and has a bustling city with many stores and amenities. It also has a MOPT facility where you can renew your driver's license. This is the place where the electricity went out right as a worker was about to enter our new driver's license identification numbers into the computer. The man wrote them down in a black-and-white composition book (the kind we had in elementary school) and said he would take care of it when the lights came back on. Apparently, he never got around to it since Rob was recently reprimanded for carrying an illegal license. So even when renewing your driver's license… results may vary.

Another thing that is awesome about San Ramón is that it is only 1 1/2 hours away from Arenal Volcano. If you are driving from San José, you'll travel straight through San Ramón to get to the volcano. It's such a lovely ride, with air so fresh and clouds so low, you'll want to get out of the car just to feel the condensation on your face.

"San Ramón is cooler, rainier and less expensive," Brooke describes. "Inexpensive houses with ocean views can be had. Some are on rough roads, others are tucked away in the cloud forest, but the ones with the best climate are just outside town."

When renting a place, here are some things to ask:

- Can I flush my toilet paper? (We will discuss plumbing a little later. I'll surely win a Pulitzer Prize for my exceptional sewer-pipe reporting.)
- Is there a phone line?
- Is cell reception available?
- Has the house ever been broken into? (This doesn't necessarily mean you shouldn't move in, because many times this can happen when a house is left empty. However, this should put you on alert.)

- Is the water reliable? Is it well water or city water?
- What is the monthly water bill? (In Grecia it was negligible; in Guanacaste it can be $100 a month depending on what development you live in.)
- Where do I dispose of my garbage?
- Has there been a mold problem?
- Is there earthquake damage to be concerned about?
- 10. If the house is within a development, who is responsible for maintaining the road? (If you're looking at a road in the dry season, it may look incredibly different in the rainy season. This is important because you might need a four-wheel drive to live there.)
- 11. Who are the neighbors? Do they own roosters or run a chicken farm? (I bring this up because I received an email from a man who moved here based on my first book and found himself living next door to a rooster that woke him up every morning at 4 a.m. He was not a happy camper.)
- 12. If you are living in an agricultural community, how close is the nearest farm? (There is a time of year farmers fertilize their land and this creates a black fly issue. Remember the scene from *Amityville Horror*? It can get that bad.
- 13. What is the elevation? It may be most important of all to consider the elevation of the home, especially if you are visiting the house during the dry season. In the rainy season it may be humid and this can damage some of your possessions. I've seen guitar necks warp and electronics fail due to the weather. Some of these things are unavoidable but worth considering if you are shipping down a lot of these expensive items. On some ridges, just a few hundred meters in elevation can make a huge difference.

These are all things to think about but are not game changers by any means. I was very content living on top of a mountain, even as the clouds rolled through, creating a carpet of mold. I watched electrical storms blow up appliance after appliance and was still happier than I've ever been. Random kinkajous came to visit, packs of coatis walked through my garden, and birds greeted me each morning with a melody of songs. It was magical and even though I didn't have all the conveniences that I did in the States, I've never lived better.

But what if you don't want to live in the Central Valley? What if the roar of the surf is calling you? Let's see what Randy Toltz has to say about living at the beach.

**Links**

Brooke Bishop: brooke@godutchrealty.com
www.godutchrealty.com

# Living at the Beach

"Is life really so different when you live at the beach as compared to in the Central Valley?"

It was a real shock for us when we moved from Grecia to the North Pacific coast. At times Guanacaste feels a little like the Wild West. There are more dusty roads with cattle running through the streets, and it's a rare day that I find everything working properly in my house. Right now my Internet is down, my oven just dropped dead while cooking a frozen pizza, and a toxic smell lingers throughout the house after one of our air conditioning units exploded. If you tried to complain to anyone who lives in this area about these problems, they would remind you that you are actually having a pretty good day. My life seems to rotate around finding the right person to fix one thing or the other.

But I think the biggest surprise to us was how much more things cost on the coast. Let's take groceries, for example. Since it requires more gas to get them here, they are about 10% to 15% more expensive. Although there are several small produce markets, they do not compare to the enormous farmers' market we had in Grecia.

The good news is that there is an Automercado located outside Tamarindo. I like to call this the Neimen Marcus of grocery shopping. I can usually find what I need, but it is very, very expensive. This is the *only* place I can buy dishwasher detergent. The last time I checked the price was $12 a box. Rob thinks this is a practical expense since it keeps me from screaming at him for never, ever washing a dish. I've concluded my husband will pay any amount of money to stop me from nagging him.

This is also the same store where my mom and dad had the infamous fight over half-and-half. My mother wanted it, not caring how much it cost, while my father thought it was an abomination to pay that kind of money for coffee creamer. Much to his dismay, my mother won the fight. After that argument, it was a real blast having them visit for a month. Especially when I reached for the half-and-half, and my dad loomed over my shoulder like I'd just lifted his bankcard. But no offense was taken since I'd probably do the same to him if he reached for my dishwasher detergent.

Another thing to consider while living at the beach is that you'll probably need to use air conditioning for some part of the day. If there is a breeze, you can get away without it. My friend Randy, a realtor in Brasilito, lives right on the beach. He doesn't need as much air conditioning because he gets a cool breeze off the ocean. I'm more inland, and I rarely get a gust of wind strong enough to cool off the house during most of the year. There are months our electric bill can be upwards of $300. It can go even higher in the dry season. In Grecia, the monthly bill was rarely over $50. Adding to the bill is our refrigerator; it never stops running. I'm sure that we are wasting a ton of money on this one malfunctioning appliance.

So why would you want to move to the beach after knowing all of this? Because it's like living within the pages of *National Geographic*. I wake up to the sound of howler monkeys outside my window, and dozens of species of birds perch themselves on branches in my backyard. Most of my best wildlife photographs come straight from my terrace. Every morning brings something new and spectacular.

The Costa Rican coast is a playground for both young and old. It's a place to gather your friends together and hunt for a new snorkeling spot. Or if the tide is right, go kayaking and follow the manta rays as they jump in and out of the ocean. However, nothing beats sitting on the beach and watching the pastel sky slowly disappear as the sun sets. You can easily fall in love here and never return home. In fact, I've met plenty of people who have done exactly that.

Rents vary quite a bit in this area. There are incredible houses that rent for over $2,000 a month, and smaller houses that rent for only a couple hundred dollars. The longer I live here the more great deals I find.

I had the opportunity to meet up with Randy Toltz and ask him why he relocated to this part of the country and what kind of housing is available around town.

"Before I start, you're never going to believe the morning I had. I went to the bank to pay the fee so that I can renew my driver's license. They said I couldn't renew it because I first had to pay a moving violations ticket."

"So?" I ask. "Just pay it."

"That's the problem. When they look up the ticket, it says zero colones. There is no such thing as paying a "zero colones" ticket. So I need to get that off my record before I can renew my license."

"You don't owe anything, but you still can't get your license? What are you going to do now?"

"I have no clue, Nadine. I've been on the phone all morning and can't get it fixed. It's driving me nuts."

It's now I notice Randy scratching his head, hard, the universal sign for knowing that a small errand, something that should have taken just fifteen minutes of your time, will now require a week or two to resolve. If you see an expat with his face buried in his hands, that means the problem will most likely take a month to fix. There is no comforting word that can ease that kind of pain.

"Okay. Enough about my license. To answer your question, I came to this area because of the weather," he says. "I'm a beach guy, and I like how close we are to Liberia Airport. We have access to over fifteen beaches within a half-hour drive! Each one is different: one may be good for surfing while another is great for paddleboarding. At the same time, we're only two hours away from cloud forests and thick jungles.

"I also enjoy our diverse community: families, schools, activities, sports, even fantasy football leagues. I've lived, worked and traveled in every part of Central America. Of all those places, I like this the best.

"Depending on your finances, there are many options. You can rent or buy. There are condominiums, houses, lots, farms, and even ranch properties suitable for horses. If you want an ocean view, we have that here as well.

"When I first came down I bought a condo one block off the beach for $22,000. It needed work but was livable. Just like in the States, you can find fixer-uppers. But you have to be careful because not everything you see here is as it appears. One of my jobs is telling people what to avoid. Local knowledge goes a long way.

"If you're buying property here, the first thing I would ask is what is its main purpose? Don't get sucked into the romance. Think about the investment. If you are not here all the time, what can it be rented for? I try to encourage people to consider homes that are easier to rent. If you do it right, you'll have a free place to stay when you come to visit."

Randy makes many good points. Part of being a good realtor is telling you what you should avoid. It's true when he says, "not everything you see here is as it appears."

After reading *Happier Than A Billionaire: The Sequel*, you probably already know that my rent is $150 a month. I was sure that our idea of moving from Grecia to the beach was going to break the bank. But Rob insisted we would find something affordable. Boy, did I underestimate his determination.

We were lucky enough to meet a nice couple who needed someone trustworthy to take care of their home while they were back in the United States. I can't express just how lucky we were to get a deal like this. It feels like we won the lottery. In return for their generosity, we treat the house as if it is our own. When there is a problem, we fix it. Rob is even planting bougainvillea bushes, and banana and mango trees in their backyard. I wake up every day feeling like I'm living in a Sandals resort.

Can you negotiate a deal like ours? I get this question a lot. I do know other people who have similar arrangements. It all depends on how long you have lived here and what kind of rapport you have with the landlords. They are trusting you with one of their biggest investments and don't want to end up with a deadbeat tenant.

The chances of getting a deal like this are better once you have your feet on the ground. It may be possible to arrange a deal with a landlord over the Internet, but there is something to be said for the power of a face-to-face encounter. My husband's determination is proof that you can make anything happen once you put your mind to it.

**Links**

Randy Toltz:
U.S (303) 719-0624
Costa Rica Cell 8705-2436
Email: rantol@me.com
www.adjustyourlatitude.com

# The Pensive Thirties or Why My Wife Won't Do It

"I'm thirty-five and feeling like I need to make a move. I work all day and rarely see my kids, and my wife is always on me about not doing enough with the family. I can't imagine doing this for another thirty years. I told my wife that perhaps we should consider a move to Costa Rica but she is one hundred percent against it. The kids need to finish school. Is there anything I can say to change her mind?"

Greg

My inbox is full of these types of emails, and they take me right back to when I was working. Sometimes they are hard to read because they remind me of the pit in my stomach I lived with for so many years. I believe many of us reach this point in our careers when we don't want to do it anymore. We just want to return to a simpler life.

Men in their thirties usually want to bail, but women are more concerned about their kids. I don't blame them. There is so much more to this move than just selling your things when children are involved. How much are private English-speaking schools? Will the kids assimilate to a totally different culture? Will they adjust to the new diet? Like I said, there is a lot to consider.

The thirties are a critical time in our careers. We are healthy enough to work crazy hours and can give a lot of energy to our employer. Of course, that usually means not being home as much. We tend to sacrifice time with our family in order to provide them with a better life. I was on the same road until my flame burnt out.

I felt this happening to my husband and me after too many hours at work and years of stress. I began looking closer at my life and realized that all the stuff I had accumulated didn't actually make me any happier. It wasn't easy for me to admit, but it was true. I found myself in a strange position: wanting less while having more. But it was also around that time I realized I had the power to change my life. I just had to figure out where to start.

I had to make crucial decisions about what was important to me. Was it a bigger house and a new car? Or did it make more sense to cut back on possessions and start planning for a simpler future? You will be amazed how much you can save when you have a goal. What's great about our thirties is we still have time to save and make huge changes in our lives. Having that in the back of your mind can help you get through those tough days at work.

As for moving here with children, it is not as impossible as it might seem. There are private English-speaking schools that are accredited. Many of these children then go off to incredible colleges. The best thing to do is come for a visit and talk with other families.

A few weeks ago I met a thirty-something from New Jersey who just purchased a condominium and plans to spend a couple months out of the year in Costa Rica. In the future, he's hoping to spend even more time, but he has two young children and understands that there is so much more involved in this decision than when I moved. His wife, Lauren, is on board so I thought it would be interesting to hear her thoughts on why she would even consider owning a condominium here while raising two children.

"For me, the desire to move is less of a hope for a new adventure and more of a hope for a better way of life," Lauren says. "Living in the States, I find myself continually annoyed, angry, stressed, and overwhelmed. When I'm driving if the person in front of me is going less than five miles over the speed limit I want to smack them. George Carlin said it best… at least I think it was Carlin… he said something like, "Did you ever notice that anyone driving faster than you is a maniac and anyone going slower is an idiot?" (Love that!).

"If I drop something I get pissed and want to kick it across the room. My three-year- old has started sighing and groaning in anger, and I realize he learned it from me. We sound like Marge Simpson over here. It's not healthy, physically or emotionally, to be mad all the time. To be wishing the day away, every day. To be waiting for when things will be better, easier, for when we'll be happier.

"I want to find happiness in smaller things, to relearn how to appreciate the little things I overlook now, things that I should cherish, like my kids' youth, or things that just seem to get in my way. We used to have tons of plants in our house… I loved the way live plants looked, but now we only have two real plants (with a bunch of dead leaves) and a bunch of fake ones. Real plants got annoying… had to water them, prune them, etc. *Plants* became annoying to me. They got in my way of getting to what needed to be done (i.e. taking care of the kids). When you're annoyed by your plants, it's time to do a one-eighty.

"I can see how some mothers get so wrapped up in the motherhood role that they lose the part of themselves that craves adventure. I think some squash it down because they expect that they'll have time later. I think others think they don't deserve it. They believe that adventure for themselves equals putting their children second, and yes, sometimes that is the case but not always.

"I think we can do this, but it may not be right for everyone. It takes a lot of thought and planning to do it in a way that benefits the entire family. I chose to have kids, and it wouldn't be fair not to put them first. But, it doesn't have to be to my detriment. We can find a way to create a better lifestyle for all of us. I still don't know if Costa Rica is the answer, but I know that my huffing and sighing and kicking toys across the room is not the behavior I want my kids to see, because I hate seeing it in myself. I'd love to be able to tap into my happier self, and I know I need to find a way to get a new perspective in order to achieve that."

I'm sure many of us can relate to Lauren's story. It's hard to acknowledge the traits we dislike in ourselves. It's easy to get wrapped up in our environment, even when it is one that is making us sick. In my own way, I, too, wanted to stop kicking the toys across the room.

Many times it's the right decision to put others before yourself. I don't want anyone to get the impression that it's a good idea to flake out on your family. It will never bring you the happiness you're seeking. But if we remember the freedom we had in our twenties, and combine it with the ability to plan for the future, it can make for a better, happier self.

There is nothing wrong with climbing into bed and telling your wife she did a great job today. Then discuss all the wonderful places you'll take her when the time is right. Never give up on your dreams, but dreams are a lot sweeter when the people you love are on board.

# Education

"I would love to move to Costa Rica, but I have two children in elementary school and one starting high school. Are there any schools in your area? Will I have to homeschool?"

It's a difficult decision to move to a foreign country, and it must be doubly difficult when you have children. I have friends who homeschool, using accredited online curriculums to ensure their children are getting a proper education. It is possible to send your child to a Costa Rican public school as well, but the lessons are in Spanish and they follow this country's accreditation standards. This could result in complications down the line if you plan on moving back to your home country.

Another option is enrolling in a private school. My girlfriend, Kim Toltz, sends her son to La Paz Community School in Brasilito. She is very happy with their curriculum and finds the environment very nurturing. It's also the same school where my friend Sandy works, and she suggests I talk with Abel McClennon.

"Abel is not only a teacher but also the school director. He's amazing and I think after speaking with him you'll have lots of great information to share," she says.

"Thanks. By the way, how is your car running?" We recently had a funeral for Sandy's car before dumping the corpse off at Claus's garage. He said there was a slight chance he could revive it by rebuilding the engine. At this point, I'm pretty sure everything in Sandy's car has been rebuilt. It's like the bionic man, but without bionic parts.

"It's not blowing blue smoke anymore," she laughs. Tragically, this may be the best news you'll get when it comes to car repairs in Costa Rica.

This morning I head out to La Paz Community School, a cute campus at the base of the Mar Vista Development. It's surrounded by beautiful landscaping and has a welcoming feel. I like it already.

A man walks toward me and introduces himself. "Hi, Nadine, it's nice to meet you. I'm Abel." Abel is younger than I thought. For some reason, I was expecting a hunched-over, gray-haired school administrator. Abel is the exact opposite with thick, dark hair, an athletic build, and green eyes that turn a shade of aquamarine when he gets excited. "I know you have some questions, but before we start, let me show you around." We walk through the campus and I discover that it's much bigger than it originally appeared.

"What are you building?" I ask, pointing to a construction site.

"I'm so excited about this. We are expanding our classrooms so we can meet the needs of the community. We already have an eight-thousand-square-foot fully equipped, purpose-built high school, a two-thousand-square-foot locker room with showers, fifteen hundred square feet of office space, and a beautiful soccer field. This new addition will provide an additional nine-thousand-square-foot primary school with a library, art room, and music room. Someone donated solar panels and they will be installed next week."

"Are all the classrooms on this campus?"

"Three through twelve are right here on site. Pre-K through second grades are located right down the street. Our kindergarten is full-day, and we have a wonderful area for the kids to play at recess that includes a big basketball gym and a yoga studio. We serve roughly two hundred and seventy-five students from twenty-seven different countries. At any given time you can hear eight to ten languages at once! I like to call it Destination Education."

"I love that. I'm sure it makes for a unique learning experience."

"I truly enjoy working here. Our class size is about fifteen to twenty-five students and our calendar runs year-round with breaks every three months. Classrooms are air-conditioned, and school starts at eight and ends at three, but some stay longer for afterschool activities. We have sports programs, with surfing and soccer being the most popular. We play against local schools, and the kids really enjoy it."

"Are school uniforms required?"

"Yes, students wear uniforms. It makes everyone feel included. We strive for a bilingual education. Having a complete grasp of Spanish as well as the English language is very important to us. There are currently scholarship programs for children from the local community. Right now the school demographic is forty percent local Costa Rican children and sixty percent expatriates. Our goal is for the student body to be made up of fifty percent of each. This is an inclusive school. That is very important to me."

"What would you say to a parent that's trying to find the right school for their children in Costa Rica?" I ask.

"It's best to ask the families that attend them. There are plenty of people in the area who will be happy to share their experiences with you. Call the school up and ask for a tour. I'm always happy to meet parents, show them around, and introduce them to our certified teachers."

"What about college? One of the biggest questions people ask is whether or not their children will get accepted to a university."

"We are an International Baccalaureate-accredited world school. Graduating seniors will have the opportunity to attend top universities. The students enjoy a unique experience growing up in Costa Rica, and their college application essays really stand out from the rest. Some of our recent graduates went on to the University of Florida, University of Colorado, American University of Paris, Stenden University-Holland, and the University of Costa Rica... to name a few."

La Paz Community School provides a lot for its students, but what impresses me most is how animated Abel becomes when describing the facility. He moves his hands around as he talks, and gets excited when discussing upcoming projects. The light in his eyes is warmly familiar: my mother is a retired schoolteacher, and her eyes still sparkle when talking about curriculum or children.

Abel is passionate about his work, this school, and his life in Costa Rica. He has children of his own and wants them to grow up in a nurturing community, one that includes every child. The best teachers are like Abel, ones that are committed to the present, but always reaching into the future.

La Paz is not the only private school in the area. Costa Rica International Academy is another popular one that is worth investigating. Ask for a tour of their campus. Every school offers something different, and I'm sure you'll find the one that best fits your child.

When I asked my friend Kim how she felt about her big move to Costa Rica, along with sending her son to a new school, she said something that really resonated with me.

"A couple weeks after moving to Costa Rica, my son said, 'Mom, we have so much more time here.' I never realized just how much time you lose with your family when you are living a ridiculously busy lifestyle. There were days in Colorado when I felt like all I did was drive one child to sports practice only to then drive another child to a music lesson. It's a pace that is hard to break, but here it's totally different. Strong family bonds and time spent with each other are a priority in Costa Rica. We are all so much closer now, and I think that's what I love the most about living here."

Someone once said that time is God's currency. If that's the case, then Costa Rica may be one of the richest countries in the world.

### Links

To find out more about the La Paz campus, tuition, and staff please check out their Facebook and/or webpage.
www.facebook.com/LaPazCommunitySchool
www.lapazschool.org/

# Landlines, Internet & Cell Phones

Things have changed a lot over the past few years in regards to phone and Internet service. However, some things have stayed the same. If your home does not have one already, it is still difficult to get a landline phone connection. I have friends who built houses over five years ago and are still waiting for one. My friend Sandy actually threw herself in front of a phone company truck, pleading with the workers to install a line. They didn't. But they also didn't run her over, so in the end it turned out to be a good day.

Fortunately, the houses I have rented over the years always had a landline. What makes this such a score is that I enjoy pretty good DSL Internet speeds. These speeds would probably make the average Internet junkie laugh (up to 1.5 Mbps), but it is fast enough to upload photos, use Skype, and stream video. The speed fluctuates a lot during the day, but overall I can't complain... when it's working. As I write this, our Internet service is down and has been for the past week. A lightning storm blew out the modem and I have been waiting every day for the phone company to replace it.

If you live in an area where they offer cable service (CableTica or Amnet), you can get Internet through them as well. I found that my friends who have cable service get the fastest Internet connections in Costa Rica. There are even some local wifi providers, like CRWiFi. Sandy just signed up with them and says her speed is excellent. Costa Rica may be years away from resembling Silicon Valley, but I can confidently say that technology is improving here.

One of people's biggest concerns about moving abroad is being able to stay in contact with friends and family back home. Skype is an excellent way to achieve this. It is a free program easily downloaded onto your computer. You can video chat for free or make low cost international phone calls using their prepaid service. It is amazing how much less my phone bill is today compared to when I first moved to Costa Rica.

The only bad news about Skype is that I had to teach my parents how to use it. It went over about as well as teaching them how to replace their empty printer ink cartridge. To this day, I still receive Skype calls from them with no video and/or audio. And if they are lucky enough to figure that out, I get to see my father sticking his pupil one inch from the camera in order to make sure I can see him. So basically, I'm talking to an eyeball for twenty minutes.

My landline phone bill cost between $26 and $32 a month. That includes high-speed Internet. It also includes the many days that it simply doesn't work. Don't try to haggle with the Costa Rican phone company, ICE (pronounced *ee-say*) about this. Just pay your bill and move on. Believe me, I've sat behind people complaining about the outages and it doesn't get them anywhere. Plus, did you really move here to sit in a government building for half a day? Pick your battles; this one is not worth the fight.

If you don't have a phone, you can get Internet using a USB stick. Just drop by any ICE office and ask for one. And while you are there, you might as well pick up a prepaid SIM card for your cell phone. (This is going to be one-stop shopping, folks. You've already saved ten dollars in gas doing this.)

In the back of many phones there is a tiny chip called a SIM. You will need one of these chips in order to obtain cell phone service from ICE. The existing SIM card that comes with your phone will need to be switched out with one that you purchase here. This will give you a Costa Rican phone number. It's all very simple.

- If you are bringing a phone with you into Costa Rica, be aware that your telephone plan usually does not work here, but they may still charge you fees for roaming service. Shut this feature off your smartphone before leaving the airport.
- You will need to have ICE replace the existing SIM card with one that you purchase from ICE. You must

also make sure your phone is unlocked before arriving in Costa Rica. While still in the States, take your phone to your provider to properly unlock it.

Now that you've made sure your phone is unlocked and that it is a brand that will take a SIM card (most smart phones do), hand it over to ICE and they will insert a new SIM card. You can get a card that is prepaid, or you subscribe for a monthly bill. The last SIM card I bought was four dollars and it included a bunch of minutes. It is a prepaid plan, so every couple months I add another five to ten dollars to it. This can be paid at any grocery store, as well as at ICE.

You are not charged for incoming calls. The outgoing calls cost 5 to 7 cents a minute. An outgoing domestic text message is about half a cent. It's super cheap and makes for an affordable way to contact people within Costa Rica, but an international text message costs close to 15 cents.

- When calling to Costa Rica from another country, dial the country code (011) then the area code (506), then the rest of the number. I will assume you are calling the contacts in this book while in Costa Rica, so I left off 011-506 before each phone number.
- When a phone number starts with a 2, that means it is a landline. If it starts with an 8, then it is a cell number.

Just in case you forgot to bring a phone, you can buy one down here. They do sell smart phones in Costa Rica but they are very expensive—80% more expensive. If your budget is tight, consider a $30 or $40 prepaid phone. We have one of these and it works fine. They don't sell them at ICE, but there is usually a store right around the corner that does. These places can even install the SIM card and activate it for you as well. Going this route can help you avoid ICE all together. I just need to warn you: don't be surprised by what your new, cheap cell phone will look like. It's a serious technological buzz kill.

If I had to describe one, I would say to envision a Barbie phone. Now imagine something even worse than that. You got it; you're going to walk around with a phone that looks like it's made out of LEGOS. It's especially funny when my husband is using it.

So now you have a cell phone and a USB stick for the Internet. Maybe you will be lucky enough to have a landline phone in your house. Things are looking up. You have conquered some of the tasks that you need to tackle when first moving here.

The next thing we should do is look for a vehicle because you don't want to keep that rental car forever. I hope you're wearing clean underwear.

**Links**

Emergency Numbers

911:  Any Emergency
117:  Police
118:  Fire
113:  Directory assistance

ICE website:  www.grupoice.com/wps/portal/

Costa Rica WiFi: www.crwifi.com

# Buying a Car

"Should I buy a car or ship mine down? If I do decide to purchase one, what type would you suggest?"

Cars are very expensive in Costa Rica. We paid $12,000 for a used Mitsubishi Montero that would have cost $6,000 in the States. I write about this experience in my first book, but for those who are unfamiliar with this escapade I'll quickly break down what happened and why Rob's favorite hiding space is his underwear.

Once we decided on the car we were going to purchase, the owner of the dealership wanted us to deposit the money into his bank account before signing over the car. Needless to say, we didn't want to do that. We knew an important transaction should be done with a lawyer present. This seemed to anger the owner of the car dealership prompting him to demand that we bring $12,000 in cash to his attorney's office. We would have walked away from the deal if we weren't paying daily for a rental car. Also, this particular Mitsubishi was in really good shape and we really wanted it.

What proceeded was running around to several different banks and withdrawing the maximum amount each would allow in order to come up with the full amount. When you consider the largest bill in Costa Rica at that time was equivalent to $20, you can imagine the huge pile of money we ended up with in the end. It was big. So big it made my husband too paranoid to carry it around in a paper bag. So, he stuffed $12,000 dollars into his underpants. It's a visual that is forever burned into my brain.

When we met the attorney, Rob excused himself to the men's room and magically returned with the money. However, the attorney informed us that the owner was angry and again refused to sell the car. I just thought he was being a jerk, but my husband imagined something far worse.

"If you think I'm leaving this office with twelve thousand dollars, you're crazy," he yelled. It was only then I understood. Someone could be outside waiting to not so politely demand we hand over the money. Honestly, I never even considered something like that could happen.

Rob put on his crazy face: a bulging forehead vein, darting eyes, and gritted teeth. It was a good thing he wasn't wearing flip-flops. Incidentally, my crazy face includes teary eyes combined with a rapid drop in blood pressure. I find remaining in a catatonic state has been advantageous for me when faced with adversity.

It didn't take long for the attorney to call the owner of the dealership. The man finally sent someone over with the car. Papers were signed, money exchanged, and we were given the title. We didn't notice until later that the guy stole a license plate off the car. But on the bright side, he also left with money that was sitting in Rob's sweaty underwear so it was a fair trade-off.

I've heard other funny stories about people buying cars in Costa Rica. Some exchanges took place in a McDonald's bathroom, others on the side of the freeway. I would suggest you do all of this in an attorney's office. Just make sure the vehicle has two license plates before driving off.

When choosing a vehicle, ask yourself a couple questions. Will you be driving all around the country? If that is the case, I recommend a four-wheel-drive vehicle. It is inevitable that you will encounter a dirt road or even one with a stream running through it. And when I say stream, I mean one that has a good chance of turning into the Colorado River during the rainy season. We wanted a vehicle that had high clearance and could weather rough terrain. In addition, we noticed that the Mitsubishi Montero is a very popular car in Costa Rica. We figured it would be easier to find parts in the event we needed repairs since they seem to be everywhere.

That said, I have friends that own less expensive compact cars, don't drive far, and avoid really bad roads altogether. Darlene and Frankie have a Nissan Sentra and they seem to have no problem getting around. In fact, when they visited our house in Grecia they drove as far as they could on the rough road. We then picked them up and drove the rest of the way in our SUV.

If buying a car gets you a little stressed, remember: results may vary. Your transaction might go without any snags. For every problematic story you may hear about Costa Rica, there is always another that didn't involve undergarments or shoving money in undignified places.

- Shipping a Vehicle

Let's consider another option. You might think that it'll be cheaper to ship your own car. Sounds a like a plan. Unfortunately, you are subject to a dizzying amount of taxes. If we had shipped that same $6,000 car to Costa Rica, it would have ended up costing us close to $12,000 in fees and taxes (the exact amount we paid).

If you do import your car, consider the taxes:

Cars:
Less than 3 years old—52.29%,
4–5 years old—63.91%
6 or more years old—79.03%

Motorcycles:
58.10%—Motorcycles 0–3 years old
46.48%—Motorcycles 4–5 years old
34.85%—Motorcycles 6+ years old

Why are taxes higher on older cars? Because they don't want an old Chevy Nova on the road here. Apparently, they frown on cars held together with bungee cords and chewing gum. But as you drive throughout Costa Rica, you will often see cars held together by bungee cords and chewing gum. In fact, I think my car is now being held together with bungee cords and chewing gum. Rob's car repair kit includes anything he can find in our junk drawer. I once saw him disappear with a glue stick. I think he fixed the lock to our hatchback with it.

Let's do some math. Let's say you bought a five-year-old used car for $10,000 and are shipping it to Costa Rica. The shipping cost is about $1,500.

Customs officials will use the Valuation Database of the Ministry of the Treasury (referred to as the "Cartica / Autovalor") to determine their cost of the car. If it is more than what you paid, they will use the higher number. But if you should place a value higher than what is recorded in their database, you will end up paying more taxes than what the car is actually worth. Thus, it is probably better to underestimate the value of the car you are shipping to Costa Rica. You can find the link to the valuation database at the end of this chapter.

Now let's say Costa Rican officials have valued your car at $12,000. The car mentioned above is five years old so we must calculate taxes according to that age.

$12,000 x 63.91% (above tax for a car five years old) = A whooping $7,669.20

After $7,669.20 in fees, suddenly shipping your car doesn't sound like such a good deal. You also need to consider the shape your car will be in when it finally arrives. I have friends that had discovered their car was damaged during shipping, and said they would never do it again. I have other friends that received their car in pristine condition.

If you are in love with your car, and it fits your needs in Costa Rica, by all means consider shipping it. When you retrieve it, it will be ready with the proper registration and inspection stickers so you can legally to drive it the moment it arrives.

Now that you've done the math, you can see this decision should not be only about the money. Many times it is just as expensive to ship as it is to buy a car here. If the car arrives undamaged, the benefit in shipping is that you know you own a great car in good working order. The peace of mind this provides is invaluable when driving on some of the more challenging roads in Costa Rica. For some, this is reason enough to go through this hassle.

- Registration

As in any other country, you need to have a proper registration (marchamo) to make a car legal in Costa Rica. This is a piece of paper that you keep in your glove compartment, with a coordinating sticker you place on your windshield. Not having a valid registration is a common reason for traffic police to pull you over and is a very big deal in Costa Rica. Fines are extremely expensive, and you, may even have your car towed.

A marchamo not only serves as one's registration, but also includes mandatory- minimal insurance that would compensate anyone who may be killed or injured in the event that you are involved in an accident. Additional insurance on a car can be provided through INS (Costa Rica insurance company). These private plans cover collision, theft, fire, etc. At this point, I actually wouldn't mind if someone stole my car since there is an ever growing graveyard of parts in my backseat. I hum the theme song from *Sanford and Son* every time an engine belt or ball bearing flies off.

Payment for the marchamo is due every December. You can easily do this at the Bank of Costa Rica or Banco National. I like that this bill is due in December; it's easy to remember. Ours costs around $200 a year. We have never bought private insurance as of yet.

- Inspection

Unlike a marchamo that is due every December, the date a car needs inspection is determined by when it was inspected last. One can determine this date by checking the inspection sticker affixed to a car's windshield. Mine expires the last day in September; yours may be in February. Remember a car must be inspected prior to paying for a marchamo. If there are outstanding tickets on a vehicle, they will show up in the computer upon attempting to register the car.

Inspection on cars is performed at Reteve, and it costs around $30. There are many of these facilities scattered throughout the country. One must first schedule an appointment via the Reteve website.

The inspection process in Costa Rica is actually a very stressful endeavor. A car can fail for just about anything. Our car has failed for everything from a strange sound coming out of the engine to being slightly low on oil.

Recently our car flunked once again because the VIN number on the frame did not match the engine block. This may raise a lot of red flags with North Americans, but you have to remember that Costa Rican mechanics are constantly exchanging parts. There is a completely different mindset here. Back in the United States, if I had that much trouble with my car, I'd eventually buy another one. In Costa Rica, they will replace practically anything to keep a car running. To correct this problem, we ended up having to contact our lawyer who eventually got it all straightened out. It was just a matter of updating the proper VIN.

It's amazing how little Rob and I knew when we first moved to Costa Rica. We were just a nutty couple with a dream and a stack of money in my husband's underwear. So many things overwhelmed me that I never bothered to investigate what was needed in order to smoothly purchase, inspect, or insure a car. In retrospect, it's probably a good thing. Sometimes having too much information can be more of a deterrent than having less. Take all of this with a grain of salt. There are plenty of people who have gone through the process and made it out the other side.

Now that you know how to purchase a car, let's take another road trip. Grab you sunblock and beach towel. We're going on a surfin' safari.

**Links**

Calculate the value of your car: www.hacienda.go.cr/autohacienda/AutoValor.aspx

INS: www.ins-cr.com/index.html

Reteve (inspection station for your car): www.rtv.co.cr/

# Road Trip: The Beaches of Guanacaste  *

Are hammocks and piña coladas in your future? Do you imagine lounging under palm trees while reading a good book? Maybe you like to surf, snorkel, or just enjoy a catamaran pleasure cruise. If any of this sounds like you, you're going to love the information in this chapter.

Guanacaste province is located in the northwest portion of the country, and is also known as the Gold Coast. Depending on traffic, it takes about six hours to drive from San José. Keep in mind that although Costa Rica is a small country, there are not always direct roads to every destination. It will usually take longer than you think to travel across the country. But these drives aren't like driving down the New Jersey Turnpike. The scenery outside your window is breathtaking.

"But Nadine, are there any volcanoes in Guanacaste?" you ask. There sure are: Orosi, Rincón de la Vieja, Miravalles and Tenorio. You can't throw a stick in any direction without hitting a volcano.

Guanacaste is the driest part of the country. If you don't like a lot of rain, then this is the place for you. Liberia's International Airport is located here and only an hour away from some of the most beautiful beaches. Definitely consider flying into this airport if you plan on visiting this part of the country. I love driving, but sometimes it's nice to fly in and arrive at your destination in the shortest period of time possible. That way you can be sitting poolside and not lose any time on your very first day.

If you will be driving from the capital, one of the first things you'll notice is a change in vegetation. The trees and flowers are different here than in the Central Valley. I'm always amazed at how one can be on top of Poás Volcano one morning, surrounded by evergreen trees, and then frolicking at the beach that evening, drinking a cocktail under palm trees.

While you're relaxing, don't forget to look up. The birds overhead are more colorful than a field of wildflowers. There are many different species, but my favorite is the white-throated magpie jay. You'll instantly recognize them since they have a big, curved feather sticking out of their heads. At first glance, it looks as if they're wearing a musketeer hat. I consider these guys the Heckle and Jeckle of the forest—scoundrels that swoop down and steal sugar packets off the table and food right out of your hand. They even chased my dog out of the backyard. I have a love/hate relationship with these birds.

There is no doubt that this is one of the most beautiful parts of the country. However, there are hiccups when living at the coast. One of them is that gas stations frequently run out of fuel. This is a recipe for disaster because Rob loves to watch the gas gauge indicator go all the way to empty, then blink red, then have the car stall before he even considers filling up the tank. This drives me absolutely nuts.

A number of times we needed to fill up only to find the gas station turning people away. We would putter home on fumes, only to putter back the next day hoping they had fuel. I'm not sure what was worse about this, the not having gas or my constant nagging at Rob for letting it get so low. It got so bad that we eventually asked the gas station for their phone number. Once again, this confirms my suspicion that we will never have a quick getaway if an emergency ever presents itself. Between the Clubs, kill switches, and empty gas tank, we're goners for sure.

Recently, a second gas station started construction on the road to Tamarindo. It's been the talk of the town for weeks.

"Have you heard? Do you think it's true?" gringos whisper, as if chatting about a neighbor's extramarital affair. I have to admit, I've never been excited about a gas station before. But now I will all but volunteer to be the majorette and throw a ticker-tape parade for its grand opening.

"They planted sod. That's clearly a sign they'll be opening soon," my friend Sandy explains. I appreciate her optimism even though the sod has been sitting there for a good three months, and the only activity I see is a sleeping security guard leaning against a dumpster. But Sandy is a successful business woman who surely knows about things of this nature. Why should I rain on her gas station parade? Plus, this is the same lady who once threw herself in front of a phone company truck. She is not easily defeated.

I have to say, the anticipation is thrilling. It's something that sneaks up on you while living in Costa Rica. You get ridiculously excited over things that would barely garner a lick of emotion while living back in the States. You know your life is getting simple when you're euphoric over a new gas station.

Now that we've gassed up, let's go on a Guanacaste beach tour. I can't possibly go through them all, but I picked a few that might interest you. Please purchase a *Frommer's*, *Foder's*, or *Lonely Planet* for additional information. These travel guides are incredibly helpful. Some of my best trips were taken after reading one and then doing something incredibly stupid, like cavorting in crocodile-infested bat caves. Although I would avoid that excursion, these books are invaluable when traveling throughout the country.

- Playa Hermosa

Playa Hermosa is a beach town about a half hour from the airport. Don't confuse it with the other Playa Hermosa near Jacó. This happens often in Costa Rica: there are usually two, three, or four towns with the same name, so make sure when booking your trip that you are going to the right area. The beach stretches for over a mile and is surrounded by lush vegetation. North of Playa Hermosa is the Gulf of Papagayo. This is a great place if you like to fish, scuba dive, surf, or snorkel.

The Santa Rosa National Park is close by and an excellent place to visit. It is Costa Rica's first national park and is home to 250 species of birds including the white-tailed hawk, ivory-billed woodcreeper, and the Pacific screech-owl. I had never been a bird-watcher until I moved to Costa Rica. I was always too busy to glance out the window, never appreciating those robins or cardinals. Nature is the biggest thing we overlook when stressed out and not in the present moment. Now my life feels like one big picture window.

Have you ever met bird enthusiasts? Trust me, they are a fun bunch of people. You'll never hear them discussing what kind of new car they're buying, or the size of their home entertainment system. These people just want to watch birds… that's it. They have a passion that is just as intense as a pro athlete's. They will hike, climb trees, and hang off platforms, all to witness a glorious white-lored gnatcatcher. In a way, they are a lot like surfers. Their enthusiasm is contagious, and it's a lot of fun to make friends with people who have such passion for the outdoors.

In between bird-watching, keep an eye out for white-faced and spider monkeys, ocelots, and anteaters. And just in case you are looking for bats, there are plenty here, including the "vampire" species. I have no idea what to make of that, but I'm sure I'll be face to face with one someday since I have an uncanny ability for exploring caves and falling into piles of bat guano. It's a graceful talent, skillfully perfected after years of participating in my husband's economical two-for-one excursions.

If you are renting a good four-wheel-drive vehicle, drive down to Playa Naranjo and look out at Witch's Rock, a popular surfing destination. It has a majestic quality, rising out of the ocean, almost daring you to come and surf its waters.

- Playa del Coco

Travel a little farther south and you'll hit Playa Coco, a popular destination for both expats and tourists. This is where many people charter fishing trips or set out for SCUBA diving. Surfers can also catch a boat to Witch's Rock from here.

Rob recently went on a fishing trip catching jacks and red snapper. Inshore fishing trips can range from $350 to $650 based on half- or full-days tours. If you're interested in big game, off-shore deep sea fishing, chartering a boat will cost approximately $600 for a half-day trip and $1,200 for a full-day trip. This may change depending on the time of year.

- Playa Ocotal

Only five minutes away from Playa Coco is Playa Ocotal. It is a calm beach perfect for relaxing or snorkeling. I've found that where there are rocky outcroppings, there are usually interesting fish. Be sure to explore these tide pools while visiting this area.

- Playa Danta

One of my favorite beaches farther south from Playa Ocotal are Playa Danta and its sister, Playa Danita. It is here you will find the Las Catalinas development—the same place where we filmed the cocktail scene from our *EX-PATS* episode with Savannah Buffett (Jimmy Buffett's daughter). You can find this episode on the Reserve Channel on YouTube. If you are the adventurous type, grab a bite at their restaurant before heading to Pura Vida Ride to rent kayaks, paddleboards, and mountain bikes.

There is a rope swing as well as a climbing rope tied to a tree. My husband loves to brag he can still climb to the top. This reminds me a little too much of gym class, where I was admonished for not being able to do one pull up in fourth grade, so I watch Rob climb up and down the rope like a monkey while I eat ice cream. Nobody reprimands me for doing that.

- Sugar Beach

I *really* like this beach; it is by far one of my favorites. There is something unique about how it's nestled into a cove. It feels intimate, familiar, a place you'll want to smooch your spouse. The waves are perfect for boogieboarding. I took my mother-in-law to this beach and watched my husband position her on the board before releasing her into oncoming waves. Over, and over, and over again! She screamed like a little girl every time. (She also screamed because the leash wrapped around her leg and she thought it was a sea snake.)

You will have to walk through Hotel Sugar Beach to get down to the ocean. It is the perfect place to stay if you are looking for a relaxing vacation. I love how you can observe the howler monkeys right from your hotel terrace and watch iguanas as they sun on balconies. We've even seen deer on their grounds. That's a rare sight in Costa Rica.

The touristy town of Tamarindo is fun, but for those on a honeymoon—or who just want to get away from it all—Hotel Sugar Beach is very romantic. The restaurant is an excellent place to watch the sun set over the water while enjoying great food and friendly service. You might even catch me here drinking an Orange Fanta and working on my next book.

- Playa Prieta

Playa Prieta is a secret little beach that is easy to miss. It's south of Sugar Beach and you'll need to keep an eye out for a steep road pointing down towards the ocean. I must have driven past this for two years before realizing the road existed.

Once you're at the ocean, you'll see little bungalows bordering the beach. It's always so peaceful here and it's never crowded. In fact, I don't remember ever seeing more than a couple people. Because of this, it's a bird-watcher's dream.

We once observed a great blue heron staring down at us from an overhead branch. He was over three feet tall and closely followed our movements as we walked underneath him. He never let us out of his sight. It felt like walking past one of those portraits whose eyes follow you around the room.

A great blue heron's distinct call sounds a lot like a duck with laryngitis. I know this because the bird let out a vociferous belch. He was either about to peck our eyes out or warning us to stop tramping through his all-you-can-eat buffet. Apparently, we walked through a bunch of purple and orange Halloween crabs that subsequently darted into the sand. You'll see these crabs throughout Costa Rica, and you can usually find them at the base of trees on many beaches.

- Playa Penca

This was one of the first beaches that I visited in Costa Rica. It is also the place where I said, "You know what? I want to move here. I'm all in." I just couldn't imagine never seeing this place again. We reluctantly returned home but started planning our exit strategy immediately.

To find Playa Penca, look for a road right next to a tiny strip of stores in Potrero, just around the soccer field. Turn down this dirt path and it will take you straight to the beach. Playa Penca has soft white sand that cradles your feet like warm slippers. This is a great place to roll out your towel, relax, and watch the ocean sparkle. In fact, I think the ocean sparkles more here than anywhere else. It's like someone has scattered silver glitter across the waves.

There are outcroppings of rocks on the north end of the beach. I wouldn't recommend swimming out to them, but if you can find yourself a kayak, this is a great place to snorkel. Unfortunately, there isn't a place to rent kayaks on this beach, but keep this spot in mind. This is one of those "in the know" places that locals talk about.

- Playa Potrero /Surfside

Playa Potrero is a long stretch of beach where many people take their morning walk. My friend Richard, when not fixing his ice maker, catches fish here, so it is not uncommon to see men walking up and down this stretch of sands with fishing poles.

Since this beach is adjacent to a few hotels and restaurants, it's a nice place to stay for a few days. El Coconut Beach Club is steps from the beach and a great place to have dinner. Their fish is fantastic. Plus, they have a pool and you know what I think of that. Why not swim and dine at the same time? Or come and enjoy a few cocktails while reclining under a starry sky.

If you're having a craving for ribs, The Smokin' Pig in Potrero serves Memphis style barbecue. You can smell this place from a block away and I guarantee you will not leave hungry. Make sure you say hello to the owner, Bobby: a Happier Than A Billionaire reader, really friendly guy, and if he's not too busy he'll share with you his Costa Rica story and why he made this country his home.

Other great places to eat are The Shack and La Perla's. In fact, most of these restaurants are just a five minute walk from each other, so have dinner at one and dessert at another!

- Playa Flamingo

Playa Flamingo is the red carpet of all beaches, perfectly positioned in a cove with incredible houses peering down from the ridges. Here you will find The Flamingo Beach Hotel. It's only steps away from the water's edge, making it an excellent place to stay if you want to have access to a beach every day. I've rented jet skis there and I highly recommend you give them a whirl. There is nothing more breathtaking than seeing Costa Rica's coast from the perspective of the ocean. It looks like one big jungle with remote rocks that spit geysers of ocean water fifty feet into the air. I've never seen anything like it.

Within walking distance is a shopping center that includes a pharmacy, a rental car agency, and the famous Marie's Restaurant. Marie is an actual person and has lived in this area before there was much of anything here. She is a really fun lady, and you might even get the chance to see her there, working the bar or assisting the waiters. Any story that I have about Costa Rica, she has a better one. I could write a book just on her.

If you're looking for the very best piña colada, walk up the hill to The Monkey Bar. Ask for Diego, the best and friendliest bartender in the area. He will prepare you one of his famous piña coladas, and you can enjoy sipping it at the hotel's swim-up bar.

If you walk south on Flamingo Beach, you will come to a small restaurant called Coco Loco. It's only open certain times of the year, and the chef is the best in the area. The drinks are not only delicious but also beautifully presented. After you drink an alcoholic beverage out of a coconut, you're going to want to call your boss and tell him you're not coming back. It's that good.

- Playa Brasilito

This is where I always see people making out in the water. I don't know why, but a lot of people get frisky at this beach. It's where one of my favorite restaurants, Dorado y Camarones, is located. It's right on the water's edge and has vibrant tablecloths that billow with each passing breeze. They serve fresh fish daily, and lots of tropical drinks that make you feel… well… frisky. You can fall in love at this restaurant. If you are planning on asking your fiancée to marry you, consider this place. Especially while the sun sets. Then go make out in the water.

Brasilito Soda is a cute restaurant just steps from the beach and offers typical Costa Rican dishes at great prices. I absolutely love their casados: dishes that include black beans, rice, plantain, salad, and a choice of beef or chicken.

Another restaurant that I enjoy is Tiki's Seaside Grille, located across from Dorado y Camarones. It's a great place to people watch and enjoy a cool drink. Try their Chicken Tiki: grilled chicken breast topped with cream sauce, bacon, mushrooms and melted cheese served with their special Tiki potato and sautéed vegetables. This restaurant is also the perfect spot to start designing your own escape plan. Just grab a napkin and start listing the pros and cons of moving to this beautiful, tropical country.

If you are looking for the perfect sunset spot, stop at The Club at Mar Vista. The views are excellent, the food is great, and you can even sing at their weekly karaoke on Friday nights. While waiting for your meal, cool off by taking a dip in their infinity pool. And who can pass up an infinity pool?

- Playa Conchal

Next door to Playa Brasilito is Playa Conchal. This is one of the more popular beaches. The Reserva Conchal development (which includes The Westin hotel) faces this beach. I have a friend who lives there and whenever I visit, I go straight to the spa and jump into their enormous hot tub. It's like something straight out of Nero's palace. And when I'm looking to exercise, their treadmills have incredible views of the ocean. I find that I'm more motivated to burn off calories when I'm watching passing sailboats. Reserva Conchal is like a fantasy camp for adults.

Many people access Playa Conchal by driving right onto the beach. Turn left at Oasis restaurant and just follow the tracks in the sand. You'll probably see ATVs heading in this direction as well. You will eventually get to a steep but short hill. Travel slowly over it since you will not be able to see anyone coming from that direction. I once encountered a bunch of galloping horses heading my way. They did not yield.

This beach has plenty of activities and you'll find both locals and tourists alike catching some rays. You can rent snorkel gear, horses, jet skis, or small boats to try your hand at fishing. You can even unwind with a massage right on the beach. If you forget to pack a lunch, there are vendors that sell food and drinks. Purchase a pipa frio: a cold coconut. It's a refreshing drink and a filling meal all in one. Don't forget to use your straw to dig out the coconut meat inside.

Save some energy and take a walk to the southernmost part of the beach. There is an excellent reef not too far offshore for snorkeling. It was our friends Ian and Sandy who first showed us this spot. We filmed one of our underwater videos here, and Rob got an up-close view with an inking octopus. Kayak over to one of the protruding rocks and watch for manta rays breaching the surface. They leap out of the sea like UFOs, the tips of their fins catching the reflection of the sun. And just as quickly, they dive back into the ocean, transforming into shadowy creatures that lurk under your kayak.

- Playa Grande

Drive a little farther south from Playa Conchal, and you will find Playas Grande and Ventanas. These beaches are situated in Las Baulas National Park, an area where leatherback turtles nest. The hatching season is October through May, and if you're lucky you might get a chance to see one lay her eggs.

Leatherbacks are the world's largest turtles weighing close to twelve hundred pounds, and they can be nearly seven feet in length. Although they have survived for 150 million years, they are now decreasing in number. Great efforts have been taken by the Playa Grande community to help preserve these turtles. Small tours can be arranged with licensed guides in order to witness them laying their eggs on the beach. No lights or camera flashes are permitted, and the guides stress that you should not get too close to the mother turtles.

Watching a turtle lay her eggs and return back to the sea is an experience of a lifetime. It will change how you see our environment, and it made me realize how much of this planet is connected in such a miraculous way. This is why I always suggest venturing away from hotels and thoroughly exploring an area. The most incredible places exist just minutes from touristy towns.

If you're a surfer, look no farther. Playa Grande offers consistent breaks and swells. It is among the best surfing locations in the entire country, but be very careful swimming here. I've personally experienced strong riptides, one of which nearly sucked my mother-in-law out to sea. After my husband brought her back to shore, she yelled at him, wanting to go back out again. She's coming for another visit in a couple of months and plans to go kayaking in crocodile-infested mangroves. That should be fun, and I can't wait to see how Rob is going to get her back into her kayak once she falls out.

As you enter Playa Grande, you'll find an attendant wearing a reflective vest standing in front of a parking lot. I believe he charges two dollars, and I would suggest you park here. To your right are a couple of picnic benches and a food stand. It's the perfect spot to grab a cool drink and watch the surfers. You can also eat at the neighboring Hotel Las Tortugas. The owner has done much to preserve the leatherbacks' habitat, so go on in and buy a soda or a plate of nachos. It's the least we can do to reward his efforts in making this world a better place. To learn more about him, be sure to check out his *EX-PATS* episode on the Reserve Channel on YouTube.

Just the other day our friends (the owners of the house we rent) returned to Costa Rica for their yearly family vacation. They always welcome us to stay in the downstairs level of the home, but there is no stove and only a small refrigerator. Eventually, our diet ends up consisting entirely of potato chips and Ho Hos.

It's one of the reasons we only pay $150 a month rent. We have to be flexible when they arrive and take on the role of caretaker throughout the year. Some of our duties include security, home repairs, and emergencies that may arise. I will also note that we're responsible for wasp removal—well… Rob is actually in charge of that. It's not that I refuse to do it, more like I'm a draft dodger sneaking into Canada. This leaves Rob playing the all-time classic… wasp nest piñata game. It's the reason I do the dishes: there is less chance of succumbing to anaphylactic shock when at the kitchen sink.

Since our house is now more secure than the US Mint, when the owners are here we all end up setting off the alarm. It's impossible to move in or outside the house without tripping one or more motion sensors. One night our landlord had to sneak downstairs while we were sleeping to grab the phone. He army-crawled across the floor just in case Rob woke up and thought there was a burglar.

"Man, was I scared. I thought I was about to get maced in the face," he said the next morning. It's nice to know that we contribute a degree of neurosis to their Costa Rican holidays.

While talking with our friend Sky Maricle, Rob mentions our Ho Hos diet dilemma. Sky is an awesome property manager and is responsible for a number of properties in the area. He proceeds to tell us about a house that happens to be available in Playa Grande for just a few days before the next renters arrive. Sky invites us to stay and we are ecstatic. We love this idea because our landlords surf daily at Playa Grande and it's a great house for them to visit, have lunch, and take a break from the sun. Sky gives us directions to a home named Casa Muy Grande.

Once in Playa Grande, we turn down a road that takes us to the Palm Estates community. It's a small enclave with houses, restaurants, and even its own tiny grocery store. Like everywhere else in Costa Rica, there are no street signs or numbers on the houses.

"Is that it?" I ask, pointing to a sign that reads Casa Muy Grande.

"It can't be," Rob says. "I mean, we can't possibly be lucky enough to stay here."

It's then a caretaker comes out and unlocks the gate. "Are you Robert?" he asks before inviting us in. Now we understand why the house is called Casa Muy Grande. It's not a hyperbole: it's actually very *muy grande*.

We are greeted by a beautiful circular driveway with a large fountain flowing in the middle. I love circular driveways; in fact, we go around a couple times just for fun. Once inside the house we discover five bedrooms, six bathrooms, and two acres of perfectly manicured gardens.

The pool has a little archway over the top directing you to the backyard that also doubles as the beach. Crabs pop their heads in and out of tiny holes in the ground. I can hear the surf rolling in and feel the earth thundering under my feet.

The grounds are alive with beautiful shrubs and flowers. I walk a little farther and find a tennis court, ping-pong table, and outdoor kitchen. An adjacent building contains surfboards, kayaks, snorkel gear, and boogie boards that are free for guests to use. I've never been to a house that provides all of this and can't help but think how great it is for a large family visiting Costa Rica. You don't even have to bother renting anything: it's all right here.

On the other side of the backyard is a tiki hut with a massage table inside. I lie down, relax, and listen to the waves smashing into shore. I can't imagine a better place to unwind so I remain here for twenty minutes. Between driving in circles in the front driveway and getting my imaginary massage in the backyard, I'm making a great first impression with the caretakers.

The caretakers end up being a sweet husband-and-wife team that live on the property. And from what I've seen so far, they do a lovely job managing the grounds. Everything is in pristine condition, and there is not one leaf or palm frond in the pool. They are here twenty-four hours a day and can assist you with anything you may need. The wife even offers to cook for us, but after seeing them work so hard, we decide to cook for them instead. I'm lucky I get to interact with Costa Ricans; their positive attitude always enhances my experience and makes me feel at home no matter where I am staying.

While I continue to lounge on the massage table, Rob decides to explore the upstairs master suite. It's surrounded on three sides by windows with a door that leads to an outdoor, covered balcony.

"Look up at that tree," Rob calls down. "There are hundreds of butterflies."

Hundreds of butterflies, even some varieties I've never seen before, have congregated around a tree with red, blooming flowers. This house is incredibly private, nestled into its environment. If I lived here, I'd probably turn into Howard Hughes and never leave.

Rob and I spend the next three glorious days at Casa Muy Grande, enjoying the pool, the tennis court, and what we decide to name the butterfly tree. We wake up every morning to howler monkeys grunting their way through the canopy and birds welcoming the day with their sweet songs. This home is big, but not just in size. It's big in keeping the natural habitat alive, a place where you can enjoy the crabs and monkeys that call it home. And isn't that why most people come to Costa Rica? A little bit of luxury, sprinkled with butterfly trees and howler monkeys. It's the right mix for a perfect holiday.

- Playa Ventanas

Playa Ventanas is a special place. There is more shade and fewer people on this beach. Where I grew up in New Jersey, the beaches were always very crowded. Now I love the feeling of wading in the water and not having to overhear how Joey Ravioli drank fifteen tequila shots at the club last night.

The ocean is calmer at this beach and it is where Rob tries to surf. I would show you pictures of my husband surfing, but it's hard to get a good shot since he spends a majority of his time on the ocean floor. He now sticks to boogieboarding.

During low tide, this is an excellent beach to explore the many tide pools. They're filled with all sorts of fish and coral. One can easily wander for hours examining all the interesting life darting in the water. Look for me here in my big, brimmed hat, pointing to sea urchins while simultaneously applying copious amounts of sunscreen. I have many memories of my husband and me walking along this beach. It seems as if every place I visit with him offers me another cardboard reel for my View-Master.

- Tamarindo

I feel that there should be theme music in the background while I write this entry; maybe Bob Marley or Jimmy Buffett. Tamarindo is one of the biggest tourist destinations in the country. It's the perfect place to begin playing your role as a beach bum. There are even signs that read, "Don't work, surf." Enough said.

There is only one road in and out of Tamarindo. You know you're at the end when you reach a circle that directs you back around. This is a great place to park your car, eat at one of the restaurants, and do some shopping. One of our favorite things to do is eat lunch at the Tamarindo Diria Beach Resort. It sits right on the beach and is the perfect spot for watching people surf.

If you are looking for gifts, this is souvenir heaven. There are people selling beautiful jewelry at stands set up all alongside the street. The craftsmanship is incredible and many pieces are reasonably priced. Since it's an easy thing to pack in my luggage, it is one of my favorite things to buy for my family. On one of our first trips to Costa Rica, Rob and I decided to buy two very large pottery vases. We busted them the minute we put them in the backseat of our car. Every time we hit a pothole, we heard another crack. We ended up giving them to our neighbor, who patiently glued all the pieces back together. It resembled more an ancient ruin than a cheesy souvenir. I doubt I will ever lug something like that around again. I'll stick to jewelry or T-shirts from now on.

The JW Marriott is only ten minutes out of Tamarindo (located in the Hacienda Pinilla development), and is a fun place to spend the day. You can purchase a day pass for $100 per person, however that does not include any food or drink. If that's too steep, try just going for their buffet: $30 for lunch or $32 for dinner.

Another fun day pass is at the Hacienda Beach Club. Like the JW Marriott, it's located in the Hacienda Pinilla development. It is $35 per person and that does not include any food or drink. You can relax by their incredible infinity pool or enjoy walking out onto the beach.

After exploring Tamarindo, you may want to relax on a less crowded beach. No problem. I have a general rule about this:

- Travel ten minutes north or south from a busy beach and you will likely find one completely deserted.

I can't stress enough how much fun it is to get out and explore the area. Take some excursions or hire a taxi driver to show you around. It's worth the money and you will find that all the magical things that people love so dearly about Costa Rica are often just a couple minutes away and are usually at the end of a dirt road.

- Playa Avellanas

Travel south from Tamarindo and you will hit Playa Avellanas. Lola's Restaurant is located here, a popular place to relax and enjoy a smoothie. Playa Avellanas is also popular for surfing and boogieboarding, so bring your towel and get ready to have some fun!

- Playa Negra

A ten-minute drive further south will bring you to Playa Negra. The entrance is one of the prettiest I've seen. A canopy of mango trees shades a cobblestone path before leading you onto the sand. One area of this beach is great for experienced surfers, while another has smaller waves perfect for intermediate surfers and boogieboarders. We catch awesome waves here, and the beach is rarely crowded.

There is usually a professional photographer perched at the end of the rocks taking snapshots of surfers. What a great souvenir to take home! If you are a surfer, definitely check out this beach and get your picture taken. That's one for the living room wall.

- Playa Ostional

It's approximately a two-hour drive from Tamarindo to Playa Ostional. It's an adventurous journey and I highly recommend a four-wheel-drive vehicle for this trip. But don't let that dissuade you—it's totally worth it. Imagine thousands of mother turtles swimming toward the beach, their heads jutting out of the water like submarine periscopes. Once the turtles get to shore, their flippers propel them forward, inch by inch, to find the perfect spot to lay their eggs. I've never witnessed anything more beautiful.

This is one of the world's most important nesting sites for Olive Ridley turtles. The nesting season is usually between August and November. It starts with a few hundred turtles, and later thousands start to come ashore (in what is known as the "arribada"). It's nothing short of amazing.

After laying their eggs, these mothers must struggle back to the ocean. With every step forward, they stop and take a huge breath. They're exhausted but little by little, they continue. Their flippers are not designed for trudging through sand, so it can take them hours before they finally reach the water's edge. But once there, they quickly disappear into the ocean.

Their babies hatch between forty-five and fifty-four days later. They dig their way up to the surface and follow the moonlight toward the surf. It's a harrowing race: vultures await. Even if they are lucky enough to make it past the birds, more predators are hiding in the ocean.

This land race is extremely important to the baby turtles. This exercise helps develop and open their tiny lungs. You shouldn't pick them up and take them to the water, but you can protect them from the vultures overhead.

Hotel Luna Azul is a wonderful place to stay in the area. Nobody knows more about the turtles than its owners. They always let me know when the "arribada" begins. Their hotel sits high on a ridge and has an incredible view of the ocean. I would highly recommend it.

- Nosara

Nosara is a short drive from Playa Ostional. It's a quiet community nestled under shady trees and is one of the prettiest towns in all of Costa Rica. "Happy molecules" float in the air and their beaches, Guiones and Pelada, are perfect gems. You'll want to bury your feet in the sand and dream about running away forever.

Getting to Nosara can be tricky: there are a few rivers to drive through. During the rainy season, these rivers can be difficult to cross, so be careful. I always recommend a four-wheel-drive when making this trip.

- Samara

If you are going to visit Nosara, make sure to stop by Samara as well. The town consists of only a few blocks, but it has that nice, slow pace Costa Rica is known for. Carrillo beach is less than five miles away and is picture perfect. Whoever designed this area should be given an award. The road is lined with palm trees and looks like a movie set.

It feels as if you can walk out forever into the surf without the water ever getting above your waist. Rob and I once walked out so far, I turned around and was shocked to see that the shore was so far off in the distance. It's a special place and worth visiting.

- Nicoya Peninsula

If you really want to get away from it all, travel the back roads from Samara all the way down the Nicoya Peninsula. It gets better and better the farther you go. Don't be surprised if you see vans full of surfers on the road—they always know where to find the best beaches.

Santa Teresa and Mal País are two popular locations at the tip of the peninsula (technically not Guanacaste, but Puntarenas Province). These places would make for the perfect honeymoon. No crowds, lots of wildlife, and incredible sunsets. Blue Surf Sanctuary is a great place to unwind, do some yoga, or surf.

I hope you enjoyed this tour of Guanacaste. It was fun showing you around the many beaches I frequently visit. Maybe now you understand why I'm so happy here. It's near impossible to get bored. If I ever start feeling antsy, Rob and I just hop in the car and start exploring. That's if our car is not at the shop.

Let's meet Claus, my German mechanic, and find out why he is the second most important man in my life.

**Links**

Playa Hermosa:

- La Gaviota Tropical Hotel : http://lagaviotatropical.com
- Bosque Del Mar Hotel: http://www.bosquedelmar.com/index.html

Playa del Coco:

- Hotel Chantel: http://hotelchantel.com

Sugar Beach:

- Hotel Sugar Beach: www.sugar-beach.com

Potrero:

- The Smokin' Pig: www.facebook.com/Smokin-Pig-7152730015271120/

Flamingo:

- Flamingo Beach Resort: www.resortflamingobeach.com
- Marie's Restaurant: www.mariesrestaurantcostarica.com
- Coco Locos: http://cocolococostarica.com/

Playa Conchal / Playa Brasilito

- Westin: www.starwoodhotels.com/westin/property/overview/index.html?propertyID=3560&language=en_US
- Hotel Brasilito: www.brasilito.com
- Tiki's Seaside Grille: https://www.facebook.com/TikisSeasideGrille/

Playa Grande:

- Las Tortugas Hotel: www.lastortugashotel.com/
- Casa Grande: www.casamuygrande.com
- Sky Maricle Property Manager: www.coastalrealtycostarica.com Email:sky@costapm.com  Office: 2653-4607  Cell: 8888-0059

Tamarindo:

- Hotel Pasatiempo: www.hotelpasatiempo.com/

- Tamarindo Diria Hotel: www.tamarindodiria.com
- JW Marriott: www.marriott.com/hotels/travel/sjojw-jw-marriott-guanacaste-resort-and-spa/
- Hacienda Beach Club: www.haciendapinilla.com/beach-club/

Playa Ostional:

- Hotel Luna Azul: www.hotellunaazul.com

Nicoya Peninsula: Mal País / Santa Teresa

- Blue Surf Sanctuary: http://bluesurfsanctuary.com/

*EX-PATS* Episode (Number 12) Featuring Rob and me: www.youtube.com/watch?v=0rd0JeMPC7Q&feature=c4-overview-vl&list=PLAD3A1AD1D428C9B1

Underwater Video with inking octopus: http://youtu.be/ndV9uBSKKlo

# Car Talk

"Did you write about our mechanic in *The Sequel*?" Rob asks. "He was acting really weird when I bumped into him at the grocery store. He keeps saying "For me" a lot more than he ever did."

Claus, our mechanic, starts off each sentence with the words "for me." It goes something like this, "For me, I vill never put a scooter horn on Mitsubishi SUV. It's bullshit." I happen to like my toy horn; it makes an adorable "toot" noise that sounds like an armadillo fart. Rob thinks it's a very unmanly sound for such a manly SUV, but I can't get enough of it. I press it as often as possible.

"I wrote about him," I tell Rob, "but there is no way he could have found out. He's German. His wife is German. He probably reads German books and watches German television shows. Sometimes he even speaks to us in German."

Later that same day, Claus comes to our house with a trailer. Our scooter is not running and Claus is kind enough to pick it up so that he can work on it at his garage. While loading the bike, Claus pauses and turns to us.

"My wife vas at a friend's house. The friend says, 'I'm reading a book, a funny book, and there is a German mechanic in it. It has to be your husband.' Now my vife looks at the chapter and reads the mechanic says "for me" a lot. This must be me, ja?"

This is quite the uncomfortable moment, one that I am sadly familiar with. Claus is the only mechanic that has been able to fix our car. In fact, he's always busy because so many expats bring their cars to his shop. Now here I am, trying to figure out how to explain myself.

During the crushing silence, I do what I do best by backing up and leaving Rob standing in the line of fire. There is no use in me going down with the ship. Plus, I'm the talent. I need unbroken fingers for typing.

I scurry into the house and watch out the window. Rob kicks a few pebbles before explaining to him that yes, he is in the book, and we just poked a little fun at him but we love the way he talks and didn't say anything bad. Claus then gives Rob a big smile and says, "For me, I love this… the famous mechanic." It appears I will not be adding him to my infamous apology tour.

What I just wrote is a cautionary tale, one in which a dopey writer almost lost the second most important man in her life: her mechanic. You'll treat him like family, bat your eyelashes and make chocolate chip cookies for him. He's that important.

In Costa Rica, labor is relatively inexpensive but parts for your car can be very difficult to find. When I lived in Grecia, we once waited a couple of days for a tie rod. At the beach, we have waited over a month for similar parts. The dirt roads in this area do nothing to help the situation. There are potholes here that will knock your transmission back into the twentieth century. This is something to consider when living at the coast. You will need more maintenance on your car than you would if you lived in the Central Valley.

Claus has come to our rescue many times since we moved to the beach. Our alternator had died and we went to a mechanic that installed one that was better suited for a Boeing 747. It almost destroyed our car. Claus found the right part and got our car running again. I love this guy. Unless you want fireworks flying out of your dashboard, Claus is one mechanic you should consider.

I would also like to add that repairs depend on who is driving the car. Rob seems to get us in all sorts of predicaments when he is behind the wheel. Not long ago our house alarm went off while we were at the bank. We quickly ran back to our car and raced home.

"Don't go too fast," I urged Rob. "I bet it's a gecko that set off the alarm."

"That's what he wants you to believe," Rob replied.

"Who, the gecko?"

"No, the person robbing our house. He's *hoping* we'll think it's a gecko."

I calmly took another sip of my iced tea and made sure my seatbelt was buckled. I've been through this before. As we turned down a dirt road close to our house, I noticed a man in a tree.

"I wonder what he's doing up there," I said.

"There's a man in a tree? He's playing chicky!"

"What does that mean?"

"Playing chicky is when your friend is the lookout for you."

Being married to Rob has inadvertently taught me new and exciting vocabulary words. Like a *fish* is a sucker, a *scutch* is a pain in the ass, and *fugazy* is something not on the up and up. It's like the Webster's Dictionary for the mentally incompetent.

After seeing the guy in the tree, and convinced that anarchy is just a gecko away, Rob slammed his foot on the accelerator and we hit the next twelve bumps going ninety miles an hour. He skidded out in front of our house, jumped out of the car, and directed me to turn the car around and prepare to run the bastards over. This is always my job: run the bastards over. It's a position I take very seriously. I even turned up the air conditioning and took another sip of my iced tea. It's important to be cool and well hydrated when running over imaginary bandits.

In the end, there was not an intruder but a gecko camping out on one of our motion sensors. It seemed like no harm done until we started driving back down the hill to finish the errands we started in the first place. It was then we discovered we had no brakes. Nothing. Nada. It appeared Rob cracked a brake cylinder during his Steve McQueen ride back to the house. I can't tell you how refreshing it is to find all this out while going down a hill at maximum velocity. Rob pulled on the emergency brake and we drove straight to Claus.

And that guy in the tree? When we passed him again he was swinging a machete and trimming the branches. Needless to say, he wasn't playing chicky.

Claus found this all very amusing and promised to have the car fixed by the end of the week.

"For me, that brake cylinder vas bullshit."
I love my German mechanic.

Claus's Telephone:  8887-1447

# Real Questions Emailed to Happier

Can I drink the water?

- Yes

Is Costa Rica's government stable?

- Yes

Do I need vaccinations before visiting?

- No, unless you are going camping for long periods of time in the jungle. But freak out your husband and tell him that he needs twelve in the abdomen. The response will be priceless.

What are Blue Flag beaches?

- Beaches that have met stringent standards for water quality, environmental management, and safety procedures. They are marked with big blue flags.

When is the rainy season?

- Typically it is from May to December. But each area of Costa Rica has its own microclimate usually due to different elevations. Guanacaste is drier while the Caribbean has more precipitation. I have found that October and November are the two months when you are most likely to get rained out.

Last time I visited, there were no yams in Costa Rica. Are there yams anywhere in this country? And why not? It's a big part of my diet and can't imagine not eating them.

- There are purple potatoes here that taste like sweet potatoes, but I've never seen an actual yam. Most likely they were stolen out of someone's car. Crime Lesson 1.

Can I work in Costa Rica?

- Yes and no. You will need to get special permits from your employer to work here legally. It is against the law to take a job away from a Costa Rican citizen. You can open a business. Please read the chapter "Can I work In Costa Rica?" for more information.

Are there bugs in Costa Rica? I'm deathly afraid of them.

- Yes, it is buggy here. There are big bugs and small bugs. Some fly and some crawl. Not much you can do about it, so get ready for some roommates.

I've heard of something called a "suicide shower." Will I see one of those?

- Probably. It is a crafty electrical device that hooks onto your showerhead so that you can enjoy hot water. Don't say I didn't warn you.

# Forties or Why We Both Can't Do It

"My wife and I are in our forties and enjoyed your books. Although we would love to do what you and Rob did, our kids will both be in college in seven years. There is no way we could do it but have a fifteen-year plan. Keep it up, it gives us all a little hope that there is something great to look forward to after the kids are out of the house. I've just been diagnosed with high cholesterol and know that eventually I'm going to have to live a less stressful life."

Adam

The midlife crisis gets a bad rap. I believe it's about the best thing that can ever happen in our lives. It's a moment of clarity that only comes from life experience. In our forties, we have a good idea what we want. The problem is we have a lot of responsibility that can prevent it from happening. There is financial fear, and that fear is warranted.

It's rare I get an email from anyone in their forties that is willing to pick up and move. Some of it has to do with their kids in college, while others are very consumed with their work, still climbing the corporate ladder, and afraid what will happen if Costa Rica doesn't work out.

If I hadn't made the move I did at thirty-seven, I'm not sure I would have done it at forty-seven. I, too, would have been preoccupied with my career. In addition, I'm not sure if I could have easily disentangled my life the way I did in my thirties. At that time, my responsibilities already felt like a big sticky ball that was growing bigger and bigger by the minute. I knew that in ten years' time, my life was going to be a bloated version of what it currently was at that moment. It was one of the things that motivated me to make the move. I was terribly afraid that I wouldn't have the courage if I waited any longer.

Another thing I notice with these emails is that it's the first time people mention their heath. It's as if all those little troubling lifestyle problems—high cholesterol, high blood pressure, high blood sugar—start to appear in this decade. It scares the bejeezus out of people. It's the first realization that time is not on our side anymore. The countdown has begun.

However, for every ten of these emails, I receive one from interesting people trying to change their life and move abroad. Some have an option of doing more work at home. If all you need is an Internet connection, then you can work anywhere there is reliable service. I've actually seen people at cafés in town working while sitting under a palm tree. That's a pretty cool day at the office.

Also, the forties is a great time to travel. If picking up and moving isn't in the cards, why not a vacation? It's the perfect way to lift your mood and feel energized again. It might even spark that adventurous spirit you had in your twenties.

Unfortunately, we all don't have those options but we should celebrate that this decade provides us the self-awareness that we didn't have ten years prior. And this self-awareness will guide our way. We finally have had enough life lessons to know that anything is possible.

Check out airfares, and surprise your spouse with a week's vacation. If possible, leave the kids at home. This trip is to celebrate all your hard work, and to remind you that there is light at the end of the tunnel.

# Road Trip: Caribbean

There is so much attention given to the Pacific coast, one might forget that this country has another shoreline as well. I love being at the top of a volcano in the morning, and then later in the day snorkeling in the warm Caribbean waters. There is nothing... nothing like the Caribbean. It calls out like a mythological Siren, enticing you to dip your toes in her waters.

There is more rain and humidity in the Caribbean when compared to Guanacaste, but it's a small price to pay for the abundant wildlife and vegetation. I've seen more sloths here than in any other part of the country. I've witnessed several in the process of climbing back up a tree. One even reached out to me as if wanting a hug.

There is less infrastructure at the Caribbean coast, but for some it's an acceptable tradeoff. Cahuita and Punta Uva are quieter towns you may want to visit, with most of the action happening in Puerto Viejo. I like to continue driving south until I hit Manzanillo: the end of the road. Each of these towns have a similar Caribbean vibe: that characteristic laid-back attitude. If you are looking to run a corporation here, you may want to reconsider unless you're willing to give your staff a three-hour siesta.

The trickiest part of getting to the Caribbean is driving through San José. It's stressful navigating an entire city with few street signs. Consider hiring a taxi to direct you. He's the best kind of GPS you will find in Costa Rica. You may also rent a GPS device with your car. Most rental agencies now have them available for their customers.

- Never rely completely on GPS. People have taken terrible beach roads, ones with many rivers to cross, because technically it was the shortest way.

From San José, you'll pick up Route 32. This road will take you through Braulio Carrillo National Park, a beautiful area that has the highest level of diversity in all of Costa Rica. I wouldn't recommend hiking in this park without a guide; there are many steep cliffs and it's easy to get lost in the thick vegetation. But if your heart is set on exploring this park, there is an aerial tram that can give you an excellent bird's eye view of the rainforest.

Continue following Route 32 all the way into Limón. If you have ever been on a cruise to Costa Rica, chances are your ship stopped here. Sadly, this is not one of Costa Rica's prettiest towns but more of a bustling city and a place to gas up if your tank is getting low. When filling up in this part of the country, I recommend super gasoline. On several occasions, our car sputtered and stalled after filling up with regular gasoline. The problem resolved itself after switching to super.

Continue straight into Limón and look for signs for the southern Caribbean beaches. You will make a right and drive south along Route 36. If you are considering exploring Tortugero, turn left. You will need to find a safe place to park your car and then hop aboard a boat destined for the northeastern tip of the country. This area is only accessible by boat or air. More and more tour companies are offering Tortugero excursion packages, and if it fits your budget, I would highly recommend it. This area is a very important nesting site for the endangered green turtle.

If it's your first time traveling to the Caribbean side of Costa Rica, I recommend you turn right at Limón and leave exploring Tortugero for another day. Turn off the air conditioning and roll down the windows. Smell that turquoise blue air. I've found that the happier I've become, the more colors I smell. Nosara's air smells like Jungle Green and Sugar Beach smells like Canary Yellow. My nose has the ability to paint a picture no matter where I travel in Costa Rica.

This stretch of coastline is everything you imagine: palm trees sleepily lean over the road, and ocean breezes affectionately hug your body, promising to wash away your worries. It's time to start whistling Bob Marley tunes because *everything is going to be all right*.

- Sloth Sanctuary

The Sloth Sanctuary is approximately 19 miles (30 km) south of Limón. Look for "sloth crossing" signs and then the sanctuary on the left. This place is a must-see.

Stop by and talk with the owners. The experience is sure to remind you that this world is full of wonderful people making a difference. They've rescued over five hundred sloths and have been featured in high-profile magazines and television shows. You'll never look at a sloth the same way again.

This sanctuary is home to the three-fingered and two-fingered sloth. Here is a fun fact: three-fingered sloths have nine cervical vertebrae instead of the typical seven most other mammals possess. This allows them to rotate their head three hundred degrees in order to scan for predators without wasting energy turning their bodies. This has Rob contemplating adding a sloth-cam to his growing Thunderdome protocol.

Sloths never have a good hair day because it grows in the opposite direction as compared to other animals. This follicle arrangement helps protect them from the environment while they hang upside down. The smile on their faces and peculiar movements makes them one of the most adorable animals in Costa Rica.

- Cahuita

Cahuita is home to the Cahuita National Park. On the day Rob and I visited, there were white-faced monkeys in the trees at the entrance. They kept watch as each visitor entered the park. I thought for sure they would jump on someone's shoulder; instead, they yawned. Even the monkeys have a laissez-faire, Caribbean attitude.

The birds are equally magnificent and are well worth the trip to this park. You'll spot a variety of herons and two types of toucans: the chestnut-mandibled and keel-billed. And if you haven't had your fill of sloths yet, you'll find many here hanging from branches overhead.

I've seen the most spectacular wildlife on rainy days, so don't let bad weather stop you from exploring. Pack a rain hat, one that is not attached to a poncho since you'll be turning your head in a bunch of directions in order to see animals. A hat attached to a poncho ends up falling off every time you look up at a sloth. I always keep a rain hat in the car. It's not even the, seventy-five-dollar mosquito-repelling hat I tried on at the adventure store before moving here. My dad, who most likely got it free from entering a Folgers sweepstakes, gave it to me.

- Puerto Viejo

From Cahuita, continue driving south until you run into Puerto Viejo, the busiest of these tiny beach towns. Vendors line the beach and sell everything from jewelry to T-shirts. You'll find Puerto Viejo has everything you need for a comfortable vacation: bank, supermarket, Internet cafes, restaurants, and affordable places to stay. It is also a popular hub for backpackers. Hostels here offer a wide variety of lodging arrangements: some rent tents, while others have more standard style of rooms. Many backpackers take a break in Puerto Viejo before continuing their journey to Panama.

Sometimes people are worried about traveling to this part of the country for fear of crime. In order to address this from the perspective of a local, I contact my friend April to weigh in on the subject:

"I've lived here for over a year and I've never been a victim of crime, but I can't say that about everyone who visits the area. Often robberies happen when people are coming home drunk from the bars. One has to be very careful when inebriated since it makes a person extra vulnerable.

"Tourists ride bicycles with laptops under their arms and iPhones in their pockets. It's unfortunate, but this is like putting a big target on your back. I would recommend hiding that stuff in a backpack.

"Also, never tell anyone what hotel you are staying at. Don't leave your things on the beach while swimming; they will likely be gone when you return. Making another copy of your hotel key can costs upward of $90, so don't lose that either.

"As with many areas of Costa Rica, there are not a lot of police. It's best to play it smart and take personal responsibility. Even with all of that, I wouldn't trade a thing. It's a wonderful place to live."

If you are looking for an active nightlife, you may want to remain in Puerto Viejo. But if you're looking to escape the crowds and experience more nature, continue driving. If you don't have a car, rent a bicycle or hire a taxi. Just a stone's throw farther south in Cocles is one of my favorite places to stay: Villas del Caribe. During low tide, an area right off the beach turns into the perfect hot tub. Thank you, Mother Nature.

- Punta Uva

Punta Uva is one of my favorite beaches in the entire country. It has awesome reefs located only a few meters from shore. I've spent hours snorkeling here. It only takes a few steps into the water before you're witnessing schools of fish swimming around you. If you're lucky enough to catch a week without rain, the water transforms into a sparkling reef tank full of life. It's so clear you'll spot even the tiniest of fish lurking in the reef's crevices. And the best part is it doesn't cost a thing! I can spend days snorkeling and never get bored.

Continue south and you'll pass the Almonds and Corals Hotel. The entrance is just before the town of Manzanillo. It's a more expensive lodging option, but looks interesting. The rooms are actually "pavilions" raised off the ground, giving guests the feeling they're on safari.

I never stayed at the Almonds and Corals Hotel, but I did do their zip-line excursion. It was a lot of fun, and at the end they served us cold drinks and a delicious plate of fresh fruit. This is a convenient place if you are interested in experiencing a zip-line excursion.

- Manzanillo

Manzanillo is literally the end of the road. It is a small town with affordable lodging options and the famous Maxi's Restaurant. Rob and I always order the seafood platter and are never disappointed. There are lots of pictures of me drinking an Orange Fanta at Maxi's. Always the sign I'm having a good time.

Digest quickly because there is another great reef for snorkeling right off the coast. Or skip the snorkeling and continue straight ahead toward the Gandoca Manzanillo Wildlife Refuge. The paths within the park quickly wind you through a lush jungle. Eventually, you'll come to a point where you can walk out onto a ledge and see the Manzanillo Rock. The scene is breathtaking and appears on countless numbers of postcards in souvenir shops. You know you're succumbing to the Caribbean vibe when a rock makes you happy.

Although it's a fun hike, I wouldn't travel too far into the jungle… which is precisely what we did. It wasn't until we saw a tent in the middle of the woods—with thoughts of *Deliverance* running through our heads—that we started turning back. We were probably in Panama at that point. It was not an Orange Fanta moment.

There are affordable accommodations in this area, and some even have air conditioning. If you're the type who enjoys more sloths than people, Manzanillo is the perfect place to escape from it all.

**Links**

Barillo Carillo Rainforest Tour: www.rainforestadventure.com/costa_rica_atlantic_tours_excursions/

Sloth Sanctuary: www.slothsanctuary.com

Villas del Caribe: www.villasdelcaribe.com/

Almonds and Corals: www.almondsandcorals.com/

# Part III: The Heavy Lifting

# Visa Runs, Perpetual Tourists & Fumigation Facials

If you do not have residency (or your "tramite" the official paper stating your residency application is processing), you'll need to leave the country for seventy-two hours every ninety days. There is much confusion—and many heated debates—over how long you need to be out of the country. Some sources say one needs to be gone for a full seventy-two hours. Others insist a couple hours will suffice and that the seventy-two-hour rule only applies if you are bringing products back into the country. Trying to find a definitive answer on this will only end with you beating your head against the wall.

All of us who have crossed the border have different experiences. While many have no problem, others get hassled because they are considered a perpetual tourist. What defines a perpetual tourist? Not sure. It's likely that if you crossed the border a couple times, you wouldn't have a problem. However, it appears at the moment that Costa Rica is focusing on people who do this consecutively for years.

My friend April recently had a frustrating experience at the Panama border. She renewed her visa repeatedly for two years. On her last run, Costa Rican border officials refused her entry into the country in spite of the fact that she had been away for three days. With persistent begging, she was given a fifteen-day visa. She then had to go to Limón and pay a fee. It was only then she was given a thirty-day extension.

"This is your last time," the lady behind the desk scolded. "You may be refused entry into the country the next time you leave Costa Rica."

I have another friend who has been going over the Nicaraguan border for years. She's never been questioned even though she only spends a couple hours there before returning. She has friends who have been detained at the same border for hours, pleading with the officials to give them another visa.

There is one thing that is certain: no matter what the rule is, the border agents are the ones who ultimately make the decision. When it comes to border crossings, once again… results may vary.

- Always check border hours (and their lunch break) before starting this trip. Remember that Panama is one hour ahead.

This is one of the reasons I decided to file for residency. I did not enjoy wondering if I'd be allowed back into the country. However, there are others who have no anxiety living as perpetual tourists. You'll need to decide which side of the spectrum you fall on with regards to this topic.

But even with the stress, visa runs can be fun! I looked at them as mini-vacations. Some of my best memories are in Bocas del Toro, Panama (also known as the Galapagos of the Caribbean) and San Juan del Sur, Nicaragua. This was the life I dreamed about while working in my office.

On one of our trips to Nicaragua, we spotted a bunch of surfers in a van. Since surfers always know the location of every cool spot, we decided to follow them. They didn't disappoint, leading us to beaches with sand so soft, it felt like walking on a bed of marshmallows.

We dined at a seaside restaurant where a little girl balancing a basket of peanuts on her head approached us. I didn't buy any peanuts but gave her a dollar anyway. She smiled—a radiant one that only an innocent child can generate—and ran into a neighboring store to play foosball. Later I saw her there playing with her brother. I was initially on edge navigating throughout Nicaragua, but it turned out to be delightful.

Never underestimate a positive attitude when you travel. It's better than a swanky resort or an elaborate buffet and can drastically shape the dynamics of a trip. A positive attitude acts like superglue for happier memories. I still remember the trials of crossing the border, and all the uncertainties of being at the mercy of border officials. But those images are in black and white. The snapshot of that little girl with the peanuts on her head is in color. Maybe that's what happiness is: little Monet paintings that float across our brain.

- Crossing By Bus

If you are considering crossing the Nicaraguan border, there are a number of options. For example, you can take a public bus from Liberia to Penas Blancas (the Nicaraguan border), for approximately two dollars. There are other private companies—such as Nica Express—that costs ten dollars and up depending on where you will be getting picked up. They can also assist you with getting your passport stamped.

If Penas Blancas sounds too hectic for you, try the San Carlos border. It's off the beaten path and known for being less populated. It's harder to find a bus that travels this route when compared to the Penas Blancas crossing. Most of the people I know who use this border live closer to La Fortuna, catching the bus from Ciudad Quesada before getting dropped off in Los Chiles. From there, they go through Costa Rican customs and walk a short distance to a dock before boarding a boat that takes them across the San Juan River into Nicaragua. These boats only travel twice a day, so make sure to check the departure time before heading out.

If you are going to Panama, Tico Express or Panama Express can take you from San José to Panama City for $40 and up. Make sure the price you are quoted is for a round-trip ticket; Panama border officials can turn away anyone who does not have "proof of onward travel."

- By Plane

Be a rock star and fly via Sansa or Nature Air. There are pluses and minuses to each airline: most of Nature Air's flights leave from their Pavas facility, a thirty-minute drive from the San José airport. Sansa has a terminal near the San José airport, but it's about a ten-minute walk to their facility.

Rob and I once flew Nature Air into Bocas del Toro, Panama. It was fast, easy, and terrifying. My anxiety was not caused by a deficiency in the plane or the pilot, but more due to it being my first time in such a small fuselage. I didn't realize I would feel every dip and pocket of turbulence. Some people love it; I find it frightening. The next time we drove.

- Driving

When I first told fellow expats that I wanted to drive across the border, whether it was to Panama or Nicaragua, they all discouraged me.

"It's too much work," some said.

"You'll have to go to the National Registry to get paperwork for your car. You'll be on one line after another and eventually give up," others chimed in. But they didn't know Rob and me. We had already come to the conclusion that if there were long lines somewhere, we'd eventually be standing in them. Preferably at lunch hour… on a busy Monday… after Rob had just sprayed himself in the eye with mace.

The National Registry rarely has copy machines, so make sure you come with copies of your passport and car title. (You will also need copies for the border, so make a few more while you're at it.) A few bucks later, you'll receive stamped papers that'll allow you to travel with your car for thirty days outside of Costa Rica. This satisfies the "Proof of Onward Travel" requirement for you and your car. What is this "Proof of Onward Travel" again and why does this keep coming up?

When crossing the border, you need to prove to the destination country that you will eventually be leaving. This proof can be in the form of an airline or bus ticket. If you do not have one of these, there are places at the border to buy one. It is also best to have a valid credit card. This satisfies your "Proof of Economic Solvency" requirement. It demonstrates that you have enough funds to enter the country. If you don't have a credit card, you can carry cash. Once again, there are uncertainties surrounding border rules. No one knows for sure, but I've read that the border officials may request proof of $200 to $500. It is hard for me to find "Proof of a Right Answer" anywhere, but if you have a credit or debit card, you should be okay.

- It's important to note that you cannot drive across the Panama or Nicaragua border in a rental car. If you're considering driving your own car across, you'll need to obtain vehicle authorization papers from the National Registry. This prevents people from avoiding taxes when selling cars abroad.

There are three different border crossings into Panama: Paso Canoas, Rio Sereno, and Sixaola. Most cross over at Paso Canoas or Sixaola. The Nicaragua border is straight up the Pan-American highway at Peñas Blancas. No matter which one you chose to drive over, it's likely to be a memorable experience.

One of our craziest adventures was at the Sixaola border on route to Bocas del Toro. If you have the chance to cross there, do it. Hold your breath as you drive over a rickety wooden bridge that is one car away from plummeting into the river below. When I expressed my concern, an official reassured me that the bridge is over one hundred years old and hasn't crashed yet. It was then I wished we flew.

After crossing the bridge, we were directed into a large bay that resembled a carwash.

"How sweet," I said to Rob. "Our car is filthy. This is a nice touch."

Seconds later, jets of sudsy, anti-fungal water shot at us like a machine gun. Apparently, this carwash was actually a fumigation station. Now, I'm not complaining. I wouldn't even mind having this done at Rapido Lube with every oil change. It's just that I like having time to roll up my window before getting sprayed in the face with insecticide. Not the nice gesture I was expecting, but my skin did remain fungus-free for twenty-four hours.

After my antifungal facial, we continued onward to the town of Almirante, where we left our car at their firehouse. They charged us three dollars a day. A taxi drove us to a small port, where we caught a boat to Bocas del Toro. At that time it cost us approximately four dollars each for a one-way ticket. Rob loved this part of the trip because the little boys on the dock thought he was Vin Diesel. Rob flexed his biceps for that entire boat ride.

All this border talk can be very confusing. You can cross one time and be asked for your proof of onward travel. The next time, you may be waved right through. Nothing is guaranteed. I learned a lot of things while going through these visa runs. The most important was keeping my mouth shut while getting my face fumigated.

Not all of these memories will be included in your View-Master, but you'll be glad you had the opportunity to take these trips. And who knows? You might end up following a van of surfers to a secret beach or make a little girl carrying a basket of peanuts smile.

Things You Will Need When Crossing the Panama or Nicaragua Border:

- A passport that does not expire within six months.
- Proof of Economic Solvency: a credit card or cash.
- Proof of Onward Travel: a bus or plane ticket if you are not driving across.
- Vehicle authorization papers must be obtained from the National Registry before driving your own vehicle

across the border. Be sure to make copies of your passport and car title.

- Most importantly, a good attitude. Even when a border official tosses your passport over his head... even after waiting for hours and watching everyone else get processed before you. Keep smiling and remain polite. You'll eventually cross over.

## Links

National Registry: www.rnpdigital.com/eng_principal/index.htm

- National Registry offices are located in San José, Alajuela, Puntarenas, Guanacaste, and Limón.

Nature Air: www.natureair.com

Sansa Airlines: www.flysansa.com

Tica Bus: www.ticabus.com/eng/index.php

Panama Express: www.expresopanama.com

Trans Nica: www.transnica.com

# The Finally Free Fifties or Why My Husband Won't Do It

"I finished your book at the same time I sent my youngest child packing for college. I feel like I just crossed the parenting finish line and now I'm looking forward to getting back to doing so many of the things that I love. Your book encouraged me to try and convince my husband to do live abroad but he is dead set against it. I'm tired of waiting, but he wants to save money for another ten years. I feel excited about the next phase of my life, and I don't see why we should wait any longer."

Judith

The fifties for women are similar to the thirties for men. At this age, women are ready to try something new. Many have spent the last couple decades raising children, and this is the first time—in a very long time—they are not guiding the hand of a little one. Once the empty nest feeling subsides, a surge of adrenaline rushes through their veins. They are ready for their victory lap.

I love running into women in their fifties. A contagious energy radiates from them. They remind me of all the things I still want to do, and to celebrate the things I have accomplished so far. They are driven in a way that can surprise people—sometimes even their own husbands.

It seems to be the opposite for many men. While they would have jumped at the chance in their thirties, men are more hesitant in their fifties. Having more invested now, many are not willing to leave their careers and plan to hold out until retirement age before doing anything so drastic. There can be other concerns as well. Minor health problems men had in their forties may be becoming more serious.

I understand why these men hesitate. Why would you unravel your entire life without the safety net of Medicare and social security? How do you leave the company you've been working at for over two decades? Dipping into the unknown was the riskiest things Rob and I ever did.

But occasionally, I do get emails from men whose health issues have actually propelled them to change their lifestyle and move abroad. Many times, this comes after a heart attack or serious health scare, sparking the realization that there is a good possibility they might not make it to retirement age. Life is too short for some to continue habits that are essentially killing them. But health issues are not unique to men. Working too many hours, a poor diet, and keeping up with the rat race can take its toll on women as well.

We often need to experience the bad to appreciate the good. It's strange how enlightenment often comes after falling ill. When my husband was sick and spent a week in a hospital, it was as if someone illuminated a thousand lanterns in front of me. My path didn't seem so dark anymore, even though it was still an unfamiliar one.

What would I say to a man whose wife is anxious to become an expatriate? Sit down and hear her out. If you think you have what it takes, this could be the adventure of a lifetime. And if you go all in, maybe your high blood pressure will suddenly disappear. Perhaps the only prescription you really need is rocking in a hammock next to your wife.

# How to Make a Living: Going Fishing with Rick and Jamie  *

"If you love what you do, you never have to work a day in your life."

Are you the type who dreams of running away with a fishing pole in hand? Possibly creating a business out of something you are already passionate about? Meet Rick Graham, a man who did just that. He opened a fishing charter business and now lives a life he once only dreamed about. Rick explains why he chose to buy an existing business, the benefits that came with that, and why he is happier than a billionaire in Costa Rica.

"Jamie and I have been best friends for over forty years. We've fished big together, dreamed big together, and now own Dream On Sport Fishing. Opening a business like this one is something we've talked about for many years. It started to get serious when our boys began getting older. The more we spoke about Costa Rica, the more serious our talks became. Five years ago we were ready to pull the 'chute and float our way into Costa Rica. Then life happened, as it always does.

"My dad had been diagnosed with Alzheimer's disease. Along with that, Jamie and his wife, Leanne, decided that they should wait until their son finished high school. After these things were sorted, the talks were back on! I came down in April of 2013 with my son, Alex, and spoke with Randy, Dream On's previous owner. We asked if he was interested in selling his business. Alex and I hopped on the boat, met the crew, and it was all looking good. I reported back to Jamie and he threw out the idea of starting fresh rather than purchasing an existing company. We listed the pros and cons of both options. In December of 2014, Jamie, Leanne and I came back to Costa Rica for a closer look. We all went out on the boat, fished, and in the immortal words of Victor Kiam, 'We liked it so much we bought the company.'

166

"As I mentioned previously, there was much discussion as to whether we should start fresh or build on Randy's efforts. Ultimately we decided on the latter. It became clear very quickly that we made the right choice. We discovered everything was easier on the path we chose. A lot of gringos come and go. They start a business, many fail and eventually leave. We noticed an obvious advantage right away when other local businesses promoted us. They were comfortable doing so because we were already an established fishing charter.

"Another benefit was in the adaptation to our new country's rules and ways. We were able to continue with the same lawyer, Alfredo Gallagos, accountant, Manuel de Jesús Venegas Zuñiga, and crew, Captain Adelso and First Mate Mario. The corporation was established and the transfer of shares was a breeze.

"Another benefit of owning an established corporation is in regards to obtaining residency (inversionista category). Within two months of arriving, the paperwork was already in process. I did not have to do any border runs to keep my visa current. Large sums of money on deposit or proof of guaranteed income were things I did not have to provide. Our immigration lawyer, Lissa Arroyo, handled it all for us. The cost was fifteen hundred dollars plus some government fees and I'm in the system! No lines, no mistakes, no trips to San José.

"In terms of daily operations, there is a lot more to applying your skills to a business down here compared to in the United States or Canada. Not because of bureaucracy (there's even more of that back there), just in the way Costa Rica does business. Rules are different, there is a language barrier at times, and there is always the acceptance from the community or competition from other businesses. Looking at how things have gone so far, I couldn't imagine having to figure out everything from scratch. We were able to bring our areas of expertise with us and focus just on that. Going this route, without all sorts of other distractions, enabled us to do our thing and drive the numbers through the roof. Since taking over we have improved the company's performance threefold. We've been able to contribute to the local economy and improve the lives of many people around us.

"Selling our things, quitting our careers, and moving down here has been the best decision we ever made. Rob and Nadine's adventures, through their books and videos, were a huge motivating factor and sources of valuable information. I can honestly say that without the *Happier Than A Billionaire* series of informational media, I might not be here right now having the time of my life.

"I love life again, and I am happier and healthier than I've been for a long time. I can't imagine moving back to Canada or the United States. Sometimes I wonder, what if I had to? When that happens I just shake those thoughts away to avoid the ensuing anxiety. It's an old saying and one my Nan used to say all the time: 'If you love what you do, you never have to work a day in your life.' I wish she was still here for me to thank her for that and to say, 'Yes, you were so right... and doing it in Costa Rica makes it even better!'

"We love paradise... We're truly 'Happier Than a Billionaire' too!"

Dream On Sport Fishing: Where angler's dreams come true!

Rick Graham & Jamie Braun
Pro-Staffers/Contributing Writers for Coastal Angler magazine/Costa Rica Edition

CR Tel: (506) 8704-8210 or 8735-3121
Toll Free USA / Canada 1-844-312-1122

**Links**

Read our reviews on Trip Advisor :
http://www.tripadvisor.com/Attraction_Review-g309243-d3388480-Reviews-Dream_On_Sport_Fishing_Private_Charters-Playas_del_Coco_Province_of_Guanacaste.html

http://www.dreamonsportfishing.com

# Fifty Shades of Residency *

"This wasn't the first time that Willow found herself in Mr. Gabriel's office. She seductively slid her residency application across his desk. Mr. Gabriel reached out, placing his hand on top of hers. Her pulse raced as he lifted each of her fingertips and placed them onto the fingerprint scanner. It was at this moment that the machine suddenly stopped working. She waited five more hours in Mr. Gabriel's office while it was being repaired, surely thinking this was his plan all along."

If residency talk gets you hot and bothered, now is a good time to pour yourself a glass of wine. I'm bringing the sexy back to Costa Rican residency rules.

Residency is like an evil leprechaun: he shows up every few months, taunting you with a new quest or challenge—one week saying your paperwork is incomplete, and the next week insisting you must drive to immigration with documents you've already cheerfully provided. If he's really in a joking mood, he'll lose your application and you'll have to start the process all over again. But for some, there is a pot of gold at the end of this residency rainbow; it just takes a lot of patience and perseverance.

The following are the three current categories for residency with their corresponding requirements. Keep in mind that Costa Rica is constantly changing the rules.

Pensionado

- Requires that applicants have a monthly pension of at least $1,000. Only one pension is necessary for a married couple.

Rentista

- This category is a little more complicated. It requires that an applicant show proof of unearned income. The current minimal requirement is $2,500 per month for two years ($60,000). This amount will apply to the applicant, spouse, and children under twenty-five years old.

- The applicant must provide a bank letter stating he or she has at least $60,000 in a "stable and permanent" manner. One of the most common forms of unearned income is a certificate of deposit.

Inversionista (Investment)

- The category requires a higher level of commitment. The applicant is required to invest at least $200,000 in a business, the purchase of a home, commercial real estate, or land used for preservation purposes. You can also invest in a teak farm. I think it's funny how that just gets tossed in. Please don't ask me if it's a good investment. Besides some patio furniture, I'm not sure what else you make out of teak.

- The property value of your investment must be registered with the local municipality. The assessed value of the property must be at least $200,000.

No matter what category you fit into, you will need to gather the following notarized documents: birth certificate, marriage certificate, police record, and a bank letter stating you have the necessary funds. I know what you're thinking, "This seems easy enough. I never even needed to purchase *The Costa Rica Escape Manual*." So why does everyone make a big deal out of this? Because nothing is at it seems in *The Matrix* of residency submissions. Let's use my own application as an example.

In order to gather and authenticate my documents, I returned to the city where I was born: Elizabeth, New Jersey. If you've never had the pleasure of visiting this town, you're missing out. It's home to the Bayway Oil Refinery, where, in December 1970, a large explosion occurred shattering windows as far away as Staten Island. It's been said that I sat up in my crib and screamed, "What the hell was that?"

It was a wonderful way to welcome in my first Christmas while simultaneously introducing me to genetically altering levels of benzene fumes. It was an enchanting time when big business considered carcinogens as harmless little fairy particles. And why would we have questioned them? We were swaddled in toxic flammable blankets while sleeping in lead-painted cribs. Little did we know we were one cigarette ash away from exploding as well.

In order to obtain a current birth certificate, I had to go to Elizabeth's City Hall. A nice lady provided me with a new one, which I then mailed to the New Jersey Secretary of State for an Apostille stamp. You are going to hear a lot about this stamp, so you might as well learn why all of your papers will require it.

The United States is part of The Hague Convention, along with a long list of other countries. This agreement, although better known for dealing with war crimes, also states that one country will honor the foreign documents of another. When I received my birth certificate back from the New Jersey Secretary of State, it came with a formal letter proudly displaying a shiny Apostille stamp. It looked like I had won a spelling bee.

My next step was retrieving our marriage certificate from Pennsylvania. I contacted the courthouse, and a clerk mailed me the certified document. I sent this paper to the Pennsylvania Secretary of State in order get its own corresponding Apostille stamp. I repeated this process with the notarized letter from my bank.

Then there was my New Jersey police record. Trying to get this really tested my patience. A lady behind a plate of glass at the police station, who I would categorize as having a very bad day, would not notarize it. She was a notary but didn't want to take the time to go get the stamp from her office. Or at least, that's the only reason I can imagine why she wouldn't do it. No matter how much I tried to persuade her, she wouldn't budge.

I actually had to pay a traveling notary.

To stand there and notarize the document.

In front of another notary.

At that time, police records older than three months were not accepted for residency. The current rules allow you *six* months to gather all of your documents. However, the time passes fast and you should be diligent in your pursuit. Another thing that has changed is that all my documents needed to be sent to the corresponding Costa Rican consulates after they were authenticated. This is no longer necessary. Hurray!  This step will save you time and money. I contact Javier Zavaleta from Residency In Costa Rica to confirm this and explain a little more about the residency requirements:

"If an applicant's country of origin is a signatory member of The Hague Convention—such as the United States, United Kingdom, and most Western European countries—the proper corresponding authority will issue the Apostille stamp," Javier says. "For the United States, the proper authority is the secretary of state where each document is issued. Because the United States and Costa Rica are both members of The Hague Convention, the Apostille stamp will be accepted by Costa Rica immigration.

"Please note that Canada does not issue Apostille stamps, and any document (birth certificate, police letters, income, pension, etc.) originating from Canada must follow the old rules for the legalization of documents, including taking the document to a Costa Rican consulate and to Relaciones Exteriores in San José."

Sorry, Wayne Gretzky. If you choose to come out of retirement and join the underserved Ice Hockey League of Costa Rica, even a famous Canadian like yourself will have to take that extra step.

Rob and I had such a hard time gathering all the documents for residency, we ended up personally delivering the paperwork to the Costa Rican Embassy in Washington, DC in order to make the deadline. My anticipation grew as I drove past large, impressive European embassies. Surely we would be offered beverages, snacks, and perhaps an invitation to a formal ball or two once we arrived. Unfortunately, the entrance to the Costa Rican embassy was more like a Brooklyn basement apartment than a fancy ballroom. It had bars on the windows and no numbers marking the address. It was as if it never existed at all. I was surprised to find that they *did* have a Xerox machine, which at that moment was infinitely more useful than chocolate-covered strawberries.

We are at the end of this chapter and I bet you are wondering where the sexy part comes in. Hmm… I might have been slightly misleading with my "Fifty Shades of Residency" title. The only sexy thing about this whole experience happened at the San José police station. One of the final steps of the residency process requires that you be fingerprinted. The woman helping Rob wanted to seduce him fifty different ways before introducing him to her extended family. The woman assisting me—who (like the lady at the New Jersey police station) I would categorize as having a very bad day—wanted to murder me fifty different ways before disposing my body in a parking lot dumpster.

Apparently, the language of love was lost on me.

Here is a summary of authenticated documents you will need regardless of what residency category you are in. All documents must be obtained, notarized, authenticated, and submitted to Costa Rica immigration within six months of the date that the application was filed.

- Birth Certificate
- Marriage Certificate
- Police  Record
- Copy of Passport

Other Documents you may need:

- Pensionados will need proof of their pension, social security, IRA, or annuity.
- Rentistas will need proof of funds (unearned income) in the amount of $2,500 per month for two years. This will cover an applicants family with the exception of children over twenty-five. This letter must be written and notarized by your bank before being submitted for further authentication.
- Inversionistas must provide proof of their investment.

## Links

Residency in Costa Rica: www.residencyincostarica.com

# Road Trip: Arenal

Lake Arenal always makes me want to ride a bicycle. Not any kind of bike, but one with a white basket and plastic flowers fastened to the front. Throw in a thumb bell and you might never see me again.

Don't miss out on visiting this area. If you are driving from San José, it's about a three-hour ride. Once you arrive, you'll be on the eastern, touristy side of the lake. This is where the town of La Fortuna and the volcano are located. If you're driving from the beaches of Guanacaste, you will hit the west side of the lake first. It's going to be another hour-and-a-half drive to get to the volcano.

Once you are here, you'll want to ride a bicycle, too. The lake, and the surrounding area, is intensely lush and beautiful. We are currently renting a house for a few weeks in Tronadora, a small town on the west shore of Lake Arenal. It is a quiet village with a sky full of birds. As I type this chapter, a flock of toucans are perched in my backyard, tossing berries back and forth like a badminton game. However, what is most impressive about this town is its well-mannered dogs. Let me explain.

Riding on the back of a scooter with Rob is an adventure all unto itself. In addition to an abundance of bugs in our teeth, it all but guarantees that every passing dog will chase us. Little unassuming Chihuahuas have frequently nipped at my toes and irritable German Shepherds dreamed of sharpening their teeth on my husband's tibia. Rob likes to call this "extreme scootering." I like to call it "extreme mauling."

In Tronodora, things are different: these dogs prefer to watch us like a bunch of old men sitting at a Dunkin' Donuts counter. Yesterday we drove past fifteen dogs that all but tilted their cap and said, "Good day." I'm falling in love with a place, solely based on their hospitable dogs.

In addition to their polite canines, I'm amazed at how many birds inhabit this area. The climate is wetter than at the beach, and this attracts species I've never seen before. Judging by the view out my window, toucans appear to thrive here. Their bright, yellow necks and multicolored bills make it impossible for them to hide in the trees. If there were a beauty pageant for birds, surely toucans would win first place.

It's hard to comprehend how a toucan can fly with such a huge bill. However, it turns out its bill doesn't weigh much at all. It's filled with honeycombed bone allowing air to flow through. This acts as the bird's own personal thermostat by regulating body heat. They also use it like a fencing sword, wrestling their neighbor to demonstrate dominance. But what I like most about toucans is their mating ritual: their foreplay consists of tossing fruit at one another. It looks fun and seems like an excellent way to enjoy snacks while getting frisky. I'll try flinging a grape at Rob tonight and see what happens.

Toucans are usually found in flocks of six that vocalize throughout the day. In fact, these birds never shut up. You can hear their frog-like calls from morning until night. I love how the many sounds coming from the forest don't become irritating like city noise. Forest sounds become so familiar, so normal, that I can't imagine ever going back to the din of a busy town.

We are all familiar with the medicinal properties of rainforest plants, but I believe there is an equal measure of healing that emanates from a forest's melody. I would love to test someone's blood pressure before and after a trip to Costa Rica. If they spent anytime near a rainforest, I can bet that it dropped at least ten points.

The Arenal area is not only a great tourist destination, but also a wonderful place to live. It's so much cooler than at the beach; my pasty skin doesn't feel like it's resting on a barbecue anymore. And how about this for something spectacular: I've seen three rainbows today. Rainbows, guys! You know what I want to do when I see a rainbow? Ride a bicycle right underneath it.

This brings me to Stacy and Bob Lux, readers of my books who heard I was visiting the area. Stacy is a property manager and Bob is a local realtor in Nuevo Arenal, a town halfway between Tronodora and the volcano. They are of retirement age and want to tell us why they call this area home. When we pull up to their gate, Stacy is waiting anxiously.

"I'm so happy to meet you guys!" Stacy exclaims. "I hope you don't mind but I have a problem I need to deal with. I have to go to one of the properties I manage right away."

"Sure. Jump in our car and we'll go straight there," Rob replies.

Five minutes later, we pull up to a house with broken shards of glass everywhere. At first glance it looks like a robbery, but as I peer through a window, I see a coconut in the middle of the floor.

"Son of a… It's from that tree up there," Stacy points.

We look up an embankment and identify the perpetrator: a palm tree full of coconuts. Apparently, one fell, rolled down the hill, and smashed straight into the sliding-glass door. You couldn't have bowled a better strike.

Those of you who have read a little about my husband already know he has an unreasonable fear of falling coconuts. Whenever at the beach, he makes me run underneath palm trees like Joe Montana going in for a touchdown. He feels the same way about icicles. Luckily, we don't have to deal with those anymore.

Stacy unlocks the front door and calls a local glass company. I grab a broom while Rob decides that this is another perfect opportunity to lecture me on the dangers of rogue coconuts. At this point I space out. I have a tendency to do that during any of his stories involving coconuts, Thunderdome protocol, or any Brooklyn stories that include his friend Tommy Walnuts.

After cleaning up, Stacy takes us out to lunch, where we meet her husband. The Luxes share with us why they choose to live in this part of Costa Rica:

"The funniest thing about living here is that almost all of the gringo men in this town are named either Bob, Tom, Jim, Mike, Bill or Dave," Stacy laughs. "If you have one of these names, we will give you a nickname so everyone will know who we are talking about."

"I was at the bank the other day and was introduced to three other Bobs," her husband says. "It was like a comedy skit. "Hi, Bob, I would like you to meet Bob. Nice to meet you, Bob; have you met my friend Bob?"

"This is a fun place to live and your books describe Costa Rica so perfectly," Stacy continues. "Bob and I are like an older version of you two. When we first arrived here, after selling everything in the States, we had only two suitcases each. We bought a car, rented a tiny studio, and began the process of getting residency.

"The people here are happy. You can see it in their faces. One of my favorite things about Costa Rican people is that when you ask where something is, they actually go out of their way to walk you there. I think this is amazing. Maybe they do this because they know explaining it would just confuse me.

"When it comes to overcoming the obstacles of living in another country, and learning the ins and outs, I believe there are three factors: time, patience, and what my niece taught me. Something she learned in the military in basic training: adapt and overcome.

"I think the secret to being a content expat in this tiny town of Nuevo Arenal is to always remember that you are a visitor. If you are having trouble finding an item that you are used to having, simply drive into San José, or have the item mailed to the next person who will be visiting. If you are going to live here long-term, you should get your residency in order to avoid leaving the country every ninety days.

"Listen to five different versions of how to get something accomplished, and then pick one. Don't walk up to people and just state your business. Start with a warm greeting in Spanish, and a handshake.

"Enjoy the view, sun, rain, rivers, volcanoes, animals, rainbows, and beaches. Embrace the importance of family, the fresh food, and the helping hands you will find all around you."

Stacy and Bob are similar to us in many ways. They remember to take note of the good things and make them count. Bad things will come; they always do. But to be happy as an expat is to give weight to all the great experiences and let the unpleasant ones roll away like coconuts down an embankment.

- Putt-Putting Around the Lake

Don't let it fool you: this lake is big. It was actually enlarged by the electric company in order to build a hydroelectric dam which now provides electricity to twelve percent of the country. It's encouraging to see green energy being used on such a large scale. The lake is also an excellent place to wind and kite surf. The best times to enjoy these sports are between December and March. The winds are much stronger during this period, which help propel the surfers to incredible speeds. No matter where you go in this country, people are surfing. Maybe we should attach a turbine to their backs and let them generate some electricity as well.

There are two ways to drive around the lake, but people rarely use the southern route. I've been told that it is more of an off-roading adventure than an actual road. Stick with the paved route, and you should be fine.

Driving around Lake Arenal on a sunny day is a wonderful thing. It's even better on our scooter since we travel at the meandering speed of an arthritic go-cart enthusiast. Before we left the beach, Rob decided to stuff the scooter into the back of our car, and I'm glad he did. It turns an ordinary ride into a high-definition movie.

The road around the lake is not unlike traveling Route 66, with similar roadside attractions urging you to pull over. I can't help but love this since I'm attracted to anything kitschy. I'm mesmerized by overpriced keychain emporiums with a force as strong as my dad's ability to avoid every last one of them.

We drive past signs for "The Number One Bakery in Costa Rica" and the "Best Coffee Straight Ahead." It appears that the "best" of everything is located around this lake. But my favorite is for a restaurant named Toad Hall. Their sign reads, "Voted Best Fish Tacos On The Planet." This piques my interest. It's not every day the total population of earth comes together to vote on something as important as a fish taco survey.

As we continue, we notice wooden posts carved into the shape of monkeys and frogs. We turn into the driveway and find it's actually an art gallery. A German woman who came to Costa Rica thirteen years ago greets us. Her paintings are on display in her house, large canvases hanging in every corner. This is a great place to be inspired. The longer I live here, the more I meet people who are following their passion. I'm also realizing there are a lot of German people living in Costa Rica.

After the enjoying the German art gallery, we stop by Café y Macadamia and enjoy a piece of pie and a cup of hot chocolate garnished with cinnamon designs. We relax on their outdoor patio and watch yet another rainbow forming over the lake. I can see why the Luxes settled here.

- Arenal Volcano

The word "majestic" comes to mind when describing Arenal Volcano. It's a young one, less than 7,500 years old. A baby when compared to other volcanoes.

La Fortuna is one of the more touristy towns in Costa Rica and is located at the base of the volcano. You will find an endless list of fun things to do: horseback riding, rafting, ATVing, hiking, bird-watching, waterfall rappelling, night bug tours, and fishing. There are several zip-lines to enjoy in the area as well, including Sky

Adventures and Arenal Mundo Adventura. The latter actually allows you to zip-line over the La Fortuna waterfall.

However, the star of the show is definitely the volcano. It's now in a resting phase so you may not get to see lava flowing from the crater. This will make fifty percent of visitors upset, while making the other fifty percent extremely happy. Not everyone wants to be at the base of an active volcano. Still, you may still feel some rumbling under your feet, just a reminder that Mother Nature is still the boss around these parts.

It would be a shame to define this area solely by the volcano; there is so much more to see and do here. The forest is so dense and green, you can't help but think this is what the world looked like before shopping malls infested the planet. When you spend time around Lake Arenal, you feel the magnetic pull of time. Remarkably, you can still find primary forest here. Very little vegetation grows on the forest floor due to the thick canopy overhead that prevents sunlight from reaching the ground. It's spooky yet fascinating walking through a forest that hasn't changed in a million years.

Not far from the volcano is the Arenal Observatory Lodge. We rented their White Hawk Lodge, a separate house on the premises that is located extremely close to the volcano. It was a blast, no pun intended, lying in bed while watching molten boulders shoot out the top.

Arenal Observatory Lodge is a great place to stop and take pictures, but be aware it now charges an entrance fee. But even if you are staying for just ten minutes, it is totally worth it. In the mornings you'll see magnificent Montezuma oropendolas eating fruit off the observatory deck, while coatis aimlessly waddle throughout the grounds. You can walk across an Indiana Jones-style hanging bridge or hike a trail into the shadows of the forest. Or you can just stare up at the volcano that looms over like a protective parent. It's *really* close, and if you are a photographer, pack your wide-angle and zoom lenses. It's way too beautiful for just a point-and-shoot.

After leaving the Observatory Lodge, take a left and head towards El Castillo. This little town may surprise you.

- Butterfly Conservatory

Near Arenal Observatory Lodge is one of the largest butterfly conservatories in Costa Rica. It is located in the small town of El Castillo with a collection of butterflies that will satisfy any insect lover. To ensure that the visitor will see a large variety and to make sure the butterflies stay healthy, the conservatory is divided into several habitats. I had no idea that in nature the blue morpho butterfly is found in the highlands, whereas the harder-to-see clear-winged butterfly prefers a deeper forest habitat.

And for those of you who like amphibians, the Butterfly Conservatory also has a frog exhibit. You'll be treated to some of the most dazzling frogs native to Costa Rica: the green-and-black poison dart frog, strawberry dart frog (blue jeans frog), and the photogenic red-eyed tree frog. The red-eyed tree frog is often seen printed on postcards, paintings, and billboards all throughout the country. In fact, Costa Rica should add him to their currency. He's that pretty.

I had the privilege interviewing the owner, Glen Baines, for our upcoming cooking/adventure show. He is a retired engineer and the most knowledgeable person I've ever met in regard to butterflies. He moved to Costa Rica years ago and decided he would build a butterfly garden. Shortly after arriving in El Castillo, the volcano emitted a strong eruption. While many would have taken this as a bad sign, it convinced Glen that this was where he was meant to be. El Castillo is a place dear to his heart.

While touring the conservatory, Glen enthusiastically points out the owl butterfly—one with a design on its wings that resembles the eyes of owls. I'm fascinated by this adaptation; the eyes look large and realistic. This must certainly deter predators. Later Glen directs us to the glass-winged butterfly, a unique insect that lacks colored scales. Upon closer inspection, their wings looks like tiny sections of transparent stained glass.

Glen shows us one of the many saucers of fruit that are placed throughout the garden. Apparently, butterflies do not live on nectar alone. They also dine on fermenting fruit, and it's not uncommon for them to get inebriated from the alcohol. I notice that some are even stumbling around like college students at last call. Watching drunken butterflies is quickly becoming one of my favorite pastimes.

Before we leave, Glen tells us to check out some of the other places in El Castillo. One of which is Essence Arenal, a hostel that prides itself with sustainability.

- Essence Arenal

A short drive up the road from the Butterfly Conservatory is Essence Arenal, a hostel located on a hill overlooking the volcano. We pull into the driveway and notice a group of middle-aged women planning their day over cups of coffee. They unfold a map and circle several destinations with a red marker. I'm happy to see that hostels are not only for twenty-somethings anymore.

Essence Arenal has several types of rooms to choose from: bedrooms with private baths, tents with a shared bathroom, or if you're really budget-minded you can even camp on their grounds. There are cooking demonstrations in the evening where guests all participate in preparing a vegetarian dish. The owner, Niko, greets us with a smile. He takes particular pride in keeping a low carbon footprint. He also agreed to be part of our cooking/adventure show that is coming soon to our YouTube Channel.

"Do you want to walk up the hill and see the rest of the property? I'm building a yoga platform with the most amazing view," he says.

I never pass on an amazing view, whether I have to get it on horseback or—as I'm doing right now—by hiking a jungle trail. Unfortunately I'm wearing a sundress and flip-flops, which confirms

I'm incapable of dressing appropriately for any occasion in Costa Rica. But I'm not missing out, so I hike up the hill regardless.

Rob and I follow Niko while he tells us his background: he's a German who grew up in Spain and ultimately fell in love with Costa Rica. He bought this property and decided to make an eco-friendly hostel. Once at the top of the hill, I can see why he fell in love: I have never seen a view of the volcano like this before. I imagine the view is even more dramatic when the volcano is in its active phase, but I'm just as happy being up here when it's not exploding. It's no surprise my father loved Arenal Volcano so much; this must have been a similar view to the one enjoyed by the inhabitants of Pompeii. He's been showing me pictures of those ruins since I was a little girl.

We walk through a grassy boulevard lined with fruit trees on either side. "Isn't it strange how much money resorts put into their landscaping?" Niko asks. "Why not plant things you can eat? They are just as pretty and serve a purpose. We use all of this fruit in our kitchen."

It got me thinking about how much work and resources it takes to keep a nice, green lawn. Niko makes a great point, and when I landscape my own property I will be sure to incorporate some of his practices. Nikko and his business are excellent examples of what you can do if you actually commit to a more sustainable lifestyle.

"My next goal is to have a yoga retreat," Niko explains while pointing to a wooden platform. "Pretty cool, huh?"

I'm all but ready to perform a sun salutation. There is energy up here, a palpable electrical field that surrounds you. This is a healing spot, and a yoga retreat couldn't be more perfect.

We tour Niko's farm, one that consists of a bunch of free-range chickens. He uses their excrement as fertilizer for coffee plants. Everything has a purpose here, and it makes me wonder if my visit has a purpose as well.

"I'm buying more solar panels and trying to get off the grid completely. It's a challenge, but by trying out different things I have found the ones that work. I'm lucky that I get so many volunteers. It's a wonderful way to share what I know and learn from others as well. The volunteers come from all over the world. We provide housing and meals in return for their work."

There are so many opportunities for people who want to see the world. I ask a college-aged man, who is washing his hands with a hose, about his stay.

"I've been here for a month, and would like to stay longer. We are in the process of integrating different plants that will help combat bugs. Farmers will plant acres of the same crop, but this leads to infestations. It is better to plant a mixed crop. This helps deter insects."

This is not your ordinary group of backpackers. These have a passion for green solutions. Some have degrees in agriculture, always giving Niko new and better ideas for his farm.

Once back at the reception, we join the cook and help prepare a meatless club sandwich. Anytime I say the word hamburger, he shushes me.

"Shhhh. The animals can hear you."

I've never been more satisfied eating a meat-free sandwich. But it's more than that; I'm happy here. This is such a wonderful place and I can't wait to return.

As we are leaving Essence Arenal, Niko mentions another sustainable farm nearby that raises cattle. It turns out there is even more to see in El Castillo before the day is over.

- Rancho Margot

I've said this before: the best things in Costa Rica are usually down the worst roads. Rancho Margot is the brainchild of Juan Sostheim, a retired fast food executive whose initial intention was to run a ranch that would be carbon neutral. He has done much more than that: he's become carbon negative.

Rob and I jump at the chance to speak with this very interesting guy. Who does something like this? Who leaves a successful career to build a sustainable resort in the middle of the jungle?

"I'm not a hippie," Juan laughs. "I just know that we can do better. The technology is here, we just need to apply it."

If you are looking for a doom-and-gloom lecture, you're not going to get it from Juan. He believes we can still live with many of the same conveniences we are accustomed to; living a green life doesn't necessarily mean living without.

Juan takes us on a tour of his farm. I've never seen someone so passionate about his work. Everything has a purpose at Rancho Margot. This place is a living university, with an incredible volunteer program that is attracting colleges from around the world.

"We grow our own food, make our own furniture, and produce our own electricity. We even started making our own soap," Juan explains. "The real dream is to interweave all of the green ideas into a fun, sustainable resort. At Rancho Margot, you can go horseback riding, take yoga classes, or enjoy our pools and lakes. People feel good about traveling here, knowing they don't leave a wasteful footprint."

There are some really magical things about Costa Rica, and one of them is the fascinating people I run into. I like talking with Juan. Here is a guy actually taking green technology and applying it on a much larger scale. Juan is a big thinker and I feel good around him. He reminds me to take only what I need from this planet. This seems to be a running theme in Costa Rica. The more I apply it, the better my life becomes.

During the course of our tour, Juan describes again how everything has a purpose. We pass plants that are grown specifically to feed cows. Pig excrement is collected to provide methane gas. He even raises his own worms that eat compost later used as feed for free-range chickens. Healthy Worms = Healthy Chickens = Healthy Eggs.

"Sustainability is a necessity. We need to change the way we do things. I want to share what I've learned, and I hope I can encourage others to think differently as well."

Juan has a unique ability to convey his message better than anyone I've ever met. He comes from a business background and uses that knowledge to improve our lives, while not sacrificing the creature comforts we have grown accustomed to. He understands that the technology is out here, and it's up to governments to do what is right for all of us. We can be energy independent, we can live symbiotically with the environment, and we can feel good about it.

I hope you all get a chance to visit Rancho Margot. Take their tour, or stay for a few days. It will change the way you think. And if you get a chance to meet Juan, ask him to do some sophisticated math. I watched in amazement as he converted kilowatts of electricity into BTUs. I can barely understand how to convert dollars into colones, and then there is Juan doing long division in his head. Like I said, this is a smart guy.

Visiting El Castillo was an amazing experience. Meeting Glen, Niko, and Juan is an education in itself. They will all be featured in our upcoming cooking/adventure shows.

- Mystica Restaurant and Yoga Sanctuary

On our way back to our rental in Tronadora, we decide to stop at the Mystica Restaurant and Yoga Sanctuary for a bite to eat. Upon walking into the dining area, I notice a room with a sign overhead: the "Be Yourself Room." I instantly went inside and sat down. How can I pass this up? Considering I spend most of my life trying not to be my neurotic self, this was a real treat. I sat there for a few moments and let the insecurity and general anxiety sink in. So far it felt like a Woody Allen therapy session in here.

Rob sits down next to me, burps, and announces, "I'm hungry. Let's eat." Not surprisingly, Rob is quite happy with being himself.

And being himself is not wasting time in a "Be Yourself Room."

The reason we stopped here to begin with is their sign advertising pizza. Rob is always in the mood for pizza. In fact, I've never seen Rob not in the mood for pizza.

Aside from the pizza being fantastic, this is a great place to get it together. You know what I mean. Did you ever sit in your car on the ride home from work and say, "I really have to get it together?" This sanctuary has a treehouse where you can get a massage while overlooking the magnificent Arenal Volcano. I bet you're getting it together just reading this.

I'll definitely come back here in case I need to be myself or just for an excellent margarita pizza. And guess what? We saw another rainbow.

## Links

Stacy and Bob Lux Real Estate: www.moranlakearenal.com

Arenal Observatory Lodge: www.arenalobservatorylodge.com

Arenal Mundo Adventures: www.arenalmundoaventura.com

Sky Adventures: www.skyadventures.travel

Butterfly Conservatory: www.butterflyconservatory.org

Essence Arenal: www.essencearenal.com

Rancho Margot: www.ranchomargot.com/

Mystica Yoga Sanctuary: www.mysticacostarica.com

Rio Tropicales Rafting Tours: www.riostropicales.com

# You Have the Right to an Attorney

Gilferd Banton Beckford is about the most honest attorney you'll ever find. Before I inform you of all the things he can help you with, let me explain some of the things he will not do for you: launder money, alter your passport, or assist you in transcontinental arms trading. Please don't bother him if you are participating in any of these things. This may seem like an odd statement, but I've heard some of the strangest things on more than one occasion. My husband was once cautioned at a Swiss bank about signing a certain paper.

"Don't sign this if you're looking to kill your wife," the man said.

It's not every day a bank representative discusses murdering one's spouse, especially when that said spouse is sitting in the same room. But I appreciated being included in the conversation, and I shook my head like I understood how troubling that could be for my husband. I mean, if a man was plotting to murder his wife, who needs a pesky paper trail? For the next hour, I made sure to finish the complimentary Swiss chocolates and planned on avoiding any hikes that led to yodeling on precipitous cliffs.

Gilferd is not going to have these conversations with you. He will not help you with scandalous endeavors, but he will certainly shake your hand and wish you a good day before escorting you out of his office. This guy always does the right thing. Believe me, you'll want someone like this in your corner.

I've had the privilege of hearing many of his childhood stories. He grew up on the Caribbean coast. His memories include going on picnics, drinking out of coconuts, and swimming in the warm turquoise waters just steps from his home. He describes how the Caribbean heat would sneak under his door and slip through every crack in the floorboards. I try to imagine such a childhood: surfing instead of riding bicycles, climbing mango trees instead of evergreens. Every time I hear someone describe their childhood, I can't help but be reminded of my own.

What type of things should you use an attorney for? Everything. Some of the simplest things can become incredibly complicated in Costa Rica. For example, large purchases such as buying property or a car are usually placed in the name of a corporation. You will need someone to help you navigate the tricky waters of these transactions.

It's also important to call Gilferd before purchasing a vehicle. If we knew him back when we bought our SUV, I'm sure Rob wouldn't have run around with $12,000 in his underpants. Although, it's comforting to know that we can cram that much cash down there if the need presents itself. Gilferd will search the car title and make sure all the necessary taxes have been paid, and as we already discussed in an earlier chapter, import taxes on cars are exorbitant. You do not want to purchase a vehicle only to find out later that the title is not completely clean.

He will also help you purchase property. Gilford makes sure every "t" is crossed when handling your contract. An uncrossed "t" can cause immeasurable trouble down the line. And remember, all the paperwork will be in Spanish. If you want to know what anal cramps feel like, sign a contract in another language.

Gilferd doesn't file residency applications anymore. Coincidently, he decided this after working on ours. It appears people quit a lot of things after dealing with the Pisanis.

"It's not you," he explained. "It's not easy dealing with immigration and all the issues that inevitably come up. It just takes too much time to do it correctly."

I remember an incident where Gilferd had to show receipts to immigration proving we paid a certain fee.

"You deposited the money into the wrong account," the clerk told Gilferd.

"But that is the account number on the immigration form. I just followed procedure," he replied.

"We decided that we are not going to use that account anymore. This will take a couple weeks to straighten out. You need to make another appointment and return."

Thankfully, Gilferd took the necessary steps and it all worked out, but there are only so many times you can make an appointment to fix things you thought you had already fixed. After a while, it makes you loopy. I want to mention that at the beginning of the residency process Gilferd quoted us a price. Although it ended up being a lot more work, with many more trips to immigration than he had planned, he honored our original agreement.

If you do contact Gilferd for his services, please tell him I said hello. I really love this guy, and his wife is very sweet as well. Gilferd is a wonderful man and is the type of person that makes Costa Rica a great place to live. I'm glad I can call him my friend.

Lic. Gilferd Banton Beckford
Attorney at Law
Grecia, 250 Metros Sur De La Municipalidad De Grecia, Costa Rica

Cell phone 8896-7910.
Office phone 2494-3493

# Obtaining a Driver's License

"I heard the laws have changed. Do I really need to be a resident in order to get a Costa Rican driver's license?"

Unfortunately, you can't get a Costa Rican driver's license anymore without a cedula. They won't even accept your "tramite" (the document stating your residency is being processed). This has caused headaches for many people, and I'm hoping that this decision will be reversed. I've seen several laws pass only to be reversed a short time later. There have been many occasions when I thought something was written in stone, only to find out that the stone had been stolen out of the back of someone's SUV. Crime Tip Reminder: don't leave anything in your car.

You will need to go to the La Uruca facility (COSEVI) to get your first driver's license. After that, you can renew it at various MOPT (Ministries of Public Works and Transportation) agencies around the country: Liberia, Limón, San Ramón, etc. You will know when you are near the La Uruca Motor Vehicles because you will see people holding up signs for medical exams. You read that right: medical exams. You'll need one in order to obtain a license. And sometimes they are conducted in the most unusual places.

I remember pulling into a parking lot after seeing a man holding up a dirty piece of cardboard. I thought it read "stranger danger" but Rob insisted it was directing us toward a medical office.

"How bad can it be?" Rob said after parking the car. We then walked through the garage bay to find a waiting room in a dark corner. Next to a row of plastic chairs stood a decapitated mannequin wearing dirty, corduroy shorts.

"Stop worrying," Rob urged. "We found the right place."

He was right; I was overreacting. I tend to do that when imagining someone wearing my skin as a cape. Happily, the office visit did not involve dumping my body into a twenty-foot hole.

Hannibal Lecter was actually a nice doctor who swiftly made sure I met the rudimentary requirements to drive a car.

The exam only lasted ten minutes. The physician smiled, explained that I passed, then shook my hand like a banker would after approving a commercial loan. I felt important. Apparently, finding out you are not blind and can sit at a ninety-degree angle is quite the accomplishment.

When we renewed our license three years later, we needed to also provide proof of our blood type. Some medical facilities don't do this so we went to a doctor's office in the center of Grecia. We thought it was going to be a pinprick, but they ended up taking enough to fill San José's blood bank. For as tough as my husband thinks he is, he cannot stomach the sight of blood. It seems to cause the same anxiety as walking under a palm tree full of coconuts. It was sweet how all the young Tica women came to his assistance and all but rocked him to sleep. I barely got a Band-Aid and was told to sit in the waiting room.

The renewal process is much easier than getting your first license, or at least that was what we thought at the time. A year after getting it renewed, we went to Motor Vehicles in Liberia to see if Rob could get a separate motorcycle license. We had learned that he needed one to drive the scooter legally.

The clerk informed Rob that his driver's license was illegal and quickly confiscated it. We ended up spending the whole day trying to rectify the problem. It took us a little while to figure out what had gone wrong. As I previously mentioned, when we'd renewed our licenses in San Ramón, the electricity had shut off just as the clerk was putting our information into the system. So instead of typing it into the computer, the man wrote down our new license numbers in a composition book, similar to the one I had in elementary school where I wrote my crappy essay on what I did over the summer. "Pura vida," he said, after promising that he would enter the information into the system once the lights came back on. He didn't, and thinking back, I remember that he was doodling in the same notebook. That's never a good sign.

In the end, we ended up fixing something we didn't even know needed fixing. We never got the motorcycle license but have recently found out that you don't need one anymore for scooters under 125cc. I got this information from the most reputable authority: the guy who rents scooters to tourists. A deliveryman in the post office also confirmed this. You'll find that much of the advice you get here is like an urban legend: a friend who has a cousin, that has a girlfriend, who has an aunt that dated someone at the government office. It reminds me of Rob's Brooklyn pal Tommy Walnuts: a guy who knows a guy, who knows another guy, who overheard that you can buy a cheap Rolex behind a dumpster on Avenue U.

One can conclude that the reason there is confusion is that laws are made and later overturned all the time in Costa Rica. This is good and bad. When the Costa Rican government finds a law is not working, they can quickly overturn it. That's the good part. The bad part is when the government does not relay this information to the public. Perhaps they could use a town crier.

The most important thing to take from this chapter is that it will all work out. Once you get your residency, you will be able to get a legal Costa Rican license. You'll drive these pothole-ridden roads with impunity and may even need to be pulled out of a ditch or two. But don't worry, I know a guy, who knows a guy, who knows *the* guy who can help you out.

Tips When Obtaining Your Driver's License:

- Bring copies of your cedula and your medical exam. Make sure you have proof of your blood type.
- Be sure to have some colones. You will be given a piece of paper and asked to pay a fee at the bank. Banco Nacional is right next door so this will not be a problem.

- You must provide a valid email address.

**Links**

CONSEVI: www.csv.go.cr

MOPT: www.mopt.go.cr

# Rob Loses His License

My husband has a trait that has remained constant since the day I met him: he loses things. It's the reason I carry the passports, money, boarding passes, and anything else of any importance when we are at the airport. If I did not, we may never have made it down to Costa Rica in the first place. Rob has lost jackets, hats, wallets, and scooter keys. I would estimate that a third of my marriage has been spent either watching him search for something, or listening to him complain because he couldn't find it.

It's most amusing when he misplaces things around the house, convincing himself that I moved them. "Where's my toothbrush? Did you hide it?"

This affliction flares up most often while Rob is standing in front of the refrigerator. He has not found a bottle of ketchup or mustard since 1995. Anything that he is looking for—if not dangled like a disco ball in front of his face—is all but nonexistent. If Rob was a superhero, all the villain would have to do is hide in our refrigerator... preferably behind a condiment. My husband would never find him.

Today Rob returns from doing errands and I immediately ask him to hand over his wallet. And when I say wallet, I mean a sandwich-sized Ziploc bag. I don't dare complain since this is a massive improvement from the secret spot in his underpants.

"Where's your driver's license?" I ask.

Rob grabs the bag back and goes through its contents. "It's not here? Did you take it?"

"How could I have taken it when I have been home all day? Retrace your steps—where did you go?"

Rob recounts his morning: the gas station, supermarket, phone company, and bank. He calls each business but not one of them has his license. It looks like we will be going to MOPT to get a new one, the very last thing I want to do. I'm so annoyed, I consider hiding his toothbrush.

"I hope we don't have to go back to San José," I grumble. I don't mind a six-hour drive when there is something fun on the other end, like a sloth sanctuary or national park. Motor Vehicles has nothing fun to offer.

"Nah, why would you think we would have to go back there?" Rob asks.

"Because two of our friends had to, that's why."

"It's just a replacement, how hard can it be?"

"How hard can it be?" is my husband's favorite phrase, and in fact, most of the time he's right. A lot of the things we do may not be considered hard, but a lot more like irritating, grating, and migraine-inducing.

The next day we head out to MOPT in Liberia. I make sure we are up nice and early so that we are first in line. And that plan works out great, since we are the first ones in line to be told to come back in the afternoon. They are closed all morning due to a seminar.

"Let's make a day of it in Liberia. We'll have lunch, do a little shopping, then come back to get the license," Rob suggests. We kill about four hours walking around Liberia before returning to MOPT.

"We both don't need to be tortured. Stay in the car while I go inside," Rob says. This was such a nice gesture that I forgive him for losing his license. It's just like my husband, constantly trying to protect me while stopping my nagging all at once. It's his two-for-one excursion theory, only applied to his wife.

I watch Rob as he approaches the entrance, but he doesn't go inside. He is told to stand on line with a group of ten other people all leaning on a fence, their fingers clenching the chain-link like it's Guantanamo Bay. The guard slowly lets one person in at a time. It's over thirty minutes before he gets to my husband and allows him into the building.

An hour later, I see Rob walking back to the car. He doesn't look happy.

"What a nightmare," he explains. "I ask for a replacement license, and the clerk insists I go to San José."

"I knew it!" I shout. Finally, my anxiety is justified. What I heard from my friend wasn't an urban legend but very true indeed.

"I kept telling him that he was wrong," Rob continues. "I'm positive that I can get a replacement license here. I even showed him my bank receipt as proof that the fee has been paid. After that got me nowhere, I noticed the guy who helped me out last time. I walked over to him and explained my problem. We started talking Nadine, and things got a little weird."

"Oh no, did they take your cedula? Are we in trouble?" I always think I'm in trouble. I go through most of my life thinking I'm in trouble.

"He started talking about women. How much he likes them, and he asks if I like women too. In the back of my mind all I wanted was my driver's license, so I said yes… I like women."

"So, what's the big deal?"

"We talked *a lot* about them. I think I talked more about women today than I did in college or even high school. It got a little crazy. He asked me which kind of girls I liked, so I told him I liked Australian girls, French girls…"

"Okay, I get it," I laugh "Australian and French girls."

"It went *on and on*. I also said I liked Italian girls, Hungarian girls…"

"Give me a break, Rob. You couldn't even point out Hungary on a map."

Rob continues to go down a thorough and oddly detailed list of the many girls he enjoys. A venerable tour of the world, if you will. I had no idea he was so multicultural. From the number of countries he lists, I would suspect any woman who walks past Rob is a potential candidate. It's only after he finishes his inventory that he pulls out his shiny new driver's license.

"You got it? Why didn't you start the conversation with that?"

"I feel kind of guilty. I would normally never go on that way with anyone, but I couldn't imagine getting back in the car and driving six hours to San José. I just kept letting him talk and continued chatting it up like we were frat brothers. It was only after our conversation about Brazilian women that he went to the computer and processed my license. Shortly after that, I got the heck out of there."

Rob feels bad about this conversation? I feel great about it. If I'd been there I might have pulled out a world map and handed them pushpins.

"Seriously, this is silly. I did not want to go back to San José, either. You are forgiven."

"I just wanted you to know the conversation took place. Things were said."

I never worry about scandalous situations concerning Rob. He can have any conversation about any woman he wants to because he is the world's worst liar. Back when we first started dating in New York Chiropractic College, he had to break up with a girl because things were getting serious between us. She called his dorm room while I was there. Rob said a few words to her, hung up the phone, and told me it was his mother. He then walked over to the closet, stepped inside, and closed the door on himself. He stayed in there for seven minutes.

We drive home, happily knowing that we accomplished what we set out to do in one day, and that not all urban legends are correct. You can get a replacement license in Liberia. I'm also happy to say that my husband did not come home and hide in the closet. Maybe a Jersey girl is all he needs.

# Banking in Costa Rica: Where's My Free Toaster?

In my first book I wrote about my husband's crazy idea to open a bank account in Zurich, Switzerland. It was pretty ridiculous; we rode our free tourist bicycles, parked out front, and waltzed inside looking like *The Beverly Hillbillies*. There is nothing like driving your Schwinn to one of the most prestigious banking facilities in the world. This was one of the most embarrassing things my husband has ever roped me into.

You have probably figured out by now that we are not the highfalutin clients Swiss banks usually entertain on a Thursday morning. Not that I don't think I deserve trips to fancy Swiss banks. If given the chance, I'd make my $25 dollar deposit every week just so I could pull out my Kindle and relax on their leather couch.

We eventually did enjoy highfalutin treatment at the bank in the form of gassy water and chocolates served on silver platters. That experience was a lot of fun and made me realize that I'm married to a man that will try to make anything happen, no matter how stupid the idea is.

On my very first visit to Costa Rica, I went to the Banco Nacional in Tamarindo to exchange money. There were no marble staircases or bankers dressed in Armani suits. What it lacked in panache was made up for with seventy-five heavily perspiring people sitting in plastic lawn chairs. As a teller became available, every person would stand up and shift down a seat. It was the sweaty version of Musical Chairs.

While waiting my turn, I noticed a sign overhead with stick figure drawings representing people who were allowed to go straight to the front of the line. There was one that looked pregnant, one bent over holding a cane, and the other looked as if it was getting electrocuted. Was it really necessary to inform us that Mr. Crispy Kilowatt needed to go first? Let's face it, this poor schmuck was having a really bad day and it was the least we could do. This was vastly different from my Switzerland experience, but it was just as entertaining.

The lines at banks now have become increasingly shorter. Most banks have a machine that gives you a number, which makes the process a little more orderly. But don't expect to get out of there quickly: a trip to the bank in Costa Rica is still a time-consuming process.

There are two main banks in Costa Rica: Banco Nacional de Costa Rica and Banco de Costa Rica. You will find that almost any major town will have one or both of these banks. If not a branch, certainly an ATM will be available. You may want to use one of these while obtaining temporary residency. There are other banks to choose from, but these two appear to have the most branches and cause the least amount of roadblocks.

- Expect a 3% transaction fee when using an international bankcard. Check with your bank before visiting to see what they charge.

- Some businesses do not take credit cards without raised digits. If you have a card and the numbers are printed on the back, you may have to use an ATM or debit card. I know of someone that was declined at a rental card agency because his credit card did not have raised digits.

When it was time to open our bank account (as per residency requirements) we had an incredibly difficult time. Costa Rican banks will not allow anyone without legal residency to open an account anymore. Since 9/11, the United States wants to know where its citizens' money is coming from and going to. Banks all around the world are required to let the United States government know who opened an account and how much is in it. There is absolutely no way to move your money here anonymously.

When we first tried to open a Costa Rican bank account, we were refused. Even with all the rigorous procedures to gain residency (proving we had enough money, a clean criminal record, etc.) the bank was hesitant. They do not care at all about immigration: their job is to ensure the bank is not harboring money that was illegally obtained through tax evasion, drug sales, or terrorist activities. Our backs were to the wall: we couldn't get residency without a bank account, and we couldn't get a bank account unless we were residents.

We tried to open an account at several banks and were given the same explanation. Finally at the last bank we visited we mentioned that we had a safe deposit box there (our landlady had provided a letter of recommendation in order for us to receive it). The teller went through their files and eventually found the document. It was only then we were allowed to open an account. I found it amusing that our goodwill letter was sufficient to fulfill their requirement. I'm not sure how that stops terrorists, since suicide bombers probably have nice landladies that would compose a flattering letter for them as well: "He's a determined worker and never gives up on something he believes in. He also lets the other We eventually walked out of the bank with our account and were able to finalize our residency requirements. Although we did not get a free toaster, blender, or Igloo cooler when opening our account, I did enjoy butterflies and rainbows for the rest of the day. All these crazy stories seem to end like this. Living in Costa Rica promises four really glorious days for every mind-numbing one.

tenants use his barbecue. Such a sweet boy."

Bureaucratic challenges are just that: challenges. Results may vary so be prepared. Every expatriate you meet will have a ridiculous story, but the common thread is that it usually works out in the end. It may not be exactly what you want, but you usually get what you need. Never at the speed you are hoping for, but there will be some degree of progress.

When you encounter situations like this, remember why you are here. If you're like me, you love Costa Rica and are amused when white-throated magpies dart out of the trees to steal food out of your hand and speechless when the sky transforms into an orange Creamsicle at the end of the day. Don't let a bad afternoon veer you off course, since a pothole will eventually do that for you anyway.

Items to Bring to the Bank When Opening an Account in Costa Rica:

- Passport: original as well as copies.
- Driver's license: original as well as copies.
- A utility bill.
- Copies of your lease since the utility bill will be useless if it is in your landlord's name.
- Two bank statements from your existing bank no older than six months.
- A notarized letter from your current bank stating you have adequate funds in your account. They may ask you to have this notarized in Costa Rica as well.
- Bring a smile and a friendly disposition in order to reinforce the fact that you're not a money launderer, drug dealer, or terrorist.

Important Note:

- Make sure you get a printout of your deposits from your Costa Rican bank every couple months. When you renew your residency, you will be asked for proof that you deposited the necessary funds. Costa Rica banks can't give you a print out for dates past six months.

**Links**

Banco de Costa Rica: www.bancobcr.com

Banco Nacional: www.bncr.fi.cr

# Rodrigo the Repairman

Costa Rica: the Land of Misfit Appliances. Just when you think your morning is going along smoothly, a weird buzzing sound radiates from your toaster (the same one you did not get free from the Costa Rican bank). You try to remain optimistic; you may even clean out the crumb tray and jiggle its cord a little, but you are just prolonging the agony. The prognosis is terminal.

The one good thing about Costa Rican appliances is that they usually detonate in fiery spectacles no less impressive than a failed North Korean missile launch. I've already mentioned my air conditioning unit. It filled our bedroom with toxic smoke before shooting a lightning bolt across the room. I thought it was the grooviest thing I'd ever seen at three in the morning, but then again I was ditzy from the plastic fumes I had been inhaling in my sleep. I would have been impressed by anything.

I recently bought an electric coffeemaker and when my husband asked about the warranty, the cashier explained that it had a guarantee of one year. Rob pressed the issue since we had just gone through four of them in the past three months. The woman called over the manager, who took a look at the box, scratched his head, and decided that this product only had a one-month warranty. We bought it anyway and it exploded on day thirty-two. Am I upset by this? Not at all. It was a pleasure to have enjoyed those thirty-two glorious, caffeinated days.

Take my friend, Richard: he's been struggling with a cantankerous ice maker for over two years. I often see him shuffling around town dragging various lengths of PVC tubing behind him. When I ask how the project is going, his eyes glaze over as if remembering a simpler time: one where you manually filled trays with water and inserted them into your freezer. Poor Richard just can't keep this thing working for more than a couple weeks and he has probably already paid repairmen more than the ice maker is worth.

Richard is also dealing with malfunctioning lawn sprinklers. He remembers watching the workers install them and noticing that the pipes looked awfully narrow. Thinking they must know what they were doing, he didn't question them. Fast forward a couple months and a minefield of water geysers began erupting all over his lawn. One would have envied this new water feature if Richard didn't resemble someone who was suffering a massive stroke while telling the story.

This brings me to my refrigerator, which on the surface looks like a normal refrigerator. There are two doors, a stainless steel front panel, and a spacious produce drawer inside. But as with any grifter who has patiently gained your trust, appearances can be deceiving.

My refrigerator runs continually. It's like having a biker revving a Harley-Davidson in your kitchen all day long. Not only is it loud, but our monthly electric bill is equivalent to lighting up Yankee Stadium. Since duct tape does not appear to be solving the problem, Rob caves in and calls a repairman. The only one we can get in touch with is a gentleman named Rodrigo. He says he will be here by nine tomorrow morning.

When making an appointment with a repairman, you can count on your friends to start making bets. These wagers are placed on how late he will be, with a spread that covers whether or not he will show up at all. The odds are usually ten to one against you.

When I explained my predicament over the phone to Brooke, she sighed. Her refrigerator has been on the fritz for months and the repairman still hasn't shown up. On the other hand, her landscaper did for one day. He borrowed her rake and never returned.

It's the next day, and nine o'clock comes and goes with no repairman in sight. But Rob is an eternally optimistic guy that believes this guy will show up, which he does, at four in the afternoon. It is then that we spot Rodrigo the Repairman beeping outside our gate. We greet him as if Publishers Clearing House

Sweepstakes just handed us balloons and a big cardboard check. This is the universal reaction when repairmen actually show up in Costa Rica. I practically jump up and down but Rob shows restraint. A lot is riding on this.

Rodrigo heads straight to the kitchen with a serious look in his eye. I like him. He's carrying a toolbox and is wearing dungarees and sneakers.

"You see," Rob says while pointing to the man's shoes. "He's not wearing flip-flops. This guy means business."

Rodrigo presses his ear against the refrigerator like a determined safecracker. He taps on the front of it in rapid succession, pauses, and then taps again.

He nods his head. I nod too just to make sure we're all in agreement. We all stand around nodding at each other before he pulls the refrigerator away from the wall and tries to maneuver it around the kitchen island. It's only then we realize it doesn't fit past the space between the island and the wall. Unfortunately, there is no exit strategy unless we unbolt this massive granite island and move it out of the way. Rodrigo then suggests we all lift it over the structure like the three of us are some sort of beefy, appliance-lifting superheroes. I turn to Rob and he is already reading my mind. If you are looking for someone with feats of remarkable strength, don't glance in my direction. My biceps have the girth of fettuccine noodles.

Rob informs the repairman that lifting it is not an option since he doesn't want it crashing down on our landlord's tiled floor. Rodrigo pauses, scratches his head, and walks outside. It seems everyone is scratching their head in this town.

"Where's he going?" I panic.

"Stand down. Give the man some space," Rob replies. His nerves are on edge; this might be the only shot we have.

Rodrigo returns, dragging our garden hose behind him. *Interesting*, I think. According to my understanding of the physics surrounding garden hoses, they usually shoot water with maximum velocity. I can't imagine what he has in mind. And that's when I witness the most remarkable display of repairmanship that has ever occurred inside someone's kitchen. Rodrigo proceeds to spray the back of the refrigerator with an intensity that can only be compared to extinguishing an Australian bushfire.

I watch in amazement, as one would while their dining room fills with an inch of water. Occasionally he presses down on the nozzle with his thumb, splattering the coils with a blast of water. He sways to and fro, sometimes placing the hose between his legs while raising the tip up into the air. Not sure what to do—and not wanting to criticize Rodrigo—I stand there and do nothing as Rob runs into the bathroom to gather towels.

Right before my garbage pail floats downstream, Rodrigo stops and instructs Rob to turn off the hose. Things start looking up from here. Not only do I have a clean floor but the back of my refrigerator is spotless. I can't wait to show my mother-in-law when she comes back for a visit.

"How do people live with all that dust and grime back there?" I will passive aggressively say while pulling it away from the walls. She'll never complain about what shelf I put the milk on after she sees how finicky I am about behind-the-refrigerator sanitation.

Just when I think I've seen the best in show, Rodrigo surprises me and pulls out a hammer from his toolbox. He proceeds to randomly bash the side of the appliance. After the third smack, it occurs to me that I could have done this myself. In fact, I'm not at all against bashing the side of my dishwasher if that's what it takes to stop it from leaking. I will even wear Taser shoes and karate kick it for good measure. Eighty dollars later, Rodrigo seems satisfied with his work and leaves.

The refrigerator did remain quiet for a couple days but the sound eventually returned. Rob tried a few swings with the hammer, but it hasn't helped. It looks like we'll have to live with it.

When explaining this story to Brooke, she seems genuinely sympathetic.

"I know it seems crazy, but that's just how it is here. We've all been through it," she replies. "But I have to ask, do you still have your hose?"

I ran outside and found the hose neatly coiled on the front lawn. So really, Rodrigo was not that bad after all.

# Will I Be Able to Work in Costa Rica?

I received an email this morning from Kyle, a university student who had an important employment inquiry:

*Hi Happier,*

*I'm quitting college to start a career in bikini photography on the beaches of Costa Rica. Can you offer any advice? Where can I find more information? Looking forward to your reply.*

*Kyle*

I admire how quickly Kyle has found his calling in life. It took me more than a decade to realize I needed a career change. I would never discourage this young man. What twenty-something-year-old would not enjoy taking photos of scantily clad women for a living? I've already mentioned how young people have an uncanny ability to believe anything is possible, and I can't help but admire their enthusiasm.

Not everyone is like dear Kyle: most of us would be filled with fear and anxiety upon starting such a risky endeavor, and if you will be depending on an income right away, things can get tricky. Costa Rica is super protective of its citizens and does not want jobs filled illegally with foreign workers. The law states people cannot work in Costa Rica unless they have permanent residency.

There are exceptions, such as obtaining a work permit. A person's potential employer must write a letter to the Department of Immigration stating that the individual has skills for a job that cannot be filled locally. The employer must also provide notarized copies of your passport and a valid birth certificate. The potential employee will be required to go to San José for fingerprinting.

If this does not sound like an option for you, you can legally open your own business but there are stipulations involved. One being the business owner cannot perform duties that can be filled with Costa Rican workers. For example, a restaurant owner can manage the business but not be his own waiter. None of this should deter you from starting a business in Costa Rica, and I've seen many people succeed.

Bad things can happen if you try to work here illegally. Some have been escorted to the airport and kicked out of the country. Others have had a lot of explaining to do to immigration officials. If you should find yourself in this situation, please ask them if it is true that I don't need a scooter license. I'm sure they know someone who has an uncle, that has a friend, who works at Motor Vehicles.

I was at a surf shop the other day and surmised that the blue-eye, blond-haired kid working behind the register probably wasn't a Tico. His last name was Feingold and he spoke with a *Fast Times at Ridgemont High* Spicoli-accent. It seemed suspicious to say the least.

"I bet he's working here illegally," I whispered to Rob. His response was to tell me to mind my own business, which in the past I've had problems doing.

One night while I was still living in Pennsylvania, I heard an argument going on outside my window.

I peeked between the curtains and witnessed someone stab another man in the head with a screwdriver. After the police were called, I went outside to tell them what I had seen. Instantly I became their star witness. I was given an appreciative pat on the back and thanked for my community service. I was also given a not-so-appreciative subpoena four months later, when I was summoned to stand in the front of a courtroom and point out the man who had the proclivity for stabbing people in the head with carpentry tools. We moved soon after that.

One of the most common questions that people ask me is what type of business they should start. Here are a few questions you should ask yourself: What am I good at? Do I have enough capital to start such a business? And finally, what services are needed in the area I will be relocating to? The best advice I can give is to investigate the neighborhood you are considering and spend at least six months trying to find a service or product that is not already being provided.

Someone recently asked me if a kosher delicatessen would make for a successful venture. I will tell you this: it would be successful with me. Mazel tov to you and your shiny lunch counter full of dreams. I have not found a deli yet, but I know a good bagel and lox would be a nice addition to the typical Costa Rican cuisine.

Some businesses I would like to see more of include: electronics repair, plumbers, and competent electricians. I would not protest a mass immigration of German mechanics, since Claus is very busy and could use some help.

My husband's dream would be to find a local pizza parlor where he can buy a slice instead of a whole pie. He can't go a week without complaining about this. "It defies logic," he mumbles every time we get stuck purchasing an entire pizza. He always finishes the whole thing so I'll never understand his dissatisfaction with the current arrangement.

The longer you're here, the more opportunities will present themselves. Each area of the country is different, but there is room for innovative ideas everywhere you go. Hopefully you'll find the perfect solution for a common challenge. Doing so will help ensure that your business will take off.

Take our entrepreneur, Kyle for example. He has a dream and a camera. Well... I can't actually be sure he owns the camera yet. He's ready to quit college in order to follow his passion and start photographing pretty girls on the beach. I wish him luck. Perhaps he'll run into a girl under her beach umbrella, smothered in SPF 50, and smelling of bug repellant.

I'll be sure to smile for the camera.

# Jamie Peligro Bookstore

Ernest Hemingway, F. Scott Fitzgerald, Ezra Pound, and others infamously known as the "lost generation" spent many hours at the Paris bookstore, *Shakespeare and Company*. Sylvia Beach, the owner, took several authors under her wing, helping them during the leanest times of their lives. Unfortunately, she closed her store in 1941 under the cloak of darkness after refusing to sell a German soldier her last copy of James Joyce's *Finnegans Wake*.

Legend has it that Ernest Hemingway, accompanied by allied troops, liberated the shop in 1944. But Hemingway often built elaborate bravado sandcastles, these tales often filled with elegant displays of heroism. Nonetheless, I like to imagine that this one is true: Hemingway riding on top of a jeep, calling out to Sylvia, the woman who helped him at a time when no one knew his name.

We all look for places like this: ones that nurture our passions, where it's our ideals and talents that are admired not the depth of our pockets. Luckily, my neighborhood has one of these places, with an owner that is as interesting as the people who shop there.

Tucked back behind the main drag in Tamarindo, Jamie Peligro Bookstore has a large selection of books, CDs, and postcards. It possesses what every good independent bookstore should: shelves and shelves of mysteries, histories, and romances. Book lovers know that the greatest escape doesn't require us to move to a new country. When we surrender our imagination to an author, we can be transported anywhere.

This bookstore is also a great resource for music connoisseurs. There are people in this world who listen to music, and then there are people like Jim, the owner, who *really* live for music. He can rattle off the merits of the Ramones, or the best live concerts performed by the Rolling Stones. It's fun to be around passionate people like him, but what I love most about Jim is his sense of humor.

When I told him I was writing a chapter on working in Costa Rica, he immediately laughed. Weathering many storms himself, Jim has also seen many expats who have come and gone. He has witnessed business ventures that have succeeded, and others that have never even gotten off the ground. The following are some of his tales and advice after many years of working in Tamarindo.

"My first friends in Costa Rica were two Canadian brothers and their cousin. They owned and ran La Bodega, a successful indoor/outdoor nightclub in Tamarindo. After about a year, they informed me that they had sold the business. Within a week, they were gone. I was flabbergasted.

"When the global economic implosion occurred around 2008, Tamarindo became a Petri dish for Darwin's theory. Weak ones, God love'em, got washed away. Only the people with enough fortitude and passion for this place survived. Here are a couple stories from both sides of the coin.

"Sean showed up in 2003, about the same time that I did, on a one-way ticket and with a thousand bucks to his name. He is a photographer whose work has been published in *Rolling Stone Magazine*, *Healthy Living*, *Golf Digest*, *BusinessWeek* and the *New York Times*. Although he could get by working as a chef, his passion was, and still is, photography.

"Sean is also an experienced travel photographer, obsessed at times with shooting human-interest photos, and works on projects geared toward ecological preservation. He's found ways to persevere during lean times and get through nasty entanglements with girlfriends. He always comes out fine in the end, relentlessly pursuing what he loves and seemingly content with his life. After ten years of being his friend, I'd have to call him a Tamarindo success story.

"Here is a story on the flip side of the coin.

"Bill and Elizabeth came to Costa Rica from Canada, shopping for a business to retire into. Their son was grown, and they had the prospect of an early retirement package from both their employers. They fell in love with Elevations Café, which happened to be for sale —coincidentally—by another Canadian couple. Bill and Elizabeth proceeded to buy the business: a turnkey operation.

This is where the story gets loony. They decided that they wanted to put their own stamp on the new restaurant, so they basically gutted Elevations Café, changed the name, the menu, and the furniture—the whole sha-bang. Meanwhile, they rented a three-bedroom house with a pool in Langosta, paying an exorbitant monthly rent I won't even repeat.

"Five months into the venture, they returned to Canada to attend their son's wedding. At the reception, both friends and family razzed them for leaving the country.

"'Well, now that Jon's married, you know what comes next, right?' a friend smirked. 'Are you really planning on being those long-distance grandparents we've heard about? I suppose you can always see your grandchildren at Christmas.'

"To add to the stress, they were both offered their old jobs back… with signing bonuses. None of these new events were known to any of us here in Tamarindo at the time. When they returned to Costa Rica, they put the business up on the chopping block. We were truly aghast when, three weeks later, they liquidated everything in the restaurant, pulled up stakes, and bailed. In my conservative estimate, they had bled about $100,000 in less than half a year.

"My advice to anyone considering a move here or starting a business is to visit at different times of the year. Make sure you have enough capital to exist for a year and a half without any revenue from the business. Make sure you are legally employed and employ legal residents. Most importantly, find yourself a niche. Rather than reinventing the wheel by going into competition with an existing business, find a way to fill a need. And make sure it is something you have a passion for. If it were financial success I was looking for, I would have stayed an operations manager at a Napa Valley winery.

Contentment and being my own boss were primary goals for me, along with gearing down into a less frantic lifestyle. This is my formula for success and I'm happy to say I've found it here."

When I first visited Jim's bookstore, I brought along a few copies of my first *Happier* book. He was kind to me and graciously included them in his inventory. Jim even gave me a nice display spot. I remember that moment: seeing them for the first time on his shelves. I think I arranged the books a dozen times, lining them up, dusting them off, making sure they appeared attractive to potential buyers. I believed my life couldn't get any better. It is still one of my fondest memories.

Much has happened since my first meeting with Jim, but he is still my Sylvia Beach. And I promise that if his store ever needs liberating from Nazis, Rob and I will come riding up on our scooter armed with rocks, sticks, and a can of mace. It's the least we can do.

There is a lot to be said for those authors and artists who picked up and moved to Paris after WWI. Whether they were looking for a more affordable place to live, or just a chance to see the world from a different perspective, I don't believe any of them were ever "lost." So often, people think that moving abroad means one is wandering through life without a sense of direction.

It turns out I felt more lost while working in my office back in Pennsylvania than I ever did while traveling on a dirt road in Costa Rica.

**Links**

Jamie Peligro Bookstore:
www.facebook.com/TamarindoJaimePeligro

# Losing Weight, Getting Healthy & Sun Salutations

One of the best things about living in Costa Rica is an abundance of fruits and vegetables. The produce is incredibly affordable and it's great incentive to eat better when a box of Froot Loops cost seven dollars. When deciding whether or not to buy junk food here, our conversation sounds more like a seminar on fiscal policy.

"Do you think we should?" I'll ask nervously. If you notice a woman in the cereal aisle sweating and punching a handheld calculator, that's me. The guy in the black tank top mindlessly throwing items in our cart is my husband.

"Why not? We haven't splurged in a while. Let's go nuts. Look, there is even a toy inside," Rob replies. My husband has an Italian appetite and has absolutely no reservations about purchasing expensive items once in a while. Just the other day he walked into the house with a birthday cake, all because he felt like having a slice. I couldn't get annoyed with him for spending the money since it's his laid-back attitude that I love most. And maybe he's right: why shouldn't we enjoy birthday cake more than once a year?

This is an active country and you'll see many people walking, cycling, or playing soccer. When I first moved here, I went to breakfast with my Tico neighbor and I'll never forget his reaction. I had ordered the "American Breakfast": eggs, bacon, toast, and pancakes. My neighbor couldn't believe it.

"Don't you get tired after eating that?" he asked.

His breakfast was very simple: a plate of fruit accompanied by a small side of beans and rice. And he was right, I was sleepy a half hour later. Since then, I've adopted much of my Costa Rican neighbor's diet and I've never felt better.

It turns out all those expensive imported items in the grocery store are a blessing. It reminds me that I did not move to Costa Rica to replicate my life back in the United States. Beans, rice, fruits, and vegetables support a healthier lifestyle than Pop Tarts and frozen pizza. Why pay so much for junk food when a pineapple is less than a dollar?

It didn't take long for Rob to lose the forty pounds he had gained while working. I didn't have a lot of weight to lose, but just getting the chemicals out of my system did wonders for my attitude. You don't realize what all that sugar is doing to you until you wean yourself off it. Everything becomes clearer, and a pleasant attitude ends up replacing depressive mood swings.

The more my diet improves, the more I want to exercise. And the more I exercise, the better my diet becomes. I do yoga every morning and find that it calms my mind, creating the tranquility that I was desperately lacking. Now it's hard for me to even remember the stressed-out person I was before moving here.

My girlfriend, Colleen, is a local yoga instructor in the Flamingo area. She's one of those people who has such good energy and you'll love being around her. Happiness radiates from Colleen, and she also does a lot for the community, especially concerning animal welfare.

Her classes are full not only with local residents, but with tourists as well. Each morning she meets people in search of an escape from their hectic lives. They visit Costa Rica hoping to experience some of the serenity they have read about. I recently met up with Colleen and asked her if her students seem to adopt a healthier lifestyle as easily as I did.

"People get off the plane and initially feel great," Colleen says. "But many times in a month or so something happens to them. When you come down to a slower pace, it's not uncommon to have illness strike. When changing your routine, your body needs a chance to calm down as quickly as your mind has. It can take thirty to sixty days to come off the high of working. It is very important to listen to your body during this period.

"Landing here is not a silver bullet to good health; you must take charge of your own diet and lifestyle. Like you always say, it is actually less expensive to eat healthy here than to continue eating processed foods. Once you get off a junk food diet, your mind begins to clear and this is the perfect time to start yoga.

"Being surrounded by green mountains, roaring howler monkeys, and the sounds of the ocean make for an uplifting experience. Many of my students had never taken a yoga class before, but they end up loving it! They feel good and begin to connect with their surroundings. We resonate when practicing in a place so close to nature. Every time a wave rolls in, you can feel the thunderous energy from the earth below. I can only describe this feeling as bliss.

"So many of my students had been advised to try yoga. Doctors and psychologists have been recommending it for years, so the seed is already planted. It's just making the time to find a class or instructor they connect with. Once they make the decision to step through my door, they feel the healing begin.

"Not everyone is able to move to Costa Rica, and I have many students who are just here on vacation. They visit this country to try new things and get healthier, both mentally and physically. My favorite experiences are with people being introduced to yoga for the first time. At the end of their holiday they proudly tell me they are going to continue to practice at home. This makes my heart sing.

"I absolutely love having my practice outdoors. Watching the sunset while doing child's pose is incredibly grounding, and being grounded is of utmost importance to yogis. In my class, you have room to breathe. Unfortunately, I've been to some classes where they cram many people into a small studio. Outside, one's body can move more freely. It's a completely different experience.

"Overall, I have found what I need in Costa Rica. Yoga is life-changing. Being an expat is life-changing. The combination of both is magical."

Colleen has helped many people with her yoga classes. She's witnessed people who have balanced their lives, made healthier choices, and let go of the rat race. I agree with her when she says landing in Costa Rica is not a panacea for all that ails you. Adopting a healthier lifestyle takes a little work and some flexibility. But what I've learned most from my adventure is that life is a seesaw: you're usually up or down, and rarely in between. But if people work together, with someone surprising you with birthday cake and another inviting you to a yoga class, you could end up balancing in midair. And that's a great place to be.

**Links**

Colleen Ouellete:
http://sattvayogacostarica.com/
www.facebook.com/CRSattvaYoga

# How to Make a Living: The Crazy Cookie Lady  *

Meet Brian and Julie. You'll probably see them at their stand, The Crazy Cookie Lady, if you visit any farmers' markets in the Flamingo/Tamarindo area. What started out as a hobby now has Julie and Brian taking orders and making gluten-free products for expats and Ticos alike. They will surely inspire anyone who is thinking about changing direction and starting a new life abroad.

"Julie and I visited Costa Rica for the first time in 2010. When we stepped off the plane, I told Julie I was going to live here someday. She told me I was nuts! She wasn't leaving her friends, family, or our new forever home we had built. We visited a total of five more times, and every time she felt more of what I had felt along. It was a calling for us to come to Costa Rica. We listed our home in March of 2014 and arrived in Costa Rica in September 2014 with three pallets of stuff from the States along with two cats and a dog.

"We kind of stumbled into baking for the farmers' market. Julie makes a delicious flan de caramello, and we started to sell it along with whoopie pies at the ferria on Saturdays. Logistically, flan was difficult to transport because the caramello needs to be kept cold. But after being at the market and listening to people, we noticed that many were looking for gluten-free baked goods. Julie is gluten intolerant and has lots of experience baking these items. She makes her own gluten-free flour blend which allows her to take any recipe that calls for all-purpose flour and substitute it cup for cup.

"As a result, there is no limit to combination of recipes. She now bakes for three different farmers' markets in the area along with special and business orders. I have since taken over the whoopie pie baking, our only product that isn't gluten free. We sell an average of three hundred whoopie pies per month. We have even added gluten-free white bread to our list of baked goods and the response has been overwhelming. It tastes great!

"We also find time to volunteer at our local Beach Community Church in Brasilito. We also help out at Abriendo Mentes, a local non-profit that teaches English as a second language to children and adults in Playa Potrero.

"Funny story. Julie was cleaning one day before our friends arrived from the States for a visit. She picked up what was she believed was a gecko egg dud. As she picked it up, the egg hatched and out popped a gecko into her hand. She screamed, so I came running into the room to find out what happened. She proceeded to inform me of the drama that had just played out with the baby gecko sitting in the middle of the floor. Panic instantly turned to laughter as we could not control ourselves. It was a wonderful introduction to our new life in Costa Rica."

# Land, Villas or Condominiums

"Are real estate prices going up? Should I buy now?"

If you're thinking about buying a piece of property in Costa Rica, I'll have to introduce you to my old realtor Martin. He uses the controversial but engaging "extreme sport of realtoring" method. He'll hike you through a jungle, across crocodile-filled streams, and into fields of angry bulls. All of which to show you things that probably aren't for sale or can only be accessed by a hot air balloon.

Martin liked to speculate on a lot of things, but I have found it is near impossible to speculate on real estate in Costa Rica. You can hardly speculate on whether you are going to have electricity that day. However, there seem to be more people interested in moving here and wondering if they should buy now or wait.

When looking on the Internet, there are times when the prices don't look all that different than where you are living. That cute little Costa Rican house on the ridge may cost you the same as one in a subdivision in the United States or Canada. But here that cute little house on the ridge comes with a 180-degree view and flocks of parrots that will greet you every morning.

If you travel about a half hour from any tourist town, or even a busy town like Grecia, you'll notice that prices come down quite a bit. Many people are hesitant to look any farther than in towns where all of the expats are living, but a small distance away may suit your budget a lot better.

The reason so many people stick to their asking price is that holding onto a piece of property here doesn't cost that much. Real estate tax is only .25%. Did you see the point before the 25? So if your land is valued at $100,000 your real estate taxes are $250 per year. This is something you need to take into consideration when moving to Costa Rica and planning your budget. I have a friend in New Jersey who pays $12,000 a year in taxes on her house, and it's not even that big of a house. But let's be modest and say you spend

$5,000 a year on real estate taxes. This is one bill that will be substantially less here. One thing you need to be aware of when buying a home is the new Costa Rican Luxury Tax. You'll read more about this in my upcoming tax chapter.

With each blog post I write I always include a cost-of-living update, and at times people will criticize me for eating a sandwich that cost six dollars. "I can get it cheaper around the corner at my neighborhood deli," they say. Take into consideration I'm eating this sandwich at the top of a mountain while watching the sunset over the ocean. I could go to a nearby soda (small eatery on the side of the road) without a view and pay much less. And if I pack a lunch I could save even more. It's the same with real estate. If you want that ocean view, it will be more expensive.

It appears the most popular type of real estate transactions at the moment are condominiums; some are priced under $100,000. There are deals here, but with a good deal there may be risk. It's best to have your feet on the ground in Costa Rica while you are looking.

I recently met a pair of brothers that got a very good deal on a condominium in the exclusive Reserva Conchal development. They are planning on renting it out and using it as a vacation getaway. They happened to come down at the right time and fell in love with this two-bedroom, two-bathroom condominium. It's a perfect start for their family, and now they are looking for a larger piece of land.

Living here helped me to realize how little I actually need. Happiness is all around. For some it's an ocean view high on a mountaintop, or a five-thousand-square-foot mansion. For others, it's a modest farmhouse in the country. Each has its charm and I like them all. Go with what you can afford. I know plenty of people who are happy owning their home, and others who wish they had only rented. Everyone's situation is different so don't base your decision on someone else's dream. Only you know what is right for you, and there is nothing wrong with taking your time, renting in different parts of the country, and doing your research.

**Links**

Resources for purchasing or renting a home:

www.costaricarealestate.com

www.adjustyourlatitude.com

www.coastalrealtycostarica.com

www.costaricarentalsnow.com

www.welovecostarica.com

# Close-Enough Plumbing

I'm in the hardware store when I notice my friend Richard talking with an employee. I'm not surprised to see he is carrying a half dozen PVC elbows and three cans of adhesive. I don't dare ask him about his ice maker, since I fear his sanity is on the line. Poor Richard is stumbling through all nine circles of Dante's Hell, and it looks like Rob and I will be joining him.

We woke up this morning to find water seeping through a wall. Apparently, an underground pipe had burst overnight. Ever since the whopping 7.6 earthquake we experienced over a year ago, random pipes have sporadically started to leak. Whatever may have been loose to begin with just got the green light to cause mayhem in our house.

I'm lucky to be living with one of the original Mario Brothers. My husband never wavers when it comes to plumbing debacles. He approaches each repair with a toolbox full of glue, duct tape, and an Italian accent. For some reason, whenever he's fixing a pipe he talks like a demented guy from Sicily: "Now I take-a-the-glue, and paint-a-the-pipe, like-a-the-Michelangelo. Ciao, bella!"

As with all matters of PVC repair, I remain on the couch while Rob goes outside and begins to dig. After a few hours, and with a moderate degree of heat exhaustion, Rob returns covered in glue.

"It's fixed," he says after wiping dirt off his forehead. "Do me a favor? Go outside and shut off the sprinklers? I turned the water on to make sure the fittings weren't leaking. But be careful! Don't fall into the hole I just dug."

I get this lecture a lot, and quite frankly, it gets tiresome. I can't leave the house without hearing about my inability to manage the effects of gravity on my own body. And to prove that Rob is wrong and that I'm clearly capable of not falling into the hole, I fall into the hole.

To be fair, I didn't exactly fall but collapse. It is no less dramatic than events often witnessed at an Evangelist church altar. It's as if my body's skeletal frame has disintegrated, magnetically pulling me toward the dark abyss below. I quietly remain there, curled up like an opossum playing dead. I tend to do this whenever I suddenly find myself in a position parallel to the ground. Plus, it's at least fifteen degrees cooler underground, making it the perfect reprieve from the afternoon heat.

As I lie in the hole, Rob eventually hears my whimpering and comes running outside. I suppose I should add that the hole is only two feet deep; therefore, my husband doesn't give me the sympathy that I certainly feel is deserved after discovering his wife is lying in a hole which he himself dug. But after determining I am fine, he asks me to check all the PVC fittings while I am down there. I quickly roll into action since the fetal position creates an excellent angle for determining quality control.

This is just one of the many stories you'll hear about Costa Rican PVC fiascos. It appears a plumbing Minotaur creeps throughout this country. He'll take a bite out of your main water line in the middle of the night, or fashion geysers in the center of your lawn during a garden party. He'll have you shuffling through the hardware store, searching for a part that will magically bring back order to your home. If you think I'm exaggerating, look under any Costa Rican sink; it's bound to be a confusing labyrinth of conduit.

Since moving here, I've learned a lot regarding the fine art of plumbing, and that there are specific diameters and attributes designed for different jobs. Fifty percent of the tubing is used for hot water, fifty percent is used for cold, and one hundred percent will be installed improperly. I'm convinced that a quarter of the passengers at the airport are carrying fixtures, PVC elbows, adapters, traps, and flanges for their poor, leaking friends in Costa Rica.

I bet you never expected to read an entire chapter dedicated to PVC, but if you're planning on building a home or even just flushing a toilet or washing a dish while visiting, this may be the most important chapter in *The Costa Rica Escape Manual*. Take Richard for example: he's spending a good portion of his retirement years wedged behind an ice maker.

The following chapters will cover real estate taxes and more information about building. This may be the exact information you've been waiting for so grab your toolbox, start practicing your Italian accent, and let's get started.

# Standard & Luxury Real Estate Taxes

Warning! Nothing about this chapter will be amusing, because it is impossible to write about taxes in my usual whimsical manner. I've already used up all of my creative juices on Fifty Shades of Residency. On the flip side, if you read this when having insomnia it's going to put you out faster than listening to a Yanni CD.

The story in my first book about going to Switzerland is one hundred percent true. It was, by far, one of the funniest trips we have ever taken. My husband's thinking was that some of the biggest names in the business world utilize Swiss banks so why not us, two little business owners from Pennsylvania?

Rob uses this term, "Why not?" often. Why not pull an old piece of plastic paneling off the kitchen wall in our first fixer-upper? I'll tell you why not; it resulted in me being showered by an army of cockroaches. In retrospect, it was good practice for the tarantula that innocently decided to take a rest in my hairdryer here in Costa Rica. This time the result was me being sprayed in the face with charred spider chunks. I can honestly say, I screamed equally loud on both occasions.

In the end, a bank account in Switzerland is just like a bank account in the United States, subject to all of the same taxes for US citizens. Although we did not open any accounts, we looked at some fine watches, ate lots of Swiss chocolate, and fell off our bicycles in front of Swarovski Crystal. (I was actually the one who fell. As usual, Rob picked me up while I yodeled.)

So if you are an American citizen looking to avoid paying your taxes, I would suggest you reconsider. Let's forget about complicating our lives and do the right thing. Come here for the right reasons, and I believe you will be happier in the end.

Now let's discuss Costa Rican real estate taxes. Standard real estate taxes are .25% per year. Notice the point before that number?

Pretty incredible, especially when you are from New Jersey, where taxes can be outrageous.

Recently, Costa Rica added an additional tax. These lawmakers must have had their marketing departments working overtime because they came up with a nifty name for it: the Luxury Tax. Doesn't this make you think of eight-hundred-thread count Egyptian sheets and trips to Switzerland? Sign me up!

The "luxury" property tax is separate from standard property tax. It only applies to people whose home construction value exceeds $234,000. If the construction on your lot is valued less than that, you are exempt.

- Luxury Tax is something to consider when planning the size of your home.

The due date for both standard and luxury taxes is January 15th. Not paying either of these taxes on time will result in penalties and/or interest and if you are late on your luxury tax, your name is published in a government list of debtors. Kind of like writing a bad check at your local 7-Eleven and having them tape it to their wall.

Now let's play with these two taxes to really understand what you will be paying:

Let's say you build your dream house, and the municipality has assessed it for $200,000. You will then multiply this number by .25% and hand a check over for $500. This will cover your standard real estate tax.

Your neighbor, Jim, builds a home that has six bedrooms, a huge in-ground pool and a tennis court. You may have been jealous while he was building it, but not so much when the municipality assesses his property *(house plus land)* for $500,000. His standard property tax will be $1,250.

Luxury taxes should be thought of as a totally separate entity from the standard property tax. When deciding whether or not Jim will be subject to *luxury tax*, the municipality will look at the value of construction on his land, but *not* the value of the land itself. Once they determine that Jim is subject to luxury tax, the amount he must pay will be calculated by adding together the value of the *construction on his land plus the value of the land itself*.

Let's say the construction on Jim's property is valued at $234,000 and his land is worth $266,000. The municipality will add these two numbers together and tax Jim on the total value of his estate now assessed at $500,000.

Here is a chart that will help you determine his luxury tax:

Total Value (Construction + Land) = Tax

- $234,000 - $582,000   = 0.25%
- $582,000 - $1,168,000 = 0.30%
- $1,168,000 - $1,750,000 = 0.35%
- $1,750,000 - $2,334,000 = 0.40%
- $2,334,000 - $2,916,000 = 0.45%
- $2,916,000 - $3,504,000 = 0.50%
- $3,504,000 and over = 0.55%

Jim is in the lowest luxury tax bracket, so he will pay .25% on his $500,000 estate. ($500,000 x .25% = $1,250 luxury tax). We have now determined that Jim's luxury tax is $1,250 and that his standard property tax is an additional $1,250. By adding these two numbers together, we conclude that Jim owes $2,500 total for the year.

What have we learned from this exercise? If you don't want to pay a luxury tax, pool hopping at your neighbor's house may be a good option for you. Wait until Mr. Fancy Pants is out of town and jump in right in. Invite your friends over to use his tennis courts and outdoor kitchen.

Luxury taxes may ultimately affect how big you want to build your dream home in Costa Rica. Or maybe it won't make a difference to you at all. If that's the case, go crazy and build that extra master suite and recording studio. Heck, throw in a gym for good measure. And if you need a house sitter, don't hesitate to contact yours truly.

# Building Your Home, Architects & Water Rights

"I'm thinking about building a home in Costa Rica. How much does it cost to build a home per square foot? Will this be a difficult process?"

If Costa Rica had more open houses, I'd go to every one of them. There are areas where almost everyone has an amazing view. I've walked through gritty welding shops to find myself in backyards with sweeping mountain views. I can't help but be inspired and often tell my husband to stop in front of houses just to peek through their gates.

"Are those mango trees shading the outdoor kitchen?" I'll say while Rob yawns. Unfortunately, my husband's avoidance of open houses is as strong as my attraction to them.

"This doesn't make any sense," he groans. "We're not buying a house, so why are we looking?"

He's right. It makes the same amount of sense as his love affair with security walls. If there were open houses for barbed wire, my husband would be at every scabby one of them. He might even carry a bag of wire swatches and matching throw pillows.

"This silver shade of wire would look fabulous against the motion sensors," I can already hear him say.

One of the things I love most about the homes in Costa Rica is that they are always full with color. There is a huge Mediterranean influence in building styles; bright tiles and incredible archways, infinity pools and palm tree gardens. Many of the smaller homes are just as beautiful with popping landscapes and mature fruit trees. This gives us plenty of ideas for our own home, but until then, I'll keep dreaming of shady verandas and wraparound porches.

Building—no matter where you live—is always a challenge. There are people like Darlene and Frankie, who didn't have much of a problem. They had one issue with a subcontractor who was hired to install their kitchen cabinets but instead ran off with $200. Other than that, everything worked out and they finished on time and within budget.

Perhaps their outcome was positive because of Darlene's influence. She was there every morning walking around the construction site with a clipboard. She didn't know Spanish at that time, and her clipboard was actually just an old grocery list. But she would occasionally look over workers' shoulders giving the impression that she understood the construction process. There is a lot to be said for just being there at the site every morning. Even if you don't know what you're doing, your presence will make a big difference.

There are others who had problems from the start: builders who quote an amount that they could never stick to, or crews that do shoddy work. And shoddy is a relative term here. The lock to your bathroom door may be on the outside. Or it can be slightly more serious, as it was for my friend Sandy.

She hired an independent crew (not the people who constructed her house) to build a rancho in her backyard. It was a lovely structure that had a wooden swing hanging inside. A week later, a gust of wind knocked the whole thing over.

After the builder of her home came out to inspect the damage, it was discovered that the crew used rotten wood. It wasn't the biggest tragedy, and eventually Sandy had it rebuilt (on her dime). Luckily, she was not in her swing when the structure collapsed, and this proves that you have to be careful when choosing a builder. Always inspect all of your supplies and be at the site whenever possible.

I frequently notice that measurements can be slightly off. I've seen dishwashers in expensive condominiums that open only three quarters of the way down before hitting an edge of an adjacent cabinet. A friend had a pantry built but couldn't open the door more than ten inches. When she showed the builder, he couldn't understand the problem.

"Señora, all you have to do is *squeeze* through," he said before easily sliding through the tiny crack. It appears being slim is not only good for your health, but an actual requirement for maneuvering about my friend's house. Who needs tax on sugary sodas when we have inaccurate doorframe measurements to solve our obesity problems? I can't help but giggle when I imagine my friend squeezing through a crack every time she needs a cup of flour.

Another issue some may have when building in Costa Rica is that many homes are built without properly ventilated sewer pipes. Gases inevitably end up accumulating in one area of the home and stinking up an entire room. This can be an asset if you have friends that keep inviting themselves for a visit. A guest room smelling like the Port Authority bathroom will certainly have them checking into a Best Western.

If at all possible, it's best to be in Costa Rica so that you can oversee the building process. I know a few people who built their homes while they were out of the country, only to return to find rooms that were too small or see that finishings were installed that they never chose. These mishaps are not always due to a sinister contractor. Any time you are dealing with different systems of measurements, unreliable utilities, and a language barrier, and all from three thousand miles away, you can pretty much count on a hilarious story or two. So please supervise your construction in order that you do not return to find an Olympic sized swimming pool and learn that you are $60 million dollars over budget.

Building costs vary greatly depending on the style of finishes you choose and where you plan to build. Quotes range from sixty dollars a square foot in completed construction closer to San José, in places such as Grecia, versus $80 to $150 dollars per square foot if you are building near the beach. One reason things are more expensive at the beach is because of high fuel costs. The farther you are from San José, the more you will pay for building materials.

Some people arrange to transport their own materials from a less expensive area. This can be a hassle but may save you money in the long run. If it were up to Rob, he would throw everything on our scooter; we've witnessed people carrying rebar and roofing materials on motorcycles. I once saw a woman wrapping one arm around her husband's waist while balancing a half dozen gutters under her other arm.

Deciding whether to buy a house already built or to undergo the tedious process of constructing one will not be easy. However, purchasing an existing home will likely cost significantly more than building one yourself. It boils down to finances and how much energy you want to put into the project. If you decide to build, make sure you have the tenacity to see it through.

• Architect

The first step, and one that is required by law, is to hire an architect and engineer. I recommend you use one that is licensed with the Costa Rica Association of Engineers and Architects (Colegio Federado de Ingenieros y Arquitectos also known as CFIA). Only a licensed architect can submit your plans to the municipality. The CFIA sets the fee schedule that architects and engineers can charge.

One architect that I recommend is José Pablo Acuna Lett because he has been working with clients from the USA, Canada, UK, France, Germany and Russia for over ten years. I give José a call and ask him to describe what a person should be looking for in an architect and the fees that are involved.

"When a foreigner is looking for an architect in Costa Rica, there are some important things to consider. If a person is not very confident with the Spanish language, communication will be easier with an English-speaking architect. It's a good idea to hire one who is knowledgeable about the area where you want to build and has experience. Always make sure your architect is a member of the CFIA.

"The architect and the electrical, mechanical, structural, and A/C engineers charge a total of a 10.5% of the projected building cost of the home," José explains. "This 10.5% is broken down into the following categories: 1.5% for preliminary studies and architectural design, 4% for architectural, electrical, plumbing, structural, A/C building plans and specifications, and 5% site supervision by all professionals involved in the process during the time of construction"

"I know that many people in this area have hired you. In fact, you designed my friend Sandy's house that was featured on *House Hunters International* on HGTV. She raves about the time and attention to detail that you dedicated to her home," I tell José.

"I like to understand each client's needs and dreams. From the moment that I meet a new client (in person or by email), I pay close attention to what they have in mind. Once I have a thorough understanding of their idea, I start the creative process.

"I love all different types of architectural style, and have designed and built projects in Playas del Coco, Tamarindo, Playa Grande, Bay of Pirates, Conchal, Flamingo, Santa Teresa, and Punta Leona.

"I studied at Tecnológico de Monterrey, a very well-known university in Mexico, and I received my MBA specializing in international business. I travel a lot and this exposes me to the many different building styles all around the world.

"Guanacaste has a special place in my heart. My parents brought me to Playas del Coco for the first time when I was four weeks old. It's always been my dream to be an architect in this area. I'm living my dream now, practicing my career in this paradise.

"Ecology and sustainable development are very important to me. I love working with alternate energy sources and bioclimatic architecture. I try to establish a good relationship with my clients beyond work in order to catch their essence and express it in the homes I design. Even though professional fees may not vary a lot from one architect to another (the CFIA sets a minimum fee schedule but there is no cap on how much one can charge), I always give my clients the very best deal I can. Living and working in the same area makes it easier for me because I don't have to charge for travel expenses.

"I always respond to a client's question or concern within twenty-four hours. I'm familiar with nearly every development in the area and have been personally involved with many. I have a strong understanding of Costa Rican bureaucracy, and this helps to move things along when applying for permits."

My friend Sandy can't say enough about José, so I feel confident recommending him. She did not encounter any problems getting her permits. It's common for documents to get lost on someone's desk or be submitted to the wrong office. José makes sure that everything gets filed appropriately so that you don't find out five years down the line that you never had a building permit to begin with. A friend of mine is now facing this exact problem, and the amount of time it takes to rectify this is unbelievable.

- Builder

It is safe to say your Costa Rican home will be built using very strict earthquake codes. Our last major earthquake in Guanacaste was a doozy (7.6). It lasted for over a minute and it felt like the house was exploding around us. It shook so much I couldn't even get our key into the metal gate at the front entrance. Finally, Rob pulled the keys out of my hands and was able to unlock it. Experts say not to run out of the house since you are more likely to get killed by things falling on your head. But our instincts told us to run… so we did. I'm surprised I didn't fall into a hole on the way out. Needless to say, I was a hysterical mess. I honestly thought all my friends were dead, buried beneath a ton of rubble. Then there was the tsunami warning, which capped off the ultimate in crappy days.

Before this episode, I always wondered if a big earthquake would expose inferior construction here like it often does in other countries around the world. Would we find newspaper stuffed into supporting columns, or a lack of rebar in concrete foundations? Thankfully, that didn't happen in Costa Rica. I feel much safer than I did before and feel confident that at the very least, most houses here have solid foundations.

I contact Aaron, a blue-eyed builder at the Mar Vista development, located between Brasilito and Flamingo, to hear his thoughts on construction. He provides me with lots of great advice for anyone thinking about building a home in Costa Rica.

"A clear and solid contract with your builder is a great place to start," he says. "There are two common types of contracts: a line-item contract and a fixed-price contract. Let me explain the difference.

"In a line-item contact, the cost of labor is based on a percentage of the cost of your materials. The total cost of your project will be materials plus the agreed-upon percentage for labor. A fixed-price contract is exactly what it sounds like: the builder gives you one upfront price for the entire build.

"They both have advantages and disadvantages. One risk you take when choosing a line-item contract is that the cost of materials can fluctuate throughout the build, making it hard to predict the exact cost of the total project. The advantage of a fixed-price contract is that the client knows exactly what the home will cost. However, when creating a fixed-cost contract, builders will consider unforeseen circumstances. An estimated rising material cost will be factored into the quote, and all of this will usually lead to a higher price for the client.

"Most of my clients prefer a line-item contract, as do I. If you have a good trusting relationship with your builder, this is usually the way to go. It's always a good idea to show up at the building site often in order to keep track of quality and the materials going into the project.

"Another important thing to consider is the climate in which you are building. A good design should have lots of cross ventilation and a good plan for outdoor living. Keeping radiant heat off a house is critical, and a lot of that can be accomplished with proper landscaping.

"There are three common ways people choose to build in Costa Rica: concrete block, concrete/Styrofoam block, or steel stud. My clients can choose any of these, but I prefer steel because it goes up much faster and has an insulation rating of R19. Concrete/Styrofoam block has a R19 insulation rating as well, but it's labor intensive and costs 20% more. Regular concrete block has a very poor insulation rating, so I'd rather not use it. Electricity is expensive in Costa Rica; it's critical that a house is well insulated in order to keep air conditioning costs down.

"I also favor steel because it's economical, creates less waste in the environment, is not as cumbersome, and it's easier to make adjustments or remodel later. For example, if you want to run a simple electrical line for another outlet, it's easy when using steel. If you have a house made of concrete block, it's much more time-consuming and expensive.

"I love my job and enjoy helping people build their dream homes. Having a good relationship with your builder is essential. I hate to say that I've seen some crazy stuff: retaining walls have been built out of roof tin, and drainage has been installed sending water back up against a house. Something very common in Costa Rica is plumbing being installed without proper ventilation. This will cause sewage gases to build up in the home, which smells terrible and can even become a health hazard. Always interview your builder, as well as his clients. A good builder will have no objection letting you tour his projects.

I take pride in my work. My heart is in it and I hope it shows in the homes I have built. I only work in Mar Vista, and my clients are going to be my neighbors. There is constant contact between us for many months, and success for me is when we are all friends at the end of construction."

- Water Rights

If you've read my second book, *Happier Than A Billionaire: The Sequel*, you know that a water availability letter is what has been holding up my own, as well as many others', construction plans. It is important to be certain when purchasing a lot or home that its water system is legal. If you are buying a property in a development, be sure the well is legal and the developer has the right to deliver water to each parcel within the project. I approach Ale Elliot, the manager at the Mar Vista development and father to Aaron the blue-eyed builder. I ask him what a potential buyer needs to check in regard to water rights before purchasing any property.

"I've been a Costa Rican resident for almost twenty-five years," Ale says. "I have two sons, Trevor and Aaron that are also project managers in Mar Vista. Moving to a foreign country can be a wonderful experience, but there are things you need to be aware of before buying a home or lot here. The three most important factors when considering a property in Costa Rica are a clean title, duly registered and legal water rights, and security.

"Knowing that water rights have become such a huge issue for property owners in recent years, both my son and I have enrolled in a six-month rigorous course at the INA (Instituto Nacional de Aprendizaje). I'm proud to say, as far as I know, we are now the only non-Costa Rican water association administrators in the country. It was not fun giving up two afternoons per week for six months, but we felt it was necessary in order to manage the water resources for our Mar Vista community.

"Costa Rica takes their water issues quite seriously. By law, Costa Rica is the legal owner of all water, and even mineral rights, below the subsoil. The country has set up four ways in which a landowner may access water. This is accomplished through concessions. The four distinct type of water administrating structures are as follows, starting with the least and ending with the most secure structure.

"The first way a property owner may have been granted a concession is through individual landowners who have a legally registered artesian (hand-dug) well. This type of concession is only meant for agricultural and uni-residential purposes. In other words, this style of water system is only legal for one farmhouse on one farm. This does not allow a landowner to distribute water to others who happen to live within the boundaries of the landowner's mother farm. Beware of situations where a large landowner claims he has legal water rights due to the fact that he has a registered well on his property and has subdivided his land into smaller parcels. The question is, does this landowner have a concession for the usage of the water which is being pumped from his well, and does he have the right to distribute and sell this water to others? If such a landowner assures you he does have these rights, then a prospective buyer must require this landowner to demonstrate these rights in writing. Once a buyer has this documentation, he should have his attorney double check the authenticity against the public records held by AYA (National Water Association) in San José. If you buy an existing home with this type of water setup, there is some risk. If buying a piece of property with the intent of building on it, you are at extreme risk.

"A second scenario is when a group of neighbors form what is referred to as a neighborhood usage association. This was commonly used in the past. It's when a group of neighbors get together around one well (either artesian or machine-dug) that has concession rights. This group is responsible for maintaining water quality and the infrastructure needed to distribute water. Today this type of neighborhood association (while certainly not the strongest form of water rights) is usually *tolerated* if the neighborhood water association has been around for years, and if there are no complaints generated about the quality of the system. In other words, for all intents and purposes, these associations have been grandfathered in. Mature neighborhood associations are *unlikely* to be challenged by Costa Rica providing their wells are legally registered and they have a legal concession granted to withdraw a pre-approved quantity of water.

"A third scenario is called a condominium type of water system (either vertical, similar to a typical condo-tower, or horizontal, which most North Americans know as a subdivision). In this case, a well is registered duly to the condominium for the administration and distribution of water. Costa Rica will require the well within the condominium property to be *legally registered*, and will *also* require that the condominium is granted a concession in order to *withdraw* water from that well. To be clear, the seller needs to provide two forms of documentation: one proves legal registration of the well, and the other proves there is a concession for the use of its water.

"Finally, the best scenario for water rights is when a community has an ASADA. An ASADA (Asociación Administradora del Acueducto y Alcantarillado) is a community organization that is formed in accordance with strict rules governing the creation and administration of all registered wells and concessions within the sphere of geographic reach of the limits of the infrastructure of that ASADA.

"This ASADA may or may not be entered into a Convenio de Delegación (which translated means a delegation contract with the National Water Association). Either way an ASADA is a strong form of water rights. However, one that has entered into a Convenio de Delegación, is the most desirable form. An ASADA must *also* be duly registered. ASADAs that have entered into a Convenio de Delegación, have the full and legal right to substitute for the National Water Association as it relates to all matters concerning water generation and distribution for a community and is the most solid form of water rights a given property can have within Costa Rica. It is exactly what we have in Mar Vista.

"Again, all of the above water administration structures must grant two essential documents before you will be able to get a building permit from your local municipality. The first document is what is referred to as a Water Availability Letter. This letter is a pre-requirement of the municipality before they will even consider granting you a building permit. The final document is the actual water hook-up approval, which is granted once the property owner presents a fully stamped and certified building permit. This approval grants the user the right to purchase a water meter and to have unrestricted use of water.

"In summary, water rights can take many forms in Costa Rica. Always use a reputable Costa Rican attorney for any and all of your real estate transactions."

Building in a foreign country is always a bit nerve-racking, but with the right information there is a better chance things will go smoothly. Having honest and professional people on your side is imperative, as is understanding the Costa Rican laws that affect your investment. Arming yourself with the above knowledge is the first step when house hunting in Costa Rica.

Now that you have information in regards to building and purchasing property, what if you need a doctor? Healthcare in Costa Rica is up next. These chapters might help you decide on whether or not you'll be making Costa Rica your home.

### Links

Aaron the Builder: acberkowitzmv@gmail.com

Ale Elliot, Mar Vista Project Manager: www.marvistacr.com
Tele: 8423-4370

Architect: José Pablo Acuna Lett, MBA
JPA Architecture and Planning
Email: jpalett@gmail.com
Tele: 2271-1965  Cell: 8830-4827  Fax:2271-1964

Costa Rica Association of Engineers and Architects: www.cfia.or.cr

# Part IV: The Journey Continues

# Healthcare

There is no use in denying it: I fall down a lot, but I rarely get hurt. Although I may cry and carry on for an unreasonable amount of time, I usually get up with only minor bruises. Rob on the other hand, constantly hurts himself. He falls into bay pits, rips open hernias, or staggers into the house followed by trails of blood. Not once has he cried or carried on.

It's good to know that when you need a doctor there will be one available. In Costa Rica, if you are a resident you are automatically covered by CAJA (Caja Costarricense de Seguro Social). It's the government agency that provides healthcare for the entire country. There are approximately 250 public clinics (EBAIS) and thirty public hospitals. Their best hospitals are near San José, something to consider when choosing the area you'll be moving to.

I pay roughly $75 dollars a month, and my husband pays $100. However, I have just learned that for temporary residents now entering the system the fee maybe upwards of $200 per month. A friend of mine is going back to CAJA to see if he can get the price reduced, and apparently if you provide the proper documentation, they may decrease the monthly fee. There is a fee cap for *permanent* residents: over fifty-five years of age pay $63 dollars a month, and younger than fifty-five will pay $114.

When I was working in the United States, Rob and I had very high insurance premiums. We each had a $10,000 deductible, which was quickly reached when Rob was admitted to the hospital for a stomach ailment. After a week in the hospital, the bill came to $60,000. Health insurance covered all but the $10,000 deductible. We recently used CAJA for Rob's hernia surgery. In the end, we didn't pay a dime. I wrote extensively about this experience in my second book.

Although the surgery was a success, the hospital was lacking in many things. We didn't know at the time that Rob was admitted to one of the least funded hospitals in the country. There were many bathrooms without toilet seats, and you had to bring your own soap. It's important to point out that people who have had similar surgeries in hospitals near San José have described their experience as being closer to what you might expect from a hospital in the United States. And like I said, the surgery was a success, free other than our monthly CAJA payments, and Rob is doing well. For a short time after the surgery, he suffered from "moon pain," a unique diagnosis with a prescription that included Rob lying on the couch and asking for sandwiches. I've never seen him happier.

There are other options for those who are not residents or for those who choose to go above and beyond what CAJA care offers. Private hospitals take many different types of insurance. The INS (National Insurance Agency of Costa Rica) has medical plans that will cover you at these private facilities. Some may even accept your Blue Cross Blue Shield plan, but even if you don't have insurance most times the cost of care is very reasonable.

Pick up *Happier Than A Billionaire: The Sequel*—or as some reviewers like to call it, "Not as Good as the First"—if you want to read more about the magical story of when Rob underwent hernia surgery in Costa Rica. It's also when we had our license plate stolen off our car. Perhaps I should have included this in my crime chapter, and insisted that you take not only your luggage with you when leaving your car unattended, but your license plates as well.

### Links

The three best private hospitals:

1. CIMA hospital : www.hospitalcima.com It's affiliated with Baylor University Medical Center in Dallas, Texas, and has state-of-the-art equipment. They are known as one of the best hospitals in the country, having an excellent coronary heart facility as well as diagnostic imaging center. Many people have orthopedic operations

here. I know someone who had her baby at this hospital and raved about the care.

2. Clínica Bíblica: www.clinicabiblica.com/eng/index.php It's affiliated with Evergreen Hospital in Kirkland, Washington. Their facilities are top notch and popular with medical tourists. Their webpage banner is presently a beach scene with a starfish and suntan lotion stuck in the sand. This makes me want to get a facelift just to see what type of accommodations I'll get. Considering it's been three days without water at my house, I might check in just to get a hot shower.

3. Clínica Católica: www.hospitallacatolica.com/ This facility provides emergency care, nutritional counseling, psychiatric care, and respiratory treatments. They even have a hyperbaric chamber. I think that's the thing Michael Jackson slept in, and some believe it can keep you young forever. Definitely go over to the website and check it out. It looks delightful. You get to wear a snazzy outfit and relax in what looks like a white spaceship. I'm all in on this one.

If you plan on becoming a resident, the following are some of the best-equipped public hospitals in the country:

1. Hospital Nacional de Niño in San José: www.hnn.sa.cr/Paginas/Default.aspx This is known to be the best hospital for children in Costa Rica.

2. Hospital San Juan de Dios in San José: They have a very good cardiac care department. They also treat burns and mental health issues.

3. Hospital Rafael Ángel Calderón Guardi—San José

4. Hospital Nacional Dr Max Peralta Jimenez in Cartago: www.hmp.sa.cr

5. Hospital Mexico in La Uruca

Other important links:

CAJA: http://www.ccss.sa.cr/

INS of Costa Rica: www.ins-cr.com

# Oops, He Did It Again *

It's not every day your husband flies over his scooter after picking up a stool sample kit. Let me explain. Yesterday morning, Rob left to pick up the kit from the pharmacy to help assess why I have been having stomach trouble for the past few weeks.

About an hour after he left, I heard yelling at our front gate. "Nadine!"

"Hmm… Is someone outside calling my name?" I thought to myself before peering out the window.

If you've been following the Pisani chronicles, then you already know that I've named our residence the Thunderdome, and Thunderdome protocol calls for all gates to be locked when my macho husband is not at home to save me from marauders. There is also a provision that states whenever Rob leaves my side, I must stay in the car in case I need to run over any looting evildoers.

"OH MY GOD!" I recall saying after seeing a puddle of blood. I rushed outside and noticed Rob wasn't wearing his helmet and there was no scooter in sight. I didn't see one evildoer. There was no pillaging.

"Hurry, open the gate!" Rob shouted while keeping pressure on his bleeding hand.

"OH MY GOD!" I said once again. Or twice. Or maybe I just kept repeating it. All I can remember was Rob dripping blood all throughout the foyer, then into the kitchen, and ultimately filling the sink.

"Quick, get me paper towels, or some gauze, or anything to help stop the bleeding. Damn it, I'm going to need stitches."

"You're going to need stitches?" I yelled. He might as well have said he needed a bone marrow transplant because as long as I've known my husband, those words have never left his mouth. It was about then I started to feel woozy. In the past he has handled every emergency with a "grin and bear it" attitude. When a guy whose first aid kit consists of duct tape is asking for stitches, you know that it's going to be a long day.

Now in my defense, I tend to be a little hypersensitive in trying situations. I wouldn't be the first person you would want to call in an emergency. But I'm not the last either. You can certainly count on Nadine Hays Pisani for your blood loss needs. I may spin in circles while performing a high-pitched scream, but this could also be taken as a sign of a take-charge attitude.

"Grab me some duct tape," Rob instructed. This actually helped calm me down since it was exactly what he usually says when large amounts of his plasma are pouring down a sink drain. "I need you to go down the road and pick up my helmet and sunglasses. A little farther down you will see the scooter. Get the key out of the ignition and take everything out of the hatch. Don't forget the stool sample kit. I have to sit down for a minute and cool off. And don't for any reason try to move the scooter. It is too heavy. Just leave it where it is."

I got in the car and quickly discovered his helmet and sunglasses. As I drove a little further, I spotted the scooter lying sideways in a very deep rut. I grabbed the key out of the ignition, removed the contents from the hatch, and finally found the stool sample kit. Good thing it was empty.

But then I didn't know what to do with the scooter. It was right in the middle of the road, and even though it is not a heavily traveled one, I was unsure if someone might run it over. And should I really listen to Rob's advice? The guy who just split open his hand? On that sound argument, I grabbed hold of the handlebars and slowly lifted it upright. I suppose this would have been a good idea if I had held onto the brake while doing so. Consequently, the scooter careened out of control and into a drainage ditch. These were not pressing details so I didn't immediately share them with my husband when I returned to the house. His blood loss would definitely make his memories fuzzy and he might not even notice.

"Before we go to an emergency clinic, I want to go get the scooter back to the house," Rob demanded.

"Are you sure? I mean, why do that now? At the very least, show me your hand so I can get an idea of what we are dealing with." It was then he reluctantly removed the paper towels and showed me the gash. It was deep. I thought I saw China.

After seeing his wound, I proceeded with an impressive period of hyperventilation followed by me driving Rob back to the scooter. He acted like it was a grisly crime scene, swiftly deciphering that the victim had been moved to a second location.

"Why is it in a ditch?" he asked. "Great, now it's going to be even harder to move. And where did the ignition switch go? It's in worse shape now than when I crashed it."

I played dumb, which is undoubtedly a natural thing for me. Sometimes I'm surprised just how easily I can slip into this role. It's as if I am born to act the part.

In some adrenalized, super-Hulk-like display of strength, Rob proceeded to walk the scooter back to the house—in the sun and up a hill— while holding one arm intermittently above his head.

"Are you finally going to tell me what happened?" I asked when we were driving to find an emergency clinic.

"It's really quite incredible. If I wasn't such a good driver, I'm sure I would be in worse shape."

"Okay, I get it. You're a hero. But can you fill me in on what just occurred one hundred yards from our house?"

"It was so ridiculous. I was driving up the hill and saw a big rut in the dirt road. I know that I shouldn't get the wheel caught in one, but I was going so slow I thought that if I started to slip I could easily bail. I had it all planned in my head, neatly tucking myself and rolling with the momentum as I have a dozen times before. I'm really quite good in an emergency."

"So then what happened to your hand?"

"It was the only part of my plan that didn't quite work out. While falling off, I outstretched my palm and got ready to roll, but my hand got caught on some sharp rocks. When I stood up I thought I was fine until I saw the blood and immediately started running toward the house. That was a bad idea because then I felt like passing out, so I remained calm and began walking quickly. I didn't even take the house keys because they were covered in gas. Halfway home I realized I should take off my helmet and that's why you found it in the middle of the road. I probably should have done that sooner. When I made it back, I got down on my knees in order to conserve energy. I knew I would need it to bust open the gate in the event that you could not hear my screams."

"I can't believe this. I hope we don't have to take you to San José. If your muscles or nerves are damaged, we're in big trouble."

"Let's not jump the gun. With my superior tuck-and-roll technique, I'm sure there can't be that much damage. This is just a flesh wound."

I have to agree with my husband. He does have some mad skills when faced with adversity. I know this because as he was getting stitched up by Dr. Abelardo Venegas (luckily no fractures, nerve, or muscle damage) he turned a color that Sherwin-Williams might call Cottage Whitewash. Apparently, his blood pressure dropped quicker than our careening scooter into a ditch. But with a little bit of leg elevation and a cold compress to his head, his face returned to a rosy glow. And I have to admit, he took it all with a smile on his face.

"See that, honey? I'm like Rocky," he said while making a fist with his newly stitched Frankenstein hand. "Do you mind stopping by the grocery store? I could use some ice cream. And make sure we have enough food in the house because you will have to do all the cooking. I can't get my hand dirty."

I can't say that was our worst day in Costa Rica, but I wouldn't want to repeat it either. To think, a quest for a stool sample kit started this whole chain of events. Who knew a stomach bug would cause this much trouble?

# Links

Dr. Abelardo Venegas
Tele: 8813-3046
CentroMedico Huacas
50 meters west of Supracompro, Huacas-Guanacaste
email: emergenciahuacas@hotmail.com

Another office recently opened, Beachside Medical Clinic, and is run by Dr. Andrea Messeguer. She recently bought X-ray equipment. This excites me since it's just a matter of time until Rob will need those services.
Tele: 2653-9911 or 2653-5053
200 Meters West of the Brasilito intersection in Huacas, Towards Matapolo
Huacas-Guanacaste
www.beachsidemedicalclinic.com

# A Stomach Bug Causes This Much Trouble

Rob gets hurt a lot, and he is the one that I'm most concerned about when it comes to healthcare. However, I may have decided this prematurely. I'm beginning to get very sharp stomach pains, and it's for this reason Rob was carrying a stool sample kit when he went careening into a ditch.

I am positive I'm dying. This isn't the first time I've felt this way: I'm positive I've been dying for years. My ailments, whether they are bee stings or tension headache, always have me convinced that I should be medevaced to the nearest trauma center.

In fact, I'm just as sure that I'm going to die as Rob is sure he's going to live. For as many times as I've watched Rob bleed out all over our kitchen floor, he has never uttered a dreary word or furrowed a brow. I've all but called the Grim Reaper after experiencing a sunburn. He's been on speed dial since 1998.

I've decided it's time to see a doctor, but unlike my husband, who would wait for hours at a CAJA clinic, I make an appointment with Andrea Messeguer, a private doctor. She has an incredible reputation and I only hear good things about her.

The moment I meet her I feel at ease. Dr. Andrea has a motherly quality, as if at any moment she's going to make me chicken soup before tucking me into bed. She is that nice. Dr. Andrea questions everything from my past gastrointestinal issues to my current diet. She prescribes medication and refers me for ultrasound tests the following day. The visit lasts over an hour and her charge is $50. I've never been treated so well.

The next morning I drive to San Rafael Arcángel Medical Center in Liberia for further tests. I'm amazed at how fast things are proceeding. The facility is very clean and incredibly modern. After taking a short history, the clinician performs the procedures and the results are given immediately: I am fine. Total costs for internal and external ultrasounds: $150. It now appears that I am not as terminal as I expected.

Unfortunately, my symptoms do continue so I return to Dr. Andrea's office. She orders blood work and refers me to a revered gastroenterologist, Dr. Vargas. After being handed lab papers, I'm told to return to the clinic in Liberia. The lab is in the same building as the doctor so I can easily accomplish both in one day. I look down at the paper; practically every test on the list is checked off. This pleases me since my dreaded diagnosis will certainly be uncovered by the results of one of these tests.

Once back in Liberia, I hand over my paperwork to the lab receptionist. For as lousy as I feel, everyone continues to be incredibly kind to me. I'm directed to a little room with a desk, chair, and leather recliner. Rob hops in the leather recliner and stretches out. This is the perfect position for a guy who can't stand the sight of blood. The phlebotomist looks over the paperwork and keeps repeating something in Spanish. I can swear he is asking for flour. My head is spinning; was I supposed to bake a cake? Is this some sort of phlebotomist appreciation week?

The technician leaves the room and returns with an interpreter dressed in scrubs, possibly a surgeon that was just yanked from the operating room to translate for the dingbat who is frantically trying to find a bag of flour.

"The phlebotomist is asking you for urine. Do you have any urine?" the doctor asks.

Do I have urine? Absolutely! I can produce as much as you want. It turns out that the Spanish word for urine (*orina*) sounds a lot like the Spanish word for flour (*harina*), which is why I was about to send Rob to the bakery. But it's always been my motto that it's better to give someone a sack of flour by accident than a bag of urine on purpose. I excuse myself to the bathroom and return with a tiny Tupperware of specimen.

The phlebotomist then proceeds to extract one vial of blood after another. "Whoa, that's an awful lot," Rob mumbles.

"I appreciate you filling me in on what's occurring," I respond, "but the reason my eyes are closed is because I don't want to know what's going on."

"I mean seriously, that's like… three or four test tubes. Whoa, I don't feel so good." It's then Rob leans farther back in the recliner and grabs the remote to turn on the massage option. Remarkably, this is the same position you'll find him in at any airport that has a Brookstone massage chair in their terminal.

After the blood work, we walk to an adjacent building and wait for my appointment. I can tell Dr. Vargas had a long day: I recognize the small bags under his eyes, the exact same ones I would get on those days after seeing many chiropractic patients. I sit in front of his desk as he listens to my complaints. I explain that I have always had stomach issues, but moving to Costa Rica has helped. I don't eat anywhere near the junk I used to, and I'm living a relatively stress-free life. I can't understand why, after years of a healthier lifestyle, my stomach is suddenly causing me this pain. It is then I break the bad news to him.

"I'm dying, Doc."

"Please tell her she's not dying," Rob pleads.

"It's okay. I've accepted it," I solemnly whisper.

Dr. Vargas escorts me over to an examining table, where he proceeds to feel my neck, look in my mouth, and press all around my abdomen.

"You are not dying," he says.

"Well, you haven't seen the blood work yet. It will certainly verify it. Trust me… I'm a goner."

"Although I appreciate your diagnosis, let me first say something. If you are dying, you are the healthiest-looking dying person I've ever met," he remarks.

I have to admit, I enjoyed the compliment. It's nice to know you're looking your best while lying next to a colonoscopy machine. He then continues pressing on different areas of my gut. It feels tender, but not so bad that I want to jump off the table.

"Your symptoms are very characteristic of someone suffering from irritable bowel syndrome," he explains.

"I'm sure I have it, but it can't just be just that. I've had a bad stomach all my life. It's getting worse lately."

It's then that we hear a knock on the door. A woman enters with my blood work and hands it over to Dr. Vargas.

"Hmmm," he says.

"Let's hear it. I'm ready," I say while gripping Rob's hand. I lean back in my seat, since hypochondria is more dramatic when in a reclining position.

"You're not dying," Dr. Vargas repeats without looking up from the lab report. "There is not one abnormal finding."

I feel a rush of relief from my head to my feet. Even my gut stopped hurting after hearing the news.

"The very first thing I want you to do is control your stress levels," Dr. Vargas instructs. "It's easy to make your condition worse by thinking you are dying. And stop Googling your symptoms. I can tell you are doing that and all it's going to do is make you crazy."

Wow, this guy has me pegged. I've been starting each day with a nutritious breakfast accompanied by a side of WebMD.

"I want you to follow a very restricted diet. I suspect that your IBS is flared up, and you might even have a serious condition called celiac disease. I'd like you to eliminate gluten from your diet and follow this plan."

He hands me a paper outlining The FODMAP Diet, which is based on the premise that some people cannot absorb certain carbohydrates properly. Offending foods include fruits, beans, and many other items I thought were healthy for my stomach. Many of the things I have been eating might be making me ill.

I thank him for his advice and assume the visit is over but Dr. Vargas continues to go over the diet with me for the next half hour. He makes sure that I am well-informed of everything I must do in order to get better.

"I'm going to prescribe a month's worth of a mild medication. Follow the diet and let's take it from there. This will not be the end of your treatment, but before we do more testing let's get you some relief. Remember, you can contact me with any concerns you may have. Call or send an email. I promise you I will respond."

My appointment lasted over an hour and a half. His charge is only $80.

I start the diet and finally begin to feel better. It's crazy that my health slipped so fast, and how frightened it made me. Convincing myself I was dying probably didn't help, but I did the job so well it's a shame I have to turn in my resignation.

Since I'm not having as much pain, Rob and I decide to take a trip to watch the turtles lay their eggs on Playa Ostional. After a busy day photographing the turtles, we have dinner at Luna Azul hotel. The dining room is aglow with soft orange lighting and every table is packed with hungry customers. It's one of those perfect, romantic Costa Rican evenings with the hint of a breeze swirling around your feet.

The waiter comes over to take my order, and Rob broadcasts to the staff, the dining room, and the entire Nicoya Peninsula that his wife suffers from irritable bowel syndrome. He all but pulls out a newspaper and yells, "read all about it," while marching throughout the restaurant.

Every customer puts their utensils down and stares at me as if I am on the verge of crapping my pants. I collapse my face in my hands as my husband makes sure the waiter understands that I have to have plain chicken breast, without any dressing, without any offending vegetables or oils having ever touched it.

"The meat can in no way come in contact with anything that has gluten!" he screams as if his wife's entrails will explode to smithereens. I don't think anyone in recent history has requested a plain chicken breast the way my husband does tonight.

I'm about to reprimand Rob and tell him that he could have easily told the waiter I suffer from something less unseemly, like food allergies. At least with that diagnosis I can maintain some dignity. But my attitude changes once I receive my meal: everything is perfectly prepared and positively delicious. It turns out that when the staff thinks you might crap your pants at the very table they are in charge of cleaning, they make sure to get the order right. It's going to be the first thing I say the next time we dine out. I might even have it printed on my business card.

Happier Than A Billionaire: Stand back, she's got more brewing inside her than a few good books.

So far I'm doing well; my restricted diet seems to be working. I've even lowered my already-lowered stress levels, which basically means I'm as anxious as an anesthetized three-toed sloth.

Going the private route was a much more direct path to receiving healthcare, but I'm pleased both CAJA and private doctors are available. It feels good to know that going the private route saved valuable space in a CAJA clinic for someone needing care. I'm thankful to all the doctors who gave me such incredible service, and for my husband who loves me so much.

"I'm happy you are feeling better, but I have to say that I'm noticing your approach to healthcare was different than mine," Rob laughs.

This is true. My husband took one for the team: sat in the street while waiting for an appointment at the local clinic and went through CAJA for his hernia surgery. I avoided potentially long waits and enjoyed a toilet seat at every office we visited.

I also learned the Spanish word for urine. It makes me laugh to know that all of this time I've been telling my Costa Rican neighbor I use a cup of urine to make my chocolate cake. This might explain the uncomfortable silence when I offered her a slice.

**Links**

Dr. Andrea Messeguer.
Tele: 2653-9911 or 2653-5053
200 Meters West of the Brasilito intersection in Huacas, Towards
Matapolo
Huacas-Guanacaste
www.beachsidemedicalclinic.com

Dr. Jorge Vargas Madrigal
Hospital Clinico San Rafael Arcangel
From the Catholic Church, 100 meters east and 50 meters south
Liberia, Costa Rica
Tele: 2666-1717   Ext: 200
gastrocr@gmail.com

# Colonoscopy in Paradise

Apparently, there is nothing I won't write about. Considering that I've chronicled my husband's hernia surgery, his scooter accident, and a number of his other embarrassing moments, it only seems fair that I include this: I'm sitting in Dr. Vargas's office and about to undergo a colonoscopy.

On a side note, every time I type colonoscopy into my iPad, my spell check changes it to kaleidoscope. I wish I were getting a kaleidoscope this morning. And by "getting a kaleidoscope this morning," I mean buying one and using it for the intended purposes of visual enjoyment and not for rectal insertion. (Just wanted to make that clear.)

While Dr. Vargas looks over my file, I glance up at his diploma and notice that he performed his residency in Rome, Italy. I like that. It makes me think of St Peter's Square, accordions and gelato. In fact, the last two would make a nice addition to his office. And considering I drank one hundred gallons of laxatives last night, I could use the Pope's blessing as well.

"Your celiac tests came back negative," Dr. Vargas states while reading over my blood work. He must have been in a rush this morning since his breakfast is still sitting on his desk: an orange, a carton of lactose-free yogurt, and what looks like some sort of granola bar. I bet his colon is perfect, the Mona Lisa of digestive organs. There is no coffee, which pleases me. No one wants a jittery-handed gastroenterologist.

"That's strange because I feel better since I've eliminated grains from my diet. I could have sworn I'd be positive for celiac," I reply.

"You can still be very sensitive to grains. That's not as serious as celiac disease, but it's important to stay away from foods that are making you ill. My suggestion is you stay on the diet if it helps. And keep exercising. There are quite a few studies that suggests exercise helps relieve many symptoms of irritable bowel syndrome."

Dr. Vargas continues to go over my diet and asks more about my stress levels. I can't believe how much time he and Dr. Andrea are willing to spend with me. I've never received such thorough care before.

The only reason that I've decided to get a colonoscopy is because I'm not one hundred percent better. Rob might say I'm doing it because I'm *one hundred percent* convincing myself I have a problem. There may be some truth to that. But there also is truth in that he *one hundred percent* shot out our water pipes and caught our gun on fire in Grecia, so it appears we each have our own faults.

"This should go fast. I mean, I'm pretty small so there is not much to see?" I ask the doctor. When about to experience a digital camera in a place I would prefer to remain unexplored, my small talk often takes on a doubtful if not worrisome tone. Incidentally, it's the same paranoid small talk I use at the Costa Rican Motor Vehicles.

"Actually, it is slightly more difficult with a small colon."

This is not the answer you want to hear right before getting Roto-Rootered. The words you do want to hear are, "Wow, your colon is *huge*! I should be in and out in no time." Or even better, "Let's get a bucket of Kentucky Fried Chicken and call it a day."

I sashay my tiny colon over to the examining table, where a man, not playing the accordion, waits for me. He smiles and we begin playing the all-too-familiar game of charades. It's that same old parlor game, but the stakes are even higher today. The man holds up a paper gown as a saleslady would in Bloomingdale's.

"It's lovely," I say.

He points to the bathroom and motions for me to put the gown on, but then turns around while pointing over his shoulder. I think he wants me to change and make sure the opening is in the back. Either that, or I'm having rotator cuff surgery.

While in the bathroom, I look for an escape route but all I find are extra boxes of medical supplies. I'm not sure if I need to leave my socks on, and I spend an inordinate amount of time deciding what to do. Procrastination seems to hit me the hardest whenever I'm bare-assed in a medical gown.

When I exit the bathroom, Rob is standing there. He looks even sadder than when he fell off his scooter. This must harder for him than it is for me. He doesn't say a word, just gives me a soft kiss and leaves the room. If this thing goes south, I'm hoping an Italian or Hungarian lady is out there to comfort him.

My charades partner instructs me to lie on the table. "No," he says while pointing to the left side of his pelvis. I guess he wants me to turn over so my back faces the other side. This makes perfect sense since that's the side of the table where all the colonoscopy equipment is. I guess the doctor can't reach around with the hose like they do at the gas station.

"We are going to sedate you now," the doctor explains. And before I know it, I'm out.

After waking, Mr. Charades is helping me with my shoes. I stare at him, as one would after finding a middle-aged man tying one's sneakers. I want to pat him on the head and tip him. "Now this is service," I would say. But thankfully Rob walks back in the room before I can embarrass myself. He helps me off the table and over to the doctor's desk.

"It all went well. You have a very good-looking colon," Dr. Vargas says while smiling.

I smile back, acknowledging the compliment. I'm sure he means that my bowels are free from disease, but I'd rather believe they were actually good-looking. Just a couple months ago, I had an internal ultrasound and the doctor said I had a beautiful uterus. I always wanted to be that attractive girl who walks into a room and has every eye on her. If I could only turn myself inside out, that might actually happen.

I begin to feel uncomfortable and look down at my abdomen; it's bloated like a hot air balloon.

"Don't be concerned. You will release gas all day and it will flatten down." I love getting permission to pass gas. I let a small toot slip out just to confirm we're all on the same page.

What happens next is a little blurry, and I start asking the doctor for permission to write about him in my book. In my mind, I sound like Grace Kelly; I've never been so poised and charming. The doctor doesn't seem to understand so I repeat myself. It's then my husband interrupts. I'm a little annoyed at this, point knowing I own the Marilyn Monroe of all colons, a position that I feel should garner a certain level of respect. I let Rob finish the conversation, and we all shake hands (I shake Rob's hand as well; I may even have introduced myself). We leave the office and begin the drive home.

"Was I making any sense in there?" I ask.

"I knew what you were trying to say but no, you were not making a lick of sense."

"I just wanted to tell him how nice he's been, or something like that. Huh… what are we talking about?"

"Just lie back, and stop worrying! All your anxiety is going to kill me."

I spend the rest of the day reading magazines while Rob pokes his head in and out of the room just to make sure I don't fart myself to death. I feel good about getting the procedure done. Final price tag for the colonoscopy was $300. That's 150,000 colones (*colon-ez*), and not 150,000 colons. If the latter were the case, it would be really weird and make for more than a few awkward requests from friends and family.

I'm lucky I found a doctor who was willing to spend so much time with me. He even suggested how yoga and Pilates have helped people with irritable bowel disease. He is always trying to give me suggestions on how I can heal myself, or at the very least, keep my symptoms at bay. I'm blessed that my doctors have such a good bedside manner and genuinely appear concerned. I'm in good, un-jittery hands.

People come to Costa Rica for a number of reasons. Some come for a vacation while others may come for a facelift or dental veneers. But what if they came for a colonoscopy? It might not be the usual excursion during one's vacation, but there is nothing better than taking care of oneself. Having a colonoscopy in paradise might just be a hit. Perhaps I should pitch it to the Costa Rican Tourism Board. It certainly sounds better than a colonoscopy in Detroit.

Dr. Vargas has become the third most important man in my life. Claus my German mechanic still holds the second spot. But after this experience, my gastroenterologist might move up a notch. I can live without an alternator, but I use my colon every day. And I'll never know when it'll need a tune-up.

I'm so pleased with this experience I might even include this memory in my View-Master reel. It's not every day a kaleidoscope makes someone so happy. *Cha-click*.

# The Retiring Sixties: I Finally Made It!

"That's it: Today was my last day at work and I'm so excited to start this next phase of life. My wife and I are both retired and we are not waiting another day to enjoy our lives. I can't believe we finally made it and are looking into living abroad for a few years. Where do we start?"

I love people in their sixties. They have a permanent smile plastered across their faces, and it's as if they broke out of jail after thirty years of hard labor. This is a group that wants to enjoy life, and I've been at parties with them that quickly turn into a scene from *Animal House*.

Many of these folks have no desire to remain in the same home, or the same town for that matter. Forget about moving to Florida, and don't even mention a retirement community. This group is looking for adventure. And why shouldn't they? Retirement doesn't have to mean sitting home in a recliner night after night.

There are bustling communities all over this country filled with retirees. Some live closer to San José so they are closer to healthcare, while others don't mind driving an hour or more for an appointment with a physician. Some even go back to the States for their medical checkups, but there is one thing they can definitely count on: their health usually improves. Costa Rica practically demands that you become more active. Between hiking, boogieboarding, kayaking, and dancing there is too much fun here to stay inside.

So kudos to all you sixty-somethings out there! Celebrate your retirement by visiting Costa Rica. Go zip-lining and horseback riding. Hike to the top of that incredible waterfall. Trust me, you can do this and there will be plenty of people your age doing the exact same thing.

Just look for the group of people with a permanent smile; they're the ones who also just received a get-out-of-jail-free card. They would love for you to join them.

# How to Make a Living: The Restaurateurs  *

"My husband and I came to Costa Rica in 2001 to celebrate our fifteenth wedding anniversary. It was a surprise vacation and my only instructions were to pack warm clothing. Yippee! Finally a week alone and away from our very young children aged three, five and six.

"I was looking forward to a week of relaxation, beaches, and flipping mindlessly through trashy magazines while drinking piña coladas. My husband—whom I love dearly and who never does anything without a hidden agenda (women, you know what I am talking about)—had a much different idea of how this week would go. We spent the entire week looking at properties all over Guanacaste. Apparently, he had been researching Costa Rica for months. This surprise vacation was really a real estate tour and not the relaxing holiday I envisioned.

"Ultimately, we both fell in love with the area and ended up buying a condo in Reserva Conchal by the end of the week. This is a decision we never regretted. We started spending more and more time in Costa Rica, eventually moving here permanently in 2007. My husband was dabbling in real estate, and I was a busy mom with three kids in Country Day School, which was located across the street from Reserva Conchal.

"One day I went to a school meeting at a friend's house located on Potrero Beach. The view was spectacular and I told my friend that I thought his house would make an amazing beach bar.

"'Yes,' he replied. 'People have been telling me that for ten years, but I have no interest in opening a restaurant.'

"A couple months later he contacted me to say he was returning to the United States. He then asked if I would like to lease his house for a restaurant.

"'I meant it would be an amazing restaurant for you to open,' I replied.

"I mentioned it to my husband and he laughed, 'Are you crazy? We are not opening a restaurant.' I told him to go check it out anyway. We always loved Woody's Waterfront Café and Beach Bar in St. Pete, Florida and dreamed of opening a Woody's of our own.

"My husband went to our friend's property and immediately fell in love with the place. We signed a lease and began construction. The building process wasn't bad because it only needed renovations. Getting reliable suppliers was a different story. There was the language barrier, and we felt that companies in Costa Rica are not as eager to do business as the suppliers we had dealt with in North America.

"I should mention that my husband and I have been in the restaurant business our whole lives. We met while working at a restaurant after graduating high school; I was a bartender and he was a bouncer. We then franchised a sandwich chain in Canada, and later managed over two hundred restaurants. We knew the business inside and out. Having experience is even more important in Costa Rica. You want to train your staff, not have your staff training you.

"My advice for anyone starting a business in Costa Rica is to know your trade well before even thinking about it. Things can be difficult here, especially if you are not fluent in the language. The hardest part of running a restaurant anywhere in the world is finding good employees. Costa Rica is no exception. It has taken us many years to build our great staff. Part of the pura vida lifestyle is that nothing is ever urgent. Our North American culture dictates fast service. Tourists want to enjoy their meal and then quickly get on to their next activity. Serving the check in a timely fashion has been an uphill battle.

"In addition to constant training, you need to keep an eye on everything. Theft in the restaurant business is common. You need to have cameras, check lists, and keep impeccable inventory of your food, liquor and supplies.

"Costa Rica has very stringent labor laws. What you think is inexpensive labor is really not when you factor in all of the employee benefits. Workers are entitled to fifteen paid vacation days per year. They also receive a bonus of 12 percent of their yearly salary in December. If they work for you for a full year it works out to thirty days' bonus pay. Employers must also contribute to employee health care and social security each month.

"Today I have an excellent staff, and I love them all. My husband and I now own three restaurants, and I love talking to customers. Every day, tourists are telling me they want to do the same thing and move to Costa Rica.

"'How lucky you are!' they say. I replay I feel very blessed to look out at the ocean every day and feel the warmth on my skin. But all I did was move! They can move too and be just as lucky as me. What's the worst thing that can happen? Planes go both ways… you can always go back!"

**Links**

https://www.facebook.com/TheBeachHouseBarAndRestaurant
https://www.facebook.com/TikisSeasideGrille

# Road Trip: Pacific Coast Highway

I've mentioned that the drive to the Caribbean is the prettiest in the country. Nothing but palm trees and salty Bob Marley breezes swirling around your body like sugar in a cotton candy machine. However, I may have spoken prematurely: the drive down the Pacific coast is just as beautiful and takes you through some of the most spectacular parts of this country. If you're flying into the San José airport, getting to this part of the country has become much easier since they finished the Autopista del Sol Highway (also known locally as the Caldera). You can take this road all the way down to Orotina.

Once you pass Orotina, look for the Jacó and Tarcoles exit and merge onto Route 34, the Costanera Sur. This coastal highway is one of my favorite drives in the country. Traveling with a dense forest to your left and an ocean to your right invites daydreams. I'm most creative during these drives, especially when the windows are down and Rob is humming a tune. There is no use playing with the radio dial since that broke long ago. There is still a charming cassette deck but unless you feel like climbing into my parents' attic to retrieve my Night Ranger tape, I'm not sure what to do with it. In fact, I once looked inside to find an abandoned wasp's nest. Or at least I hope it's abandoned.

As you pass through Tarcoles, you'll notice a bunch of tourists looking over a bridge and taking pictures of crocodiles. This is a popular place and many people will stop and get out of their car to look, but remember crime rule number one: take all your belongings with you. This is a common place for thieves to snatch a bag while you're off taking pictures. Now there is usually a police officer stationed there, so things have gotten a lot better. Please take note of your belongings if you consider getting out of your car.

- Jacó

Continue traveling south and the first touristy town you'll come to is Jacó. Popular for its proximity to San José and the Central Valley, it's also known for its active nightlife. If you are on this journey to party, Jacó may be the spot for you. You'll find the typical tourist activities: fishing, horseback riding, and ATV tours.

Jacó is full of hotels, restaurants, and souvenir shops. Rob and I like to stop for a bite to eat before continuing south. There is a scenic bluff just past the town where you can take incredible pictures of the Pacific.

- Playa Hermosa (the southern one, not the beach in Guanacaste)

One of my favorite beaches south of Jacó is Playa Hermosa. It's where I first witnessed scarlet macaws flying overhead. Costa Rica is constantly unfolding its beauty, often at times I need it the most. Nature has a way of fixing the things in me that need fixing and reminding me to slow down and look around. After seeing those birds, I knew I'd be living in Costa Rica for a long time.

- Playa Bejuco

Playa Bejuco is one of those beaches you can easily miss. We spent a couple days here, and it's where I took the cover picture for my first book: that cute little doggie waiting for his owner to come back from surfing. In a way, I felt like this dog while working in my office: waiting for something, a different kind of life that would surf straight toward me. Unfortunately, that didn't happen. I finally realized that life wasn't going to surf to me; I had to paddle out toward it. Once I made that decision, I've been paddling ever since.

- Playa Palo Seco

Once you drive through the town of Parrita, watch for a turn-off to your right for Playa Palo Seco. This beach is on a small peninsula that borders the ocean on its front and an estuary to its back. This barrier isle is not to be missed. It reminds me of *Gilligan's Island*, with rows of shady palm trees and scores of sand dollars peppering the beach. This tract of land is so narrow you feel as if you can skip a stone right over it from the estuary to the sea. If you are looking for a quiet place, one where you rarely see anyone on the beach, this tiny piece of paradise should be added to your itinerary.

- Manuel Antonio

Do you like monkeys? Do you feel like there's not enough of them in your life? If that's the case, Manuel Antonio is the place for you. Monkeys run this town.

This area is most famous for its park: Manuel Antonio National Park. It's not the biggest park in Costa Rica, but what it lacks in size, it makes up for in wildlife. You'll see three out of the four types of monkeys that reside in Costa Rica: howler, grey-capped titi (squirrel), and white-faced (capuchin). The latter are the most mischievous. Don't be surprised if a white-faced monkey pickpockets you while you are staring up at the canopy. They'll steal anything: cigarettes, money, and—their favorite—keys. It's not uncommon to see a frantic tourist tracking a monkey as it swings from tree to tree waiting to get his keys back. Can you imagine sitting in on that phone conversation with a car rental company? "Um… a monkey stole my keys. Yes, you heard me correctly. That's not covered under insurance? I signed a monkey crime waiver? Son of a… "

When visiting the park, don't forget to pack a swimsuit. There are several white sand beaches that provide the perfect place to unroll a towel and relax. It was at one of these beaches Rob and I were robbed by a couple raccoons.

After Rob and I dashed into the water, we watched as these bandits leisurely sifted through our beach bag, backpack, and sneakers. They scampered off with a few Ritz crackers and mixed nuts. From what I hear, they are still on the run.

The park is also an excellent place to see sloths. I love sloths. Who doesn't? They don't do much, get to hang out upside down in a tree all day, and from what I've witnessed are not part of the raccoon and monkey crime syndicate.

It's best to hire one of the park's guides so that you don't miss out on any of this. The last time we were there, we opted for a private tour. Our guide pointed out woodpeckers, motmots, and toucans and identified many plants. He even spotted sloths snuggling up high in trees. There is so much more to this park than meets the eye.

Enjoy the moment but remember to hold onto your keys.

- Dominical: The place to get a good night's sleep

Approximately forty-five minutes from Manuel Antonio is Playa Dominical. If you are a surfer, you probably already know that this tiny beach town is popular for its dependable waves. It's also a place where you can see the same animals that are up north, but with a twist. Red iguanas lounge on sunny branches over head, and fiery-billed toucans dine on palm fruit all along the coastline. It's as if Dominical is sprinkled with paprika; every animal is a little jazzier than its counterpart found in other parts of the country. Every time I'm in Dominical, I'm amazed at what I'll see just by looking up.

The town is made up of only a couple unpaved streets, lined with restaurants and shops. I've never seen anyone rushing here. And why would they? This town is designed for relaxation and surfing.

Dominical is the perfect town to take a break from a road trip and spend a few days. When I mention this to my friends Kelley and Daveed, two realtors in the area, that I am writing a guidebook and am searching to include properties that could deliver the "wow" factor, they are excited to suggest some of their favorite places.

The first place they recommend is Canto del Mar, a complex of villas overlooking the bay of Dominicalito. Not only do we have an incredible ocean vista, but our villa also borders a luxuriant forest. Perched high above the trees, we have a bird's-eye view of all the amazing creatures living in the canopy. This place is a photographer's dream. While Dominical offers amazing natural wonders around every corner, you do not need to leave this beautiful villa in order to capture incredible snapshots of the sea or animals that inhabit the area.

I never sleep better than in Dominical, and I always wake up refreshed. Rob and I spend lazy mornings watching iguanas climb trees and toucans flying overhead in search of breakfast. Surfers paddle off in the distance, hoping to land that perfect wave, and fishermen prepare for their day by catching bait in the bay before heading out to sea. This is—by far—the sweetest way to start the morning. It's so incredibly peaceful that it's hard to remember how rushed I used to be, how anxious my mornings were. Maybe that's the reason I sleep so well in this small town: I know I'll be waking up to a masterpiece.

Dominical smells good too, like a forest and fresh-cut grass. It smells alive and hopeful. It softens your hard, pointy edges created by years of stress, sanding them down little by little before ultimately creating a smooth curve. Stress sits perfectly on pointy edges, but with curves it has nowhere to rest. Bad days thoughtlessly slip away.

Our stay at Canto del Mar is amazing. We are ready to explore further down the coast when Kelley tells us about a place with an even bigger "wow" factor. She describes a big, beautiful home with such passion and surprises us by saying that it runs on solar power. It is one of the first houses in the country powered by alternative energy, and the president of ICE (the electric company) was there for its inauguration. This is a home I have to see so we move down the block to Villa Pacifica.

I know these type of homes exist but have never had a chance to stay in one. Villa Pacifica has six bedrooms, an outdoor kitchen, and a tower of towels positioned near the most amazing infinity pool. I stare out over the pool for what seems like hours while Rob runs around the house in disbelief. This place is perfect for family reunions, weddings, or just large groups of friends who love spending time together. And if you don't want to spend time together with your friends or family, three of the six bedrooms are tucked away around the side of the house. Kelley has recently completed an extensive renovation on them, and they are a perfect hideaway for when your drunk Uncle Benny starts his impromptu karaoke with an empty wine bottle.

I still can't get over the size of Villa Pacifica's pool. My dad feels like you have made it if you own one. It doesn't even have to be an in-ground pool with an infinity edge; it could be an above-ground model with a plastic ladder. If he had a chance to see this one, he might go a little nuts, celebrating by buying expensive, imported Kellogg cereal and half-and-half. I can see us now, clinking our bowls of Frosted Flakes before pouring pricey cream into our coffee.

Once again, I sleep well. I don't do my usual tossing and turning or yell out, "Pancakes!" I don't know why I do this, but it has happened on more than one occasion. Rob completely freaks out thinking someone has broken into our house and is cooking flapjacks in the kitchen. He ultimately runs around only to find no one there. He ends up cooking pancakes at four in the morning, since he's already up and now it seems like a good idea.

I'm treated to some amazing sunsets in Dominical: orangey-red with blue mixed in between. The afterglow lasts a long time, with purply clouds resting on the horizon before surrendering to the night. Costa Rica is never shy when unveiling its loveliness.

Dominical is delicious, a little paprika-sprinkled town nestled along the shore. An easy place to rest one's head and let go of collected worries. I left quite a few of mine there, right next to a sleepy red iguana.

**Links**

Jaco:

- Jaco Laguna Resort and Beach Club: www.jacolagunaresort.com/
- Hotel Nine: http://hotelnine.com
- Los Suenos Marriott Ocean & Golf Resort: www.marriott.com/hotels/travel/sjols-los-suenos-marriott-ocean-and-golf-resort/

Playa Bejuco:

- Hotel Playa Bejuco: www.hotelplayabejuco.com

Manuel Antonio:

- Hotel La Mariposa: www.lamariposa.com
- Si Como No Resort: www.sicomono.com
- Hotel Costa Verde: www.costaverde.com

Dominical:

- You reach Kelley at: www.costaricarentalsnow.com/
- Canto del Mar Villas: www.costaricarentalsnow.com/vacation-rentals/canto-del-mar-20/
- Villa Pacifica: www.costaricarentalsnow.com/vacation-rentals/villa-pacifica/

# Firearms in the Fireplace

So you're thinking about hiding a gun in the fireplace? Good. You and Rob will get along fine. Maybe you'll even want to shoot out the water pipes in your backyard. I'm already planning a barbecue so we can get to know each other better.

I've only shot our gun once. I didn't hit any of the flowerpots Rob lined up as targets, probably because I had my eyes closed and was screaming hysterically. I thought I might as well reenact what would actually happen if someone broke into my house and I was in charge of protecting my husband.

When we moved to Costa Rica, it was possible to buy a firearm even without permanent residency. We went to San José to start a corporation (real estate, firearms, and car purchases are often incorporated), get fingerprinted, and provide a criminal record. That was all it took at that time.

But like everything else in Costa Rica, the laws are always changing. Today you must be a permanent resident and follow stricter rules in order to obtain the weapon. The steps are as follows:

1. Fill out an application with the Ministry of Public Security.
2. Provide them documentation regarding the origin of the firearm.
3. Provide original and photocopies of your cedula (Costa Rican residency card).
4. Have the weapon inspected. This is usually done at the gun shop.
5. Undergo a gun training course and pass the firearm exam.
6. Get fingerprinted at the Department of Arms and Explosives in San José.
7. Provide certification of a clean criminal record from the Ministerio Judicial.
8. Pass a psychological exam taken in Costa Rica.

I love number eight: pass a psychological exam. Reclining on a therapist's couch and recalling how much my parents screwed me up is time well spent. I mean, leaving Disney World early over my dad's bloody head wound? I'm surprised we're still talking.

If you are already a permanent resident, you can bring a gun into the country but you'll be opening a can of worms. If you decide to do it that way, let's go through it together because I really want to see how this plays out with customs.

Follow airline regulations by separating the gun from the ammunition in your checked luggage. There will be paperwork to fill out so make sure you contact the appropriate office with the airline you will be using. Or you can be like one of those do-ta-doos you hear about on the news, and forget you have a loaded gun in your carry-on. Who are these people? How do you forget you packed a loaded Magnum in with your toothpaste? Apparently, this happens a lot.

I recently met a man, Alan, who just moved to Costa Rica from the United States. He packed a large shipping container that included his car and all his household belongings. It made it all the way down to the Miami port before Alan realized he left his loaded gun in the glove compartment of his car. He frantically called up the movers and paid a man to climb into the container and retrieve the gun. It didn't help that the car was the first thing Alan had packed, so the shipping employee had to climb over everything to make it to the far end of the container. This ended up delaying the move and cost Alan an extra thousand dollars. His wife wouldn't talk to him for two weeks.

If you are a permanent resident in Costa Rica and have your heart set on bringing your firearm down, these are the steps you will need to take:

1. Provide the Costa Rican Ministry of Public Security with a clean police record of where you've lived the

past 6 months. Have this paperwork notarized by a Costa Rican consulate.
2. Provide proof that the firearm is registered with your Secretary of State. You must also have that paperwork notarized by a Costa Rican consulate.
3. Provide a weapon Entrance Receipt issued by a Costa Rican custom official.
4. Pass a psychological test performed by a licensed psychologist in Costa Rica.

I don't know anyone who had their firearm imported into Costa Rica, so I can't give you firsthand knowledge on how quickly this process works. In my experience, if there is a lot of bureaucracy attached to importing something, you may be better off buying it in the country.

On a side note, no weapons of war are legally allowed in Costa Rica. I'm a bit relieved because if my husband could get hold of a bazooka, I'm sure he would test it out about two feet from our living room window. The monkeys would just adore this and I'm sure we would not see them again for the next twenty years.

Don't worry too much if you do not qualify for a gun permit. There are plenty of other nifty little weapons you can use for home security. How about a machete behind the headboard? Or a few motion sensors around the house? Maximum-strength bear mace, anyone? There are many things you can do if you feel you need that kind of security. I have one friend that has a flare gun that resembles a handgun. Anyone breaking into his house is in for one hell of a surprise.

Considering that many of the people I know back in the United States have at least a baseball bat under their bed, none of this should come as a big surprise to you. Do what makes you feel is comfortable. Everyone lives a different lifestyle here: some never lock their doors; others have alarms on their houses. It's all a matter of personal preference. Live here a while and then determine what the best choice is for you.

When you have nothing better to do, Google "urban street violence paper targets." These are the targets that gun ranges hang up for clients to shoot at and are images of the scariest people you'll ever encounter. My dad was right in sending me all those awful crime newspaper clippings when I was in college. Who knew these creeps were running around town? Maybe I should get my butt to the shooting range.

If I do, I plan on logging in some serious Yosemite Sam time. I just have to remember to keep my eyes open while I shoot.

# Dental Care

"Your back molar is broken," Dr. Alan Alvarado explains to me. "I am going to have to do some work back there, but first I'll have to numb the area. Close your eyes and think of rainbows."

I lie back in the chair and do as he suggests. I begin imagining rainbows, which isn't hard to do since I just saw one this morning.

"Okay, this might be a little uncomfortable," the doctor says while approaching with a needle. "Now think about butterflies, monkeys, and sunshine. Imagine you are in a happy place."

This cracks me up since my dentist is describing my impression of Costa Rica. This is my happy place, albeit not in a dentist chair.

"Now you will taste something. It will taste like lemonade. Not sweet lemonade but tart lemonade, so imagine that. Lemonade on a hot summer's day."

Rainbows, sunshine, and lemonade? I love my dentist! I could sit in this office all day. It's like story time in here. After twenty minutes, my molar is fixed and I have one more good experience to share about living in this country.

Costa Rica is the land of aligned incisors, and most expats' choppers are similar to those you might see in Beverly Hills: perfectly white without one snaggletooth. I tend to notice teeth a lot, and oddly, I also notice toupees. I can pick one out from at least half a mile away. There has not been one artificial hairline that has gone unnoticed by me in the past fifteen years.

Dental care is less expensive in Costa Rica than in many other countries. Whether it's whitening, veneers, or even more complicated procedures you'll have no problem finding a dentist that offers these services. I picked my dentist after friends had recommended him many times, and I've been a patient of his for over three years. The last time I got my teeth cleaned, he spent forty-five minutes doing it himself. I'm not used to the actual dentist doing this, but he does an incredible job and made sure I was comfortable during the entire visit.

It's a perfect example of one of the things I love about Costa Rica: people spend more time with each other. He never appears rushed and makes me feel like he truly cares about his patients. On a side note, during my visit I couldn't help but notice that he has really nice teeth and fresh breath. It was like an Orbit commercial. And from what I could tell, he has an authentic hairline.

I had made an appointment with him right before the *EX-PATS* show. The crew came and filmed Rob and me for four days. I didn't have much time so I thought about getting that super-duper whitening process everyone gets back in the States. The one in which your teeth could be beacons for lost ships. When I asked about the procedure, the dentist explained the pros and cons of the treatment. Because I have sensitive teeth, he suggested that I brush with special toothpaste for ten days before the treatment. Ultimately, we decided bleaching trays were my best choice. The kit cost about thirty percent less than in the States. It worked out perfectly and I had a dazzling smile for my television debut.

I was so nervous during that show since it was my first introduction to that kind of professional production. The team was really kind to me and I was happy to see that Savannah Buffett came with the most amazing hair-and-makeup woman. I also had my own hair-and-makeup person—Rob. His commentary included such high notes as "You look sweaty," "That black stuff on your eyelashes is running down your face," and my favorite: "You're good."

After giving me whitening trays, my dentist injected Botox into my forehead. JUST KIDDING. He never offered such a thing. But I did have a gynecologist back in the United States who once suggested I get this treatment. Luckily, he was talking about my face. Later I discovered that he had just returned from a weekend seminar and was now going to be offering the facial procedure to his clients. I believe his sales pitch would have gone over better once his patients were out of the stirrups, but what do I know? Give me a couple more years in this sun and I'm sure I'll be considering it while getting a mammogram.

Dr. Alvarado works with an oral surgeon, so his office can handle not only common cosmetic dental procedures, but more complicated cases as well. Or you can just see him for a cleaning; he'll whisper a lovely fairytale to you while scraping plaque off your teeth. And we could all use a little lemonade and sunshine while reclining in a dentist's chair.

**Links**

Dr. Alan Alvarado: www.costadental.com/
*EX-PATS* Show: Have you seen it yet? It's here I'll dazzle you with my white smile, and you can admire Rob's beautician skills. http://youtu.be/0rd0JeMPC7Q?list=PLAD3A1AD1D428C9B1

# Real Questions Emailed to Happier

Is it true Costa Rica doesn't have an army?

- Yes.

Do I need mosquito repellent?

- Absolutely. Especially near the beach. Those sandflies are awful and you can get bit up quickly. Occasionally, there are outbreaks of dengue fever, a disease transmitted by infected mosquitos. I would recommend repellant for those reasons.

Can I watch college football if I move there?

- Yes. There are cable packages that carry all those stations. Go Rutgers.

Is it safe to drive in Costa Rica?

- Yes. It's much like the old Frogger game from Atari. If you keep it slow and watch for the occasional cattle in the road or for the… well… completely washed-out road you will be fine. Don't worry. Some nice person will plunge a stick in the gaping ditch and tie a plastic grocery bag on top to warn you. Surprisingly, this works out fine. And driving throughout Costa Rica is the best way to see it. Get a scooter, and now you are really living the dream.

I've heard that it is difficult to get lettuce in Costa Rica. Is that true?"

- What dastardly individual is spreading such lies? It's obviously the cabbage mafia besmirching the lettuce industry again. I see lettuce in every store. Sometimes it's sad lettuce (here at the beach), wilted and defeated, like they just got their backpack stolen out from their car. Or it's happy lettuce, crisp and ready to eat. It appears that the quality is determined by your location. Therefore, I just buy a head of cabbage the size of a bowling ball and use that for most of my salads. It's cheaper and goes a long way.

I'm thinking of moving to Costa Rica. I've saved up $500 so far. Is that enough?"

- No.

Is it true you don't get mail in Costa Rica?

- Considering my address is something like 500 meters south of the mango tree, I doubt if a postal worker would ever find me, or any of my neighbors for that matter. Most expats have PO boxes in both Miami and Costa Rica. They then use a mail courier service to ship their mail and packages down. Some of the most commonly used are Mail Boxes Etc., JetBox, and Aerocasillas.

# Farmhouse & Horseback Riding

Have you been thinking about writing a novel but never seem to be in the right frame of mind? Look no further; I believe I've found the perfect place to get started.

Finca Dos Rios is a lovely rustic farmhouse located just outside of a small town called Balsar. My friend Anne, the owner, invites us down for a couple of days.

"Jorge, the caretaker, will give you a tour of the property. Are you up for getting on a horse?" The answer is no. I do not want to horseback ride again considering every time I do, I find myself racing up a steep mountain or at the edge of a cliff. I can never seem to find flat ground while riding a horse.

"I'll pass on that, Anne."

"Okay, but don't you want to see the ancient sphere?" she asks.

"Wait, you have a sphere on your property?"

"Yes."

"A real one?"

"Yes, but the best way to see it is by horse."

Oh boy, this is a game changer. Spheres are one of the biggest archeological mysteries in Costa Rica. They date back to at least a thousand years, and no one is certain how they were carved. They're usually found by workers clearing fields, and now I have a chance to see one not in a museum, but right where it has been sitting for ages. I'll certainly get on a horse for this.

Anne's farmhouse is approximately forty-five minutes south of Dominical. We turn left at kilometer marker 196 and drive up a dirt road leading to another dirt road. The more dirt roads you encounter in Costa Rica, the better your chances of seeing something *really* good.

As per Anne's instructions, we stop by her caretaker's house. He's out working on the farm, so his wife calls to let him know we've arrived. A few moments later, we hear the clickety-clack of horseshoes against the stones in the road. Two riders approach: Jorge and his five-year-old son. The child's head is held high; his small hands hold onto the reins, steering the horse without any trace of fear in his eyes. He's so little that his legs barely fall past the bottom of the saddle. It makes me feel silly for fearing something this child is confidently managing. I think I just found a way to crack everyone's phobias: watch a child do the very same thing that they themselves are afraid of.

Jorge grabs a key from his wife, instructs us to follow him, and gallops away like the Lone Ranger. He goes so fast our Mitsubishi can't keep up and he disappears in a cloud of dust. Eventually we find him up the road, unlocking a large gate with two metal carvings of cattle welded to it. We follow him as he trots up the driveway and it's only now we understand why Anne was so eager for us to visit: the property is divine.

As we step out of the car, parrots pass overhead and land on an adjacent tree. One stretches his wings above us like a holy man giving a benediction over his flock. It's as if I'm walking on sacred land.

These parrots look different from the ones I usually see in Guanacaste. They seem bigger, louder, and more colorful. When one flock flies away, another group lands. There must be hundreds.

Rob collects our bags and carries them inside the house. As Anne suggested, we plan a horseback tour of the property with Jorge. He promises to show us the sphere and gallops back home.

"It's really hot today," I say while putting on one of Anne's cowboy hats.

"She said it'll cool off tonight," Rob replies while tying a GoPro camera around his neck.

"Why are you wearing that around your neck?"

"I can get video footage with the GoPro while simultaneously freeing my hands to take pictures. It's genius."

Jorge returns to the house with two additional horses. Mine has satiny brown hair and blue eyes, looking more like a Hollywood horse than a working farm one. Jorge gives me a boost and hands me the reins. Here I go again on another horseback-riding excursion, but at least this time it's for fun and not to look at a piece of property that requires my friends boarding a helicopter to visit.

As we enter the woods the air cools ten degrees. Trees surround us, and all the obscure sounds of the forest become more recognizable: birds in the trees, melodic frog calls, and the rustling of a forest floor full of life and decay. The sun manages to peek through branches, piecing the air with golden lightsabers.

"I can't believe how wonderful this is! Take a picture," I yell back to Rob, but he is too busy getting smacked in the face with the GoPro. It's genius: every time he goes over a bump, the GoPro socks him in the nose. He attempts to let go of the reins to take a picture but almost falls off the horse. I swiftly turn back around and pray that I won't need to use my YouTube medical degree today.

We stop by a river and Jorge explains how white-faced monkeys occasionally stop here for a drink before darting back up into the trees. They never stay on the ground long, always fearing predators, namely caiman. I don't see any monkeys here today, but I bet they're watching. This forest is full of Peeping Toms.

The three of us trot toward a herd of cattle that barely acknowledge our existence. One mother has a suckling baby and refuses to budge. The horses don't seem to care and push straight past them. My leg brushes up against the baby calf, who glances upwards, batting her eyelashes. It's amazing what you notice on a trail ride when you aren't having a panic attack.

We pass under a mamón chino tree and I watch as Jorge yanks fruit from a branch, peels off the skin, and eats the inside. He's been picking things off trees throughout the entire tour. I guess you don't need to pack a lunch when you work on this farm: just shop at the produce market dangling overhead.

The mamón chino tree is overcrowded with its odd-looking fruit. At first glance, you might shy away from eating one; its exterior has rubbery tentacles emanating from it like a Koosh ball. Remarkably, what's hidden inside is white fruit that tastes like a plum. There must be a thousand of them hanging from this tree, and an equal amount untidily strewn on the ground. It's impossible to starve if you have one of these in your backyard. They are probably a lot of fun for the children, who undoubtedly pelt each other with the fruit after school. We had snowballs growing up; they have mamón chinos, each one perfect for smacking your friend in the face when no one is looking.

Jorge takes us farther up the mountain and points into the distance. I see it: the sphere. Only the top half is excavated, the rest still buried in the same ground it's been sitting in for over a thousand years. I jump off my horse and run my hand over it. It's cold and smooth, and I can't get over how a person made this for some unknown reason lifetimes ago. Many think these spheres were created in honor of a nearby volcano they may have worshipped, but there are no volcanoes in this part of the country. Some believe that the stones these spheres are made of may not be native to this area and may have been hauled in from other parts of the country. How exactly did they do that? What kind of tools did they use?

These spheres hold many mysteries and are just as historically significant as Easter Island or Stonehenge. As I brush my hand against the sphere, I wonder if this same family of parrots stretched their wings over ancient civilizations as they have for Rob and me, or if white-faced monkeys sipped from streams while natives chiseled the rocks. Costa Rica constantly connects me to the past, always stepping Rob and me back in time with each new adventure.

The last part of our tour takes us to the very top of the mountain. I gasp as I'm greeted by a 360-degree view of the area. My horse seems equally impressed and stands at full attention. To my right I see the beaches of Uvita, and to my left is the Osa Peninsula. Down below, roofs dot the countryside like tiny Monopoly houses. I'm so grateful for this, all of it: the trail ride, my patient tour guide, and the time I'm spending with my husband. The view reminds me of how marvelous this world is, and how much more I want to see of it. I can't believe I've been in this country for seven years, and still feel like I just stepped off the plane. I often find myself here: on top of the world. However, today feels even more special.

My horse is on autopilot as we make our way back to the house. There is no need to pull on the reins, as he obediently follows Jorge down the mountain.

"Wow... look up, honey!" Rob shouts as we return to the house. A pack of titi monkeys jump from branch to branch, dropping broken twigs as they go. Titi monkeys must be some of the cutest animals I've ever seen. They have an adorable white-and-black facial mask across their faces and bounce across the treetops in groups ranging from twenty to seventy-five. Titis communicate through squeals and chirps, and when encountering a predator they let out a specific high-pitched alarm to warn their buddies before diving for cover. Their bodies are small, only about ten to seventeen inches in length, but the main reason I love them so much is because they are monogamous. After a female gives birth the father plays a large role in caring for their young.

We jump off our horses and say goodbye to Jorge. He gallops away and once again disappears in a cloud of dust. As we enter the farmhouse we are surprised to find a humongous fruit basket. I shouldn't even call it a fruit basket, but more like a fruit table. While we were gone, Jorge's wife brought us coconuts, lemons, mangos, oranges, bananas, red peppers, and mamón chinos. There is no possible way we can eat all of this in the short time we are spending here. I open the refrigerator to find a covered plate with a large wedge of white cheese inside. Who knew we'd enjoy a five-star experience in this lovely little rustic farmhouse?

As Anne promised, the cool night air sweeps away any lingering heat. There is no Internet here, but I am able to get a faint 3G signal and it is strong enough to send an email, though not fast enough to surf the web. I'm actually happy about this; I didn't come here to play on the computer all day.

We lie in bed filling our stomachs with fruit and cheese as the stars twinkle outside our window. The faint hum of an overhead fan is barely heard over the sounds of the crickets and toads. It's the perfect finale to an adventurous day; a day where I learned that I actually like horseback riding.

Rob also learned not to tie a camera around his neck while riding a horse, but I have to give him credit. He did get great pictures and video of me on that mountain, gasping at its view and feeling on top of the world. It was genius after all.

### Links

If you would like to rent the farmhouse or take the horseback riding tour of Anne's property, you may contact her on Facebook or through her email:

www.facebook.com/balsarfarm
foster0088@hotmail.com

# Wild Animal Rescue Center *

As you pass Anne's farmhouse, continue up the dirt road and watch for signs that will direct you toward Osa Mountain Village. Just before you reach this development, you'll see an entrance for Osa Santuario De Animales. It's a remarkable place with an equally remarkable owner. Many of the animals that reside here were rescued by MINAE (Costa Rica Ministry of the Environment), a division of the government responsible for protecting Costa Rica's wildlife. Some will be rehabilitated and returned to the forest. Others will spend the rest of their lives at the sanctuary depending on their condition.

It's our lucky day and we receive a tour of this center by its owner, Mike Graeber. He's a burly man who speaks with authority and intent. I imagine him riding motorcycles through South America, or logging in Oregon. However, looks can certainly be deceiving. He is a gentle man whose calling is to care for helpless animals that have no other place to go.

The center consists of large enclosures that house a variety of animals. Mike escorts us around, giving a brief history of each animal, including the conditions they were rescued from. Thankfully he only divulges some of each story, because heaven knows I can't bear to listen to the rest. There is a menagerie of sadness surrounding these creatures, but what outshines the inhumanity is this man who cares for his furry tribe with a sacred heart and scarred hands.

"Have you ever been bitten by the animals?" I ask.

"Yes, all the time. It's part of the job," Mike says.

"Any one instance that really stands out?"

"Let me introduce you to our spider monkeys." He goes inside the cage containing two monkeys. One immediately grabs his hand, while the other climbs up and wraps her spindly arms around him. "These guys gave me the hardest time when they first arrived."

What I'm witnessing now doesn't match what Mike is saying at all. "I don't understand. They look so gentle. One is even hugging you!"

"*Now* they're gentle, but you should have seen them when they came to the sanctuary. They were rescued from someone's backyard where they had been chained up with leashes around their necks. They spent most of their lives in fear of people."

Spider monkeys are endangered and are one of the smarter species of monkeys. Their long arms nearly drag on the ground as they walk; they use their tail for balance and can appear humanlike in their attempt to stand upright. Spider monkey faces are adorably hairless, and when approached by a predator they make loud barking noises in order to alert the rest of the pack. They are beautiful, and I can't imagine anyone doing something so cruel to them.

"They were terribly frightened when they arrived. And why wouldn't be they be after all they've been through?" Mike tries to put the monkey down but she climbs back up and wraps her arms around him once again. "The first day they were here, I entered the cage and one lunged at me in full attack mode. No matter how hard I tried, I couldn't get him off. Don't let their size fool you—spider monkeys are incredibly strong. I only have two hands while they can use all four limbs against me at once."

"I would have sprinted for the hills," I respond, since getting beat up by a monkey is not on my bucket list. Although as with all of my husband's whacky excursions, that scenario will probably happen sooner or later.

"It all went down so fast, I couldn't even turn around," he continues. "It was then I came to the realization this was an all-out fight. I pushed him, put up my hands like a boxer, and made a wild face. If this is what he wanted, I was ready. Then something miraculous happened: he looked straight into my eyes, backed off, and sat in the corner."

"When did you try going back inside the cage?"

"The next day. This is my job. I have to get close to these animals for feedings and medical care. I had my colleague ready to spray him with the hose while I slowly entered the cage. I was preparing for what I thought could be round two when the same monkey that attacked me walked up and grabbed my hand. Just like that, we were now friends. It was amazing. They have been very affectionate toward me ever since."

As I'm watching Mike hug the spider monkey, a red squirrel jumps on my head and decides to make a nest in my scalp.

"He's in my hair!" I scream.

"Stop yelling," Mike calmly replies. "It's no big deal. I've had that squirrel since he was a baby."

I make a stance, like Mike did with the spider monkey. This does nothing but encourage him to use my body as his own personal jungle gym.

"Get the hose!" I yell.

Mike casually grabs the squirrel and tosses him up on a branch. "I can't get rid of him. He goes off into the forest but always returns. Such a troublemaker."

We head on over to another enclosure housing two white-faced monkeys. They were rescued from a drug cartel, and unfortunately they can never be released back into the wild.

"It's very hard for white-faced monkeys to make it on their own after being pets," Mike explains. "If we let them go, another pack of monkeys will probably kill them in less than forty-eight hours. They will spend the rest of their lives here, but I will make it a good life for them."

As Mike approaches the enclosure, the monkeys maniacally jump up and down. This behavior is radically different when compared to howler monkeys. Howlers have a laissez-faire attitude, grunting at you before falling asleep seconds later. They just can't commit to that kind of energy.

I'm all but certain white-faced monkeys pop amphetamines when no one is watching. It's as if their goal in life is to cause as much mischief as possible. They remind me of my husband's Brooklyn friend Tommy Walnuts.

"I love the action," Tommy confesses, usually after playing poker for twenty-four hours straight. I'm sure if white-faced monkeys hopped a flight to the United States they'd settle in Las Vegas, double down on blackjack, and drive fancy Cadillacs.

The moment he opens the cage these guys spring into the air as if rocket launchers were attached to their feet. One jumps up on me, reaches into my pocket, and steals my hair band. He plays with it for a few seconds before tossing it over his shoulder, then jumping on Rob and pickpocketing him as well. We're all grateful that my husband is not carrying bear mace today.

"That's Pablo—what a rascal," Mike laughs. "There's only one way to calm him down: sit in that chair, and once he jumps into your lap start grooming him."

"This may sound like a stupid question, but how do I groom a monkey?"

"Brush your hand along his fur, just like you see them doing to each other. Act as if you are picking bugs off his skin."

Once I'm in the chair, Pablo leaps into my lap. I begin rubbing my hand along the fur and he reacts as if I removed his batteries: a second later he stretches out and closes his eyes. Apparently, I am the monkey whisperer and a darn good bug picker. Now that Pablo's calm, I can take a closer look, and I notice how the black cap of fur on his head looks a lot like a beret. His face is light pink, the color of bubblegum that you're likely find in a pack of trading cards. I continue grooming since I imagine that's the polite thing to do when a monkey is curled up in your lap. It doesn't take long before Pablo wakes up, and in an instant propels himself halfway across the room.

"Who's that?" Rob asks, pointing to a small animal wrestling with the monkeys.

"That's Oscar, our baby coati. Or as they call them in Costa Rica, a pizote. His mother was poached and someone brought in her babies. He is the only one out of three that survived."

The coati and monkeys chase each other like kids on a playground. He's adorable but will not stay still. We try to get a picture; however Oscar is moving way too fast. Every shot is a blur. Rob falls in love and immediately wants us to adopt a baby coati.

"If you want to see a real charmer, let me show you our anteater." Mike reaches inside a cage, and an anteater (Tamandua) about two feet in length climbs into his arms. It's as if Mike has an air of kindness that animals immediately detect. Every time he puts the anteater down, the animal extends his arms to be picked up once again.

Tamandua tongues are covered with thousands of hooks that are used to scoop up insects, and boy do they love insects. I'm even considering putting an anteater on my terrace. It would make alfresco dining more pleasurable if three-inch flying beetles weren't always landing in my spaghetti.

Mike calls out to his assistant and asks her to warm up a bottle of milk. "Wait until you see this little guy," he says while opening up another cage. Inside is a box where I imagine something must be napping.

"What is it?" I ask while Mike coaxes the animal out of its nest.

"Her name is Blossom and she is a baby Mexican tree porcupine. Do you want to touch her? Make sure you pet in the direction of the quills and not the opposite way."

Rob volunteers and delicately strokes the porcupine. "It feels like the bristles of a straw broom."

Blossom reaches up and uses her front legs to grasp the baby bottle as Mike feeds her. The milk dribbles all over her face, making this one of the cutest things I've ever seen.

"The quills are sharp, and because they are hollow it creates a suction when embedded into predators. It's not uncommon for my dog to come home with a bunch of quills in her face. It's best not to jerk them. Instead, cut the quills in half. This removes the suction effect making them easier to pull out."

I wish I had known this when trying to help Dolores (the Crazy Dog Lady from my first book) remove quills from her pet's face. My job was to hold her dog down while Rob tugged at the quills with pliers. While we were busy saving the day, Dolores spent her time searching for a calculator that was allegedly stolen by Indian spirits living inside her house.

Mike's dedication to these creatures is phenomenal. Just when I think we are at the end of the tour, he shows us another cage where a baby opossum is sleeping. Mike explains that he has to get up periodically throughout the night just to feed this little guy. Even with all of this on his plate, he plans on expanding the sanctuary so that he can care for larger animals such as Costa Rica's big cats. Within the year, the sanctuary will be relocating to a bigger facility at the Villas Alturas resort in Dominical. I can't imagine how one cares for jaguars, but I'm confident that Mike will find a way. Maybe this is one of the secrets to living a more purposeful life: finding a way.

Osa Santuario De Animales is an oasis for the discarded, and the love that radiates from this place could light up an entire city. Mike is a man that looks to the future. A future that ensures the well-being of all his furry friends. He's a man I admire, and I hope that others will take this tour, get to know him, and leave a donation as well.

Between the antics of Pablo, the energy of Oscar, and the cuteness of Blossom, this is a View-Master moment I'll never forget.

- The sanctuary has since moved to Dominical and has been renamed The Alturas Wildlife Sanctuary. It now has the space to take in many more animals in need.

**Links**

Warning: You may overdose on cuteness.

https://alturaswildlifesanctuary.org

https://www.facebook.com/alturaswildlifesanctuary

# Embassy

Do you want to feel like a rock star? Then visit the United States Embassy, located in the Pavas section of San José. There is always a long line outside, but that's not the one for United States citizens. We get to bypass the line and head straight to the front like Bon Jovi.

Once at the door, show the guard your passport. If he isn't there, press the little doorbell that's on the wall, and he will come out to escort you inside. It's all very aristocratic. Savor the moment; this doesn't happen often Costa Rica.

If you're a United States citizen and applying for residency, you will need to register with the embassy. The first step is to fill out the Smart Traveler Enrollment Program on the embassy website. Print out the profile page, and give it either to your attorney or to the immigration office.

Another important thing you can do at the embassy is get your lost/stolen passports replaced or renew a passport that is about to expire. There is even a booth inside where you can get your picture taken. How's that for service?

After getting your pictures taken, continue up the stairs and into the glass-enclosed, air-conditioned room to your right. Rob and I got our passports renewed here, and the only documents we needed were our expiring passports and driver's licenses. We paid a $110 fee and returned a couple weeks later to pick them up.

I wished everyone who was at the embassy that day had been there to renew a passport. Unfortunately, that wasn't the case. I spoke with several people who'd had their passports stolen. When I asked how this had happened, their stories were all the same: "We left our bags in the car."

I cringed when I heard this. For most of these people, it ruined their vacation… except the twenty-somethings. It appears you can't ruin anything for these guys. To them, this was just a small detour on an otherwise fantastic trip. They couldn't stop talking about all the cool things they did and how much they wanted to return. Some of the older people were more aggravated, even arguing with the embassy employees about the theft. This concerned me most because I didn't want the embassy to shut off the air conditioning, or make everyone go back outside and stand at the end of the line. The phrase, "You'll catch more flies with honey than vinegar," is nowhere more true than in Costa Rica. Sometimes you just have to know when to shut up and smile.

If your passport is stolen, you'll need to show proof at the embassy by obtaining a report from the OIJ police (Organismo de Investigación Judicial). With this and another form of identification, you can get a temporary passport that will be good for thirty days, hopefully long enough for you to catch your flight home. Be sure to tell everyone you went zip-lining and hiked to the top of a volcano.

I cannot stress enough how important it is to have a copy of your passport when you travel. Better yet, email yourself copies of your passport and driver's license. That way if anything happens, you will at least have access to copies of these documents. While you're emailing yourself, drop a note to puravida@happierthanabillionaire.com and say hello. I love hearing from you guys!

If you get a chance, chat with embassy employees. Many have great stories to share. Some have worked at embassies all around the world. One employee told me fabulous stories about her travels throughout Europe, and all the incredible places she had visited. My world has become so much larger since moving to Costa Rica. I'm constantly meeting interesting people who have taken a different path, and some to different continents.

I remember traveling to the Bahamas and meeting a woman whose job was to film tourists with her underwater camera while they snorkeled. At the end of our excursion, I asked her how she ended up with this incredible job. She explained that she used to be a banker, hated it, and decided one day to quit. She didn't want to work in an office the rest of her life so she packed up and moved to the Caribbean. She now makes a living selling these videos.

After her explanation, Rob turned to me and said, "Why don't we do something like that? It's better than working all year just to pay for the vacation she gets to live every day." This woman's story stayed in the back of our minds for years, until we finally designed our own escape plan.

**Links**

United States Embassy: http://costarica.usembassy.gov/

Canada Embassy: http://www.canadainternational.gc.ca/costa_rica/index.aspx?lang=eng

Smart Traveler Program: https://step.state.gov/step/

OIJ for reporting stolen passports: www.poder-judicial.go.cr/

# Rodrigo Fixes the Air Conditioner

In previous chapters, I've chronicled mishaps with appliances, utilities, and even PVC. But nothing compares to the issues we have had with our air conditioners. They've been under hospice care since the moment we moved in.

There are five blowers in the house, each one connected to one of two compressors located outside. It's not unusual to have one working while the others do not, or to have one compressor fail, making all the blowers attached to it useless. Coincidently, these things usually happen in the dry season on some of the hottest days of the year.

It's not just our house, either. Many of my friends suffer the same fate, always searching for a good repairman. The problem is that you can never get in touch with one. These guys must be incredibly busy since they never answer their phone. Or maybe they're just avoiding us. It wouldn't be the first time someone noticed all the cameras and warning signs outside our house and kept on driving.

The other day, there was a car of church folk leaving pamphlets in front of everyone's house. They took a quick glance at ours and sped past. They didn't even attempt to stick one between the razor-sharp barbed wire. It's a shame because we are exactly the kind of people who could use an amen.

If they would have stopped, I might have asked them to pray for our air conditioners because most of the units have been on life support at one time or another. It's been two months, and not one repairman will answer his phone. Well… there is one who is available: Rodrigo. He promises to come by nine o'clock this morning to take a look.

Don't get me wrong. I appreciate my rendezvous with Rodrigo. I just get a funny feeling I should be preparing for his visit by building an ark, or mixing and matching some cruise wear. But I shouldn't have to worry about that since the water has been mysteriously off for the past two days.

"Thank heavens," I say to myself, right before hearing a toilet flush.

"Awesome. The water is back on," Rob yells from the bathroom. Under normal circumstances, I'd celebrate by running around the house and manically flushing every toilet. Heck, I might even avail myself of bashing the side of my refrigerator a few times with a hammer. But Rodrigo is coming soon: the Aquaman of household repairs, so all I feel today is a heavy pit in my stomach.

By far, water is the worst utility to lose. I used to think it was electricity until I went a couple days without water. It was awful. My parents recently visited, staying in a lovely development down the street—one where utilities are always in working order. If there was ever a zombie apocalypse, I'd jump over their fence, hang out in the oversized hot tub, and enjoy the all-you-can-eat buffet. Rob is more than welcome to hunker down and eat canned peaches while he fights off the dead. My plan is to forfeit as quickly as possible, and I'm going to go down in style while eating shrimp cocktail until the very end.

However, the day my parents checked in, the development's water main cracked, affecting two buildings. And just my luck, it included their ocean-view condominium.

"NO WATER? What the hell am I supposed to do?" my father hollered. "I was in the army; I can handle this. But your mother? How can you do this to her?"

I didn't even know how to respond since my father was already in hysterics. He scrambled, locking every door and window just in case all hell broke loose. He even went to the sliding glass doors and scanned the horizon with his binoculars. For what, I can't be sure. Maybe to signal a passing ship. All I know is if he was given the option, my father would have returned home on the next available flight or nearby fishing boat.

For as much as he was worried about my mother's restroom choices, she didn't even pick her head up from the book she was reading.

"Can you poor me another scotch?" was all I recall her saying during my dad's visions of lawlessness.

While my mom relaxed with her drink, my dad swiftly unpacked an entire suitcase of Kellogg cereals he brought with him because it is an expansive item here. At this point I thought he had planned to trade them for water on the Costa Rican black market. It's clear the only apocalypse I have to worry about is the parent-induced one that visits me every year.

As always, Rob remained calm and headed to the pool with a garbage can. It was there he found other refugees filling their buckets with pool water to flush their toilets as well. My father was impressed with Rob's bravery, so later that night he too went down to the pool to fill up another garbage can. In all likelihood, my dad thought crazed residents would empty the entire pool—all one zillion gallons of water— by morning. Unfortunately, he underestimated the weight of the garbage can and had to wrestle it all the way back to the condominium, spilling most of the water before he ever reached the front door. The next night, the water was back on and all was right again in the world.

I have no idea why my father became *that* upset by this inconvenience, but I really can't blame him. In New Jersey, you may lose water for a couple hours if the city is working on a pipe, but it's usually turned back on by the end of the day. Learning to live for extended periods of time without running water is something you don't want to have to deal with while you're on vacation.

Rodrigo calls again to tell us he's coming this morning. And just as promised, once again, he shows up outside our gate at four in the afternoon. As far as he's concerned, he's early. Rodrigo is wearing his patented big smile while Rob shows him the malfunctioning unit in our living room. After shaking his head, Rodrigo goes outside to retrieve his tools.

He sets up a ladder under the air conditioning unit and proceeds to take it apart, piece by piece, until all that remains is a skeletal frame of electronics. It's now that Rodrigo seems stumped, as if I'm asking him to decode the mysteries that surround Stonehenge. I start to wonder if he is aware at all that this is an air conditioner and not a stove, ham radio, or pool pump.

After a considerable amount of time sitting on top of the ladder, he excuses himself and walks outside. He returns with a long metal trough not unlike something you might see on a farm. He then goes back outside and reaches for… you guessed it… the hose. He turns off the breaker before climbing the ladder and sitting on its top step. He balances the trough on his lap and asks me to turn on the water, which I do, because I'm stupid like that.

Rodrigo blasts the remaining part of the air conditioner, and I watch as his trough catches all the water. It's so crazy and unconventional that you would never see this in the United States. I can't even imagine the insurance premiums repairmen would have to pay if they were dragging hoses into clients' living rooms to spray electrical appliances. But sometimes in Costa Rica the simplest solution is the best solution. It's easy to see why suicide showers are so popular here. This is a magical country: a place where water and electronics coexist side by side. Where a mechanic is judged not by what is in his toolbox but by the size of his hose.

I admire him. Rodrigo obviously comes from the same school as Rob: the Harebrained Jerry-rigging Institute of the World. Although I feared Rodrigo would destroy every electronic in my living room, the trough actually works and everything remains dry. He must have graduated at the top of his class. Where Rob's half-baked fix is duct tape and underwear, all Rodrigo needs is a hose and a smile.

Seemingly satisfied with his work, Rodrigo instructs me to turn off the hose as he starts to reassemble the air conditioner. Only a few large parts are left over, which pleases Rob. To my husband, leftover parts are a sign of a job well done.

Seventy-five dollars later, our air conditioner works… for two weeks. The piece that broke this time has nothing to do with Rodrigo; *this* part is located outside on the condenser.

After the latest round of repairs, the owners of the house have decided to get brand new air conditioning units And just our luck, Rodrigo will be available to install them.

He'll be at our house by nine o'clock tomorrow morning.

# Road Trip: The Osa Peninsula

Are you overdue for a break from your everyday routine? A break from sitting in traffic, a break from your inbox, and a break from the many pressures that can leave you exhausted by the end of the day? If so, then the Osa Peninsula is a great place to visit. It's home to one of the few remaining lowland tropical rainforests in the world.

The crown jewel of the peninsula is the Corcovado National Park. Spanning over 103,000 acres, *National Geographic* once called this area "the most biologically intense place on Earth." Can you imagine that, a unique setting overflowing with wildlife? Costa Rica is a treasure chest, eager to sparkle once you crack open her lid.

There are a few ways to get to Corcovado National Park. One option is to stay in Drake Bay, an area on the north side of the peninsula. There are eco-lodges in the middle of the jungle, and from here it's easy to access hiking trails straight into the park. If driving from San José to Drake Bay, take the Autopista del Sol and merge onto Route 34 (the Costanera Sur). Another option is to take the Pan-American Highway from San José, continuing south to San Isidro del General. Once there, turn right and follow signs to Dominical. Dominical is a great place to stop and stretch before continuing south on Route 34. Once at the town of Charcarita, stop at the town's gas station to fill up since there will not be another one for a while. Turn right at the gas station and continue driving approximately another forty-five minutes to Rincón. Just before crossing the bridge, make another right and follow this road all the way to Drake Bay.

- Be aware that you may not be able to drive to Drake Bay in the rainy season due to several rivers that have no bridges. Even in the dry season you'll need a four-wheel-drive vehicle with high clearance, and navigating the roads can be challenging.

Another option is to use public transportation or drive to Sierpe. If you decide to drive, you can park your car at the Las Vegas restaurant. From Sierpe you will take a one-hour-and-thirty-minute boat ride to Drake Bay. Lastly, you can drive or use public transportation to Puerto Jiménez and continue around the peninsula and upward to the town of Carate. From Carate it's a forty-five-minute hike to the entrance of Corcovado National Park. Make sure you are in good health and have plenty of water if you choose this option.

If you are uncomfortable making this trek, why not just fly in? Both Nature Air and SANSA have flights that land in either Puerto Jiménez or Drake Bay itself. I always say, the best things in Costa Rica are down a dirt road, or in this case, down a dirt landing strip.

Once you are in this particular zone of the country, the air is overstuffed with oxygen. Microscopic particles of wonder buzz around you, creating a unique force field of curiosity. You'll feel like a child again, uncovering the marvels of this planet, seeing bugs and plants that you never knew existed. This part of the rainforest is one of the biggest gifts Costa Rica shares with the world.

Home to over 360 species of birds and 140 mammals, this park is jam-packed with wildlife. You'll see all four species of monkeys that reside in Costa Rica: howler, capuchin, spider, and the red-back squirrel monkey (a member of the titi family).

While looking up for monkeys, you might as well enjoy the birds. I've seen more scarlet macaws at the Osa Peninsula than in any other part of the country. Their yellow, red, and green feathers sweep the sky like iridescent kites. These birds often land in almond trees to munch on the nuts. I found this out while sitting under one and getting pelted in the head with discarded shells. Incidentally, this is exactly how Rob eats pistachios in our car.

You might get lucky in the park and encounter the endangered Baird's tapir. It's a funny-looking animal: part pig and part cow, with a splash of rhinoceros thrown in for good measure. They are nocturnal, so the odds of seeing one are small. Your best chance is to wait near a watering hole. On a hot day, you may find one submerged with only his head above the water. They are like tourists at a swim-up bar except these tourists defecate in the water to keep predators away. Sounds like a great security plan, and I can't wait to see how Rob incorporates this into his Thunderdome protocol.

Although I've never seen a tapir, I did come across a path lined with dozens of snakeskins. At first I was startled, but later I was relieved since I would much rather step on a snakeskin than tread across the actual snake. It was hard to tell which species left these skins behind, mostly because I didn't stick around long enough to find out. There are enough poisonous snakes living in this jungle to persuade me to skedaddle: coral, bushmaster, eyelash pit viper, and the fer-de-lance snake (also known as the Costa Rican landmine). When snakes are nicknamed after explosive devices, you know it's time to move on.

The way we reached the park was through one of Rob's infamous money-saving two-for-one excursions from Puerto Jiménez. He paid for a three-hour tour that included a bit of fishing before traveling up the coast. He did not divulge before the trip that when we got close to the park we would have to jump overboard, swim to a deserted beach, and hike in search of the entrance to the park. No one had a map, a compass, or even enough water to last more than a few hours. Needless to say, this wasn't the way I would have planned it, but it turned out to be a fun trip. Apparently, Gilligan is a real person and I'm married to him.

Rob and I have such good memories of the Osa Peninsula that we decide to return. This time we drive back to the place we first saw scarlet macaws flying overhead: Agua Dulce Beach Resort. It is just a five-minute drive from Puerto Jiménez, which borders the Gulfo Dulce: the bay that separates the peninsula from the mainland. It is the only resort on the beach in this area that offers air conditioning. We book an oceanfront bungalow that includes a wooden porch. Out front are two rocking chairs, perfect for relaxing, watching the sunrise.

I slop on a ton of sunscreen and immediately head out to the beach. The sand is soft; it feels like New Year's Eve confetti underneath my feet. Mother Nature must have known I was coming and arranged for two macaws to fly overhead. This is exactly how I remember it, and precisely why the Osa Peninsula is so magical.

The two birds vocalize back and forth with each other, using sounds that are not unlike a tarot card reader after her fifth Camel cigarette. I sit on a piece of driftwood and notice a pile of shells. Some are brown and shiny and look like tiny Godiva chocolates. Others are cracked open resembling angel wings. This country is always reminding me to revere the small as much as the big.

"I've scheduled a mangrove tour," Rob says while taking a seat next to me.

"I don't have to swim there, right?" Whenever my husband plans excursions, it's important to inquire whether I'll need my floaty wings to survive it.

"No, it's just kayaking. We'll have to leave soon so let's get our stuff together and head out."

Kayak Tour and Adventure is located just five minutes down the road from Agua Dulce. We pull up in front of a house where dozens of kayaks hang from a metal frame. Another car parks behind us; a father, mother, and two small children pile out. The mom has a soft-sided cooler stuffed with sandwiches, snacks, and water bottles. This is not unlike my sister's purse. On any given day I can reach in and find gummy bears, various crackers (some packaged, some loose floating), and tragically squashed juice boxes. And forget about trying to stay clean in the backseat of her car; I once sat on a pancake that was covered in maple syrup.

As I watch the mother lather her children up with Coppertone Waterproof Sunscreen, I realize I brought nothing: no water, sunblock, or treats.  Apparently, "let's get our stuff together and head out" means just getting our bodies in the car and physically there.

The father takes out his wallet and pays the guide, while little Jimmy cries because he's hungry. I want to cry, too. If my mom were here she would have packed a delicious bologna-and-mayonnaise sandwich and an UNO card game.

UNO was always available to my sister and me, my mother praying that it would shut us up long enough to give her a little peace and quiet. However, our family didn't do fun outdoorsy stuff like kayaking that would have kept two kids entertained. My parents' go-to was the Metropolitan Museum of Art to stare at broken Roman pottery vases. The only redeeming part of these trips was the Greek and Roman Art Gallery, where statues are prominently displayed with their wieners broken off. My sister and I laughed our way through the Lincoln Tunnel, and all the way home. Since I'm considered the "fun aunt," I feel it's my responsibility to take my nieces to that exact same floor where they also lapse into uncontrollable giggling fits. Then we stare at the broken pottery vases because it feels like the thing to do.

Alberto, our mangrove tour guide, piles three kayaks onto a trailer and we ride a block to the bay in the back of his pickup truck. Two dogs are playing in the water, totally oblivious to us and totally enjoying their morning. Other than that, no one is around. It's the reason Rob and I enjoy doing our Costa Rican excursions so much: we are never just a number in a crowd of fifty other people. It doesn't feel like a tour, but more like kayaking with a good friend.

Rob decides to share a two-man kayak with our guide so that his hands are free for taking pictures.

"Use my kayak," Alberto says before handing me a life vest. "I make them myself and this one is my lightest and fastest."

He's right. Rob easily pushes me off into the water and whenever I turn, I end up spinning in a circle. I'm used to my old, banged-up kayak that feels like a brick when compared to this one.

I'm also used to inflatable kayaks that deflate at the most inopportune times.

"So you actually made this?" I ask.

"Yes. It takes a long time but it's worth it. The top and bottom pieces are not only glued together, but secured with rivets as well. They are very safe."

"Safe like we're not going to fall overboard?"

"Yes."

"Are there crocodiles around here?"

"Yes."

"So it's good to stay in the kayak."

"Yes."

Alberto doesn't have to tell me twice. I'm all for staying inside the kayak. Hey, I'll sit inside it on dry land if that ensures I will never encounter a crocodile.

I look down and the water is so flat, it reflects the sky like a watercolor painting. Maybe my parents had the right idea by dragging me to all those museums. Beauty can be captured in many different places. Sometimes it hangs on a gallery wall and other times it's found while kayaking in Central America.

Our guide takes us down a narrow waterway and into a mangrove maze. The water darkens, shaded by the thick canopy overhead. I glance over at a tree and could swear the roots are moving. As I paddle closer I realize it's a carpet of crabs.

"There are one hundred and fifty species of crabs," Albert explains. "Just keep your eyes open—you'll see them everywhere."

As I peer into the forest, they're hidden in between roots, in hollow crevices, and hanging off branches above my head.

"Can you eat them?" Rob asks.

"You can, but some are better than others. My favorite are the snails. If you cook them in butter, they're delicious. They're very small so you have to collect a lot. It was fun when I was a kid, but too much work now. The government has educated the community on how everything here is part of a fragile ecosystem. And that things such as crabs and snails should no longer be eaten."

At first I didn't notice the snails, but now that I look closer they are everywhere. It's a French cook's dream. I imagine one in his white, poofy hat rummaging around the mangrove, collecting snails and singing patriotic French songs.

I paddle farther ahead and quietly glide through the waterway. Birds are stationed everywhere: blue herons, white ibis, and black hawks. Some are frozen like lawn ornaments; others cautiously turn their heads as we pass by. They are watching us closer than we are watching them. It's creepy and exhilarating all at the same time.

As we head farther into the mangroves, a fallen tree blocks our route

"Squeeze through," Alberto calls from behind.

I lean back and lift the branches overhead. From this position I see a spiderweb the size of Cincinnati, and an equally large spider in the middle of it. As I slide underneath, I notice dewdrops hanging off the web, casting reflective prisms of light. It looks like an oily New York City puddle: swirly mixes of blues, greens, and reds.

The arachnoid remains frozen as my face passes an inch from its belly. I keep my mouth shut, just in case he's curious and decides to take a misguided leap. After I'm through, I carefully place the branches back down, not to disturb the spider or break his web. "Leave nothing but footprints, take nothing but memories, kill nothing but time," is a common quote you will hear repeated in Costa Rica.

"Last time we were here we saw a pack of white-faced monkeys," Rob comments.

"Yes, they are around. They cause me a lot of trouble," Alberto replies, shaking his head.

"What kind of trouble?"

"A couple months ago, I walked into my garage and saw everything scattered all over. I immediately thought I was robbed until I realized my tools were still there, just thrown across the floor and around the room. I cleaned up, and in a couple days, the same thing happened again. The next night I stayed up late waiting to catch what I thought were kids playing a prank. But I couldn't believe it! A pack of monkeys came in and started going through my toolbox. They picked up anything shiny, tasted it, and tossed it over their shoulder. The minute I pointed my flashlight on them, they ran away."

"What did you do?"

"I installed motion sensors, so whenever they enter the garage, the lights turn on. It scares them and they immediately jump back into the trees."

"Seems like you solved the problem."

"Yes. But then I began noticing eggs missing from the henhouse. I thought my neighbor was stealing them so the next night I stayed up late waiting to catch what I thought was my thieving neighbor. But once again I couldn't believe it. I saw a monkey reach in, unlock the cage, and tiptoe inside. He grabbed an egg, backtracked and locked the door on the way out! I almost called the police on a monkey!"

As he is telling this story, I'm thinking I should update my crime chapter to include monkey theft. It could prevent a lot of premature fighting between neighbors.

"I'm glad you didn't get into a fight over it. I recently got an email from a guy who read my book, moved here, and was angry with me and his Tico neighbor over a—"

"A rooster?" Alberto says, finishing my sentence.

"How did you know that?"

"Are you the woman who wrote a book about moving to Costa Rica?"

"Yes, I'm her."

"I'm the Tico neighbor!" the guide laughs. "This man moves next door and tells me that he read a book about a lady moving to Costa Rica. It inspired him to move here as well. After a week, he starts coming over and complaining about my rooster. I could understand why he was upset, since my rooster is a little confused. He crows all night. He wanted me to kill the bird but I refused. To me, my rooster sounds beautiful. It made my neighbor so angry he went down to the municipality multiple times to complain."

"So what happened to the neighbor?"

"Oh, he moved."

"And the rooster?"

"He stayed," he says, smiling.

I can't be a hundred percent certain that I was the author the neighbor was talking about, but it does sound a little suspicious. To think that by happenstance I would be in the middle of a mangrove tour with the notorious Tico-rooster-neighbor is hilarious. I'm glad that my books are bringing people closer together, only to have them move farther apart.

We take a break from paddling and pull our kayaks up onto a sandy bank. Alberto grabs his machete, cracks opens a coconut, and slices a pineapple. It begins to rain; we are drenched in seconds. That's a funny thing about Costa Rica: you rarely get a *little* wet when it rains.

We quickly finish our fruit and pull our kayaks back into the water. Although mine was built specifically for Alberto, it fits me perfectly. For once I don't feel small but powerful as I zip through the water. Thunder claps overhead, and the water's reflection turns from a watercolor painting into a muddy mess.

When I dreamed of moving to Costa Rica I didn't foresee mangrove tours or carpets of crabs. In fact, I wasn't even sure if what I was looking for really existed. Now I have experiences like this, streaming through the Gulfo Dulce on a kayak built by a local Tico, flying past skipping fish and foamy algae that will soon by eaten by the creatures below.

The Osa Peninsula remains one of my favorite areas to visit. Traveling through a place like this is life-changing and alters the way you think. It can even clear the foggiest of heads, minds that have become compulsive hoarders of stress and worry. A lot of that anxiety gets washed away here, and what's left is a radiant clean slate. Granted, there may be a spiderweb or two, but it'll be a clean slate nonetheless.

I smile once I see land ahead, take another deep breath, and continue paddling back to shore. Back to a life that looks nothing like it used to. A life I didn't know existed, but one that surprisingly fits me perfectly.

**Links**

Agua Dulce Beach Resort: www.aguadulceresort.com
8399-0112

Kayak Tour and Adventures: www.aventurastropicales.com
2735-5195

24655460R00188